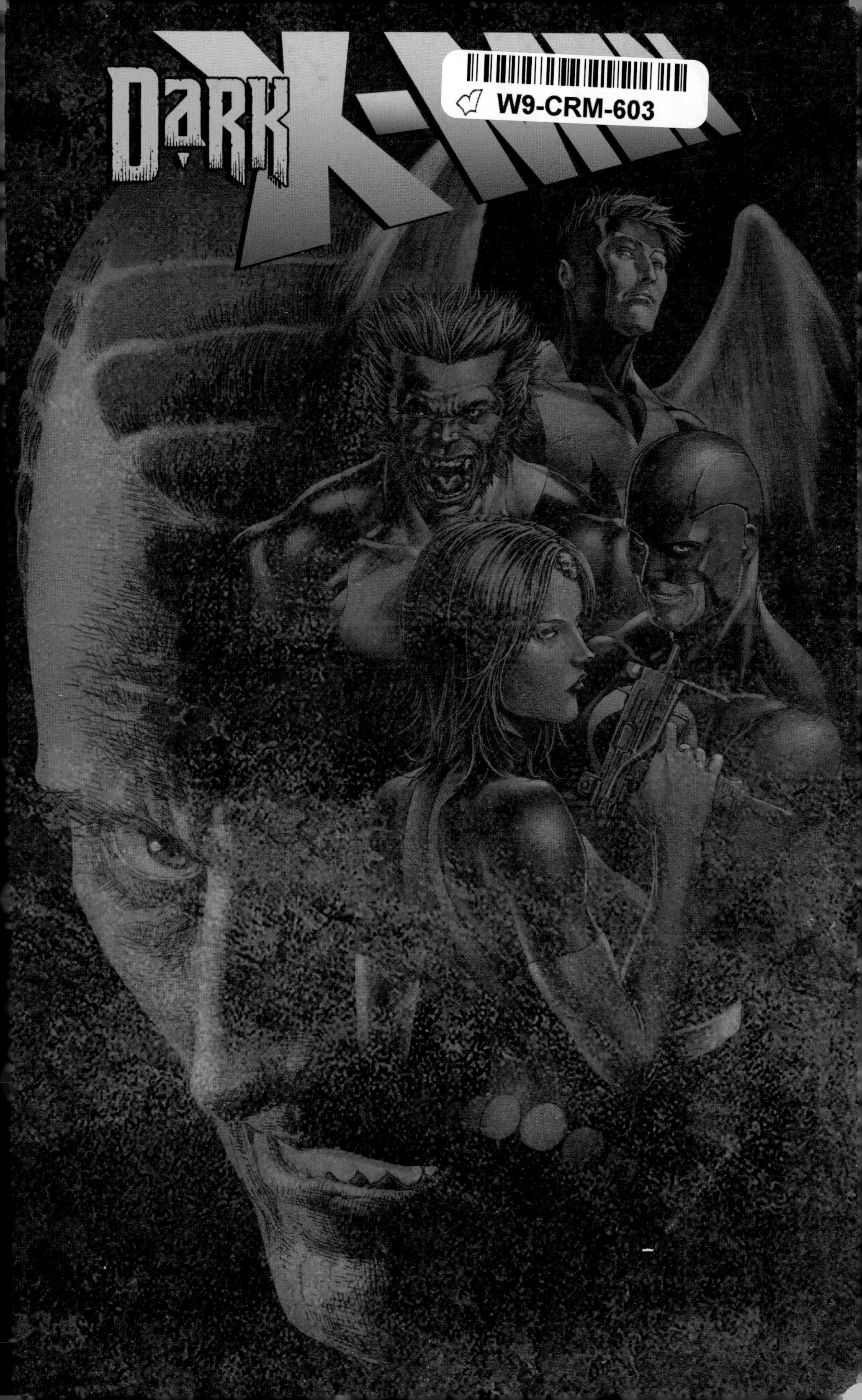
DARK

Collection Editor	Senior Editor, Special Projects	Editor in Chief
JENNIFER GRÜNWALD	**JEFF YOUNGQUIST**	**JOE QUESADA**
Assistant Editor	Senior Vice President of Sales	Publisher
ALEX STARBUCK	**DAVID GABRIEL**	**DAN BUCKLEY**
Associate Editor	Book Design	Executive Producer
JOHN DENNING	**JEFF POWELL**	**ALAN FINE**
Editor, Special Projects		
MARK D. BEAZLEY		

DARK X-MEN. Contains material originally published in magazine form as DARK X-MEN #1-5. First printing 2010. ISBN# 978-0-7851-4526-4. Published by MARVEL WORLDWIDE, INC., a subsidiary of MARVEL ENTERTAINMENT, LLC. OFFICE OF PUBLICATION: 417 5th Avenue, New York, NY 10016. Copyright © 2009 and 2010 Marvel Characters, Inc. All rights reserved. $19.99 per copy in the U.S. (GST #R127032852); Canadian Agreement #40668537. All characters featured in this issue and the distinctive names and likenesses thereof, and all related indicia are trademarks of Marvel Characters, Inc. No similarity between any of the names, characters, persons, and/or institutions in this magazine with those of any living or dead person or institution is intended, and any such similarity which may exist is purely coincidental. **Printed in the U.S.A.** ALAN FINE, EVP - Office of the President, Marvel Worldwide, Inc. and EVP & CMO Marvel Characters B.V.; DAN BUCKLEY, Chief Executive Officer and Publisher - Print, Animation & Digital Media; JIM SOKOLOWSKI, Chief Operating Officer; DAVID GABRIEL, SVP of Publishing Sales & Circulation; DAVID BOGART, SVP of Business Affairs & Talent Management; MICHAEL PASCIULLO, VP Merchandising & Communications; JIM O'KEEFE, VP of Operations & Logistics; DAN CARR, Executive Director of Publishing Technology; JUSTIN F. GABRIE, Director of Publishing & Editorial Operations; SUSAN CRESPI, Editorial Operations Manager; ALEX MORALES, Publishing Operations Manager; STAN LEE, Chairman Emeritus. For information regarding advertising in Marvel Comics or on Marvel.com, please contact Ron Stern, VP of Business Development, at rstern@marvel.com. For Marvel subscription inquiries, please call 800-217-9158. **Manufactured between 3/22/10 and 4/21/10 by R.R. DONNELLEY, INC., SALEM, VA, USA.**

10 9 8 7 6 5 4 3 2 1

WRITER
PAUL CORNELL

PENCILER
LEONARD KIRK

INKERS
**JAY LEISTEN &
LEONARD KIRK**
(ISSUES #4-5)

COLORIST
BRIAN REBER

LETTERER
ROB STEEN

COVER ARTISTS
SIMONE BIANCHI WITH
SIMONE PERUZZI
(ISSUES #1-3)
MIKE CHOI & SONIA OBACK
(ISSUE #4)
AND **GIUSEPPE CAMUNCOLI
& MORRY HOLLOWELL**
(ISSUE #5)

ASSOCIATE EDITOR
DANIEL KETCHUM

EDITOR
NICK LOWE

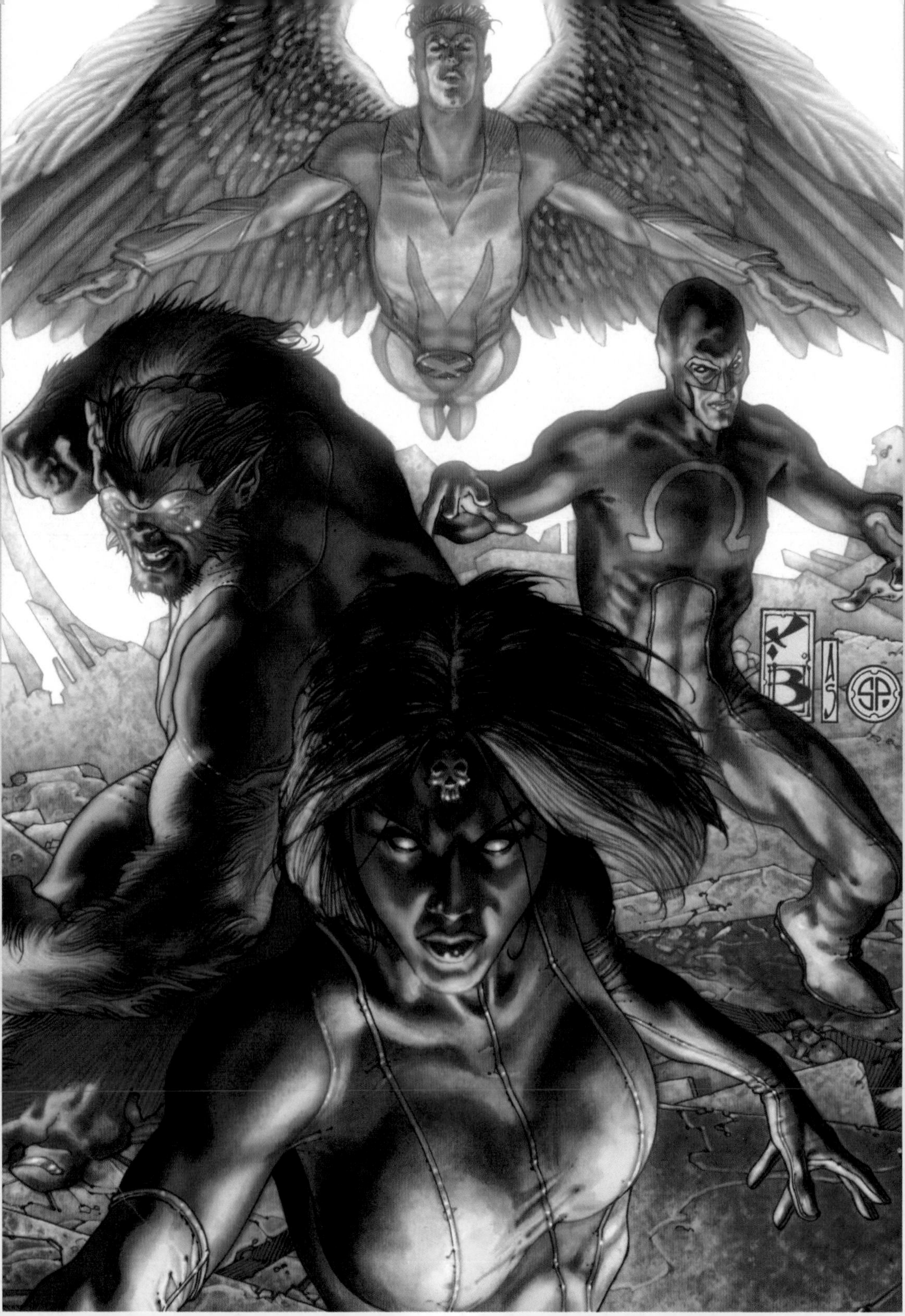

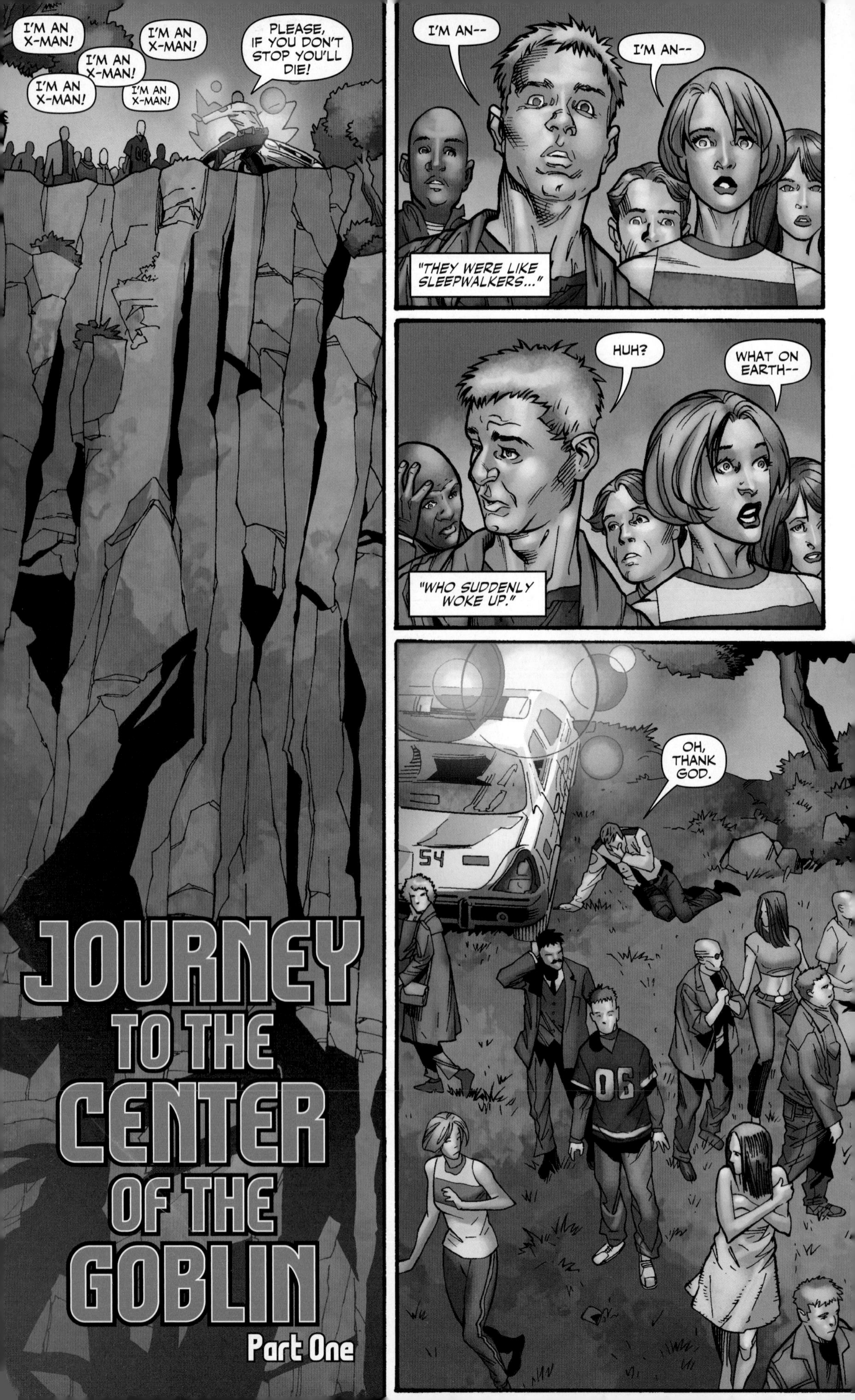
I'M AN X-MAN!
I'M AN X-MAN!
I'M AN X-MAN!
I'M AN X-MAN!
I'M AN X-MAN!
PLEASE, IF YOU DON'T STOP YOU'LL DIE!
JOURNEY TO THE CENTER OF THE GOBLIN
Part One
I'M AN--
I'M AN--
"THEY WERE LIKE SLEEPWALKERS..."
HUH?
WHAT ON EARTH--
"WHO SUDDENLY WOKE UP."
OH, THANK GOD.

DARK X-MEN

Following the failed Skrull invasion of Earth, Norman
Osborn became the Director of the national peacekeeping
organization H.A.M.M.E.R. and leader of the Avengers.
Finding himself in need of a means for policing America's
mutant population during riots in San Francisco that
involved the X-Men, Norman recruited his own team of
X-Men to be the face of law and order for mutantkind...

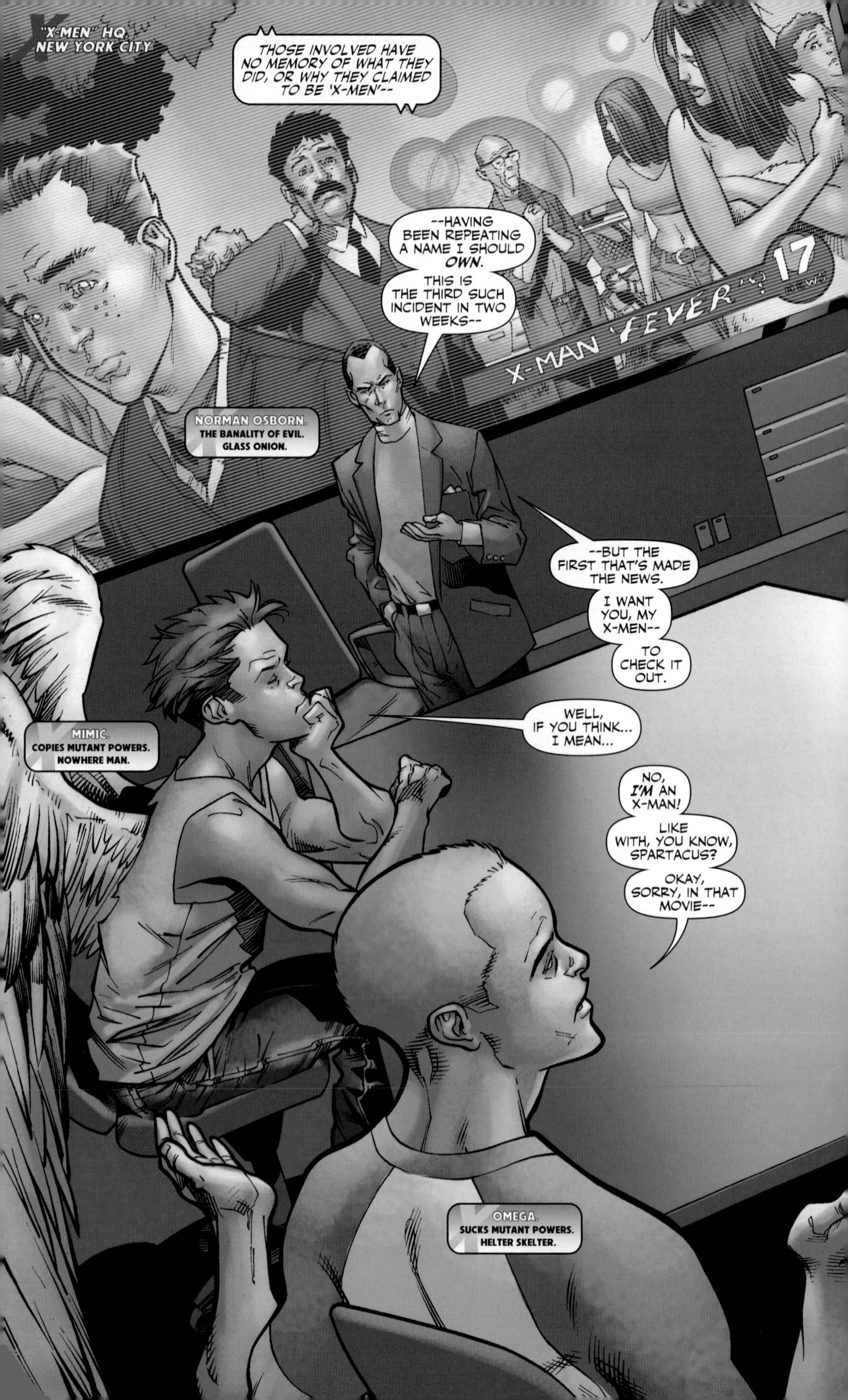

"X-MEN" HQ, NEW YORK CITY
THOSE INVOLVED HAVE NO MEMORY OF WHAT THEY DID, OR WHY THEY CLAIMED TO BE 'X-MEN'--
--HAVING BEEN REPEATING A NAME I SHOULD OWN.
THIS IS THE THIRD SUCH INCIDENT IN TWO WEEKS--
X-MAN 'FEVER'?
17 NEWS
NORMAN OSBORN. THE BANALITY OF EVIL. GLASS ONION.
--BUT THE FIRST THAT'S MADE THE NEWS.
I WANT YOU, MY X-MEN--
TO CHECK IT OUT.
WELL, IF YOU THINK... I MEAN...
MIMIC. COPIES MUTANT POWERS. NOWHERE MAN.
NO, I'M AN X-MAN!
LIKE WITH, YOU KNOW, SPARTACUS?
OKAY, SORRY, IN THAT MOVIE--
OMEGA. SUCKS MUTANT POWERS. HELTER SKELTER.

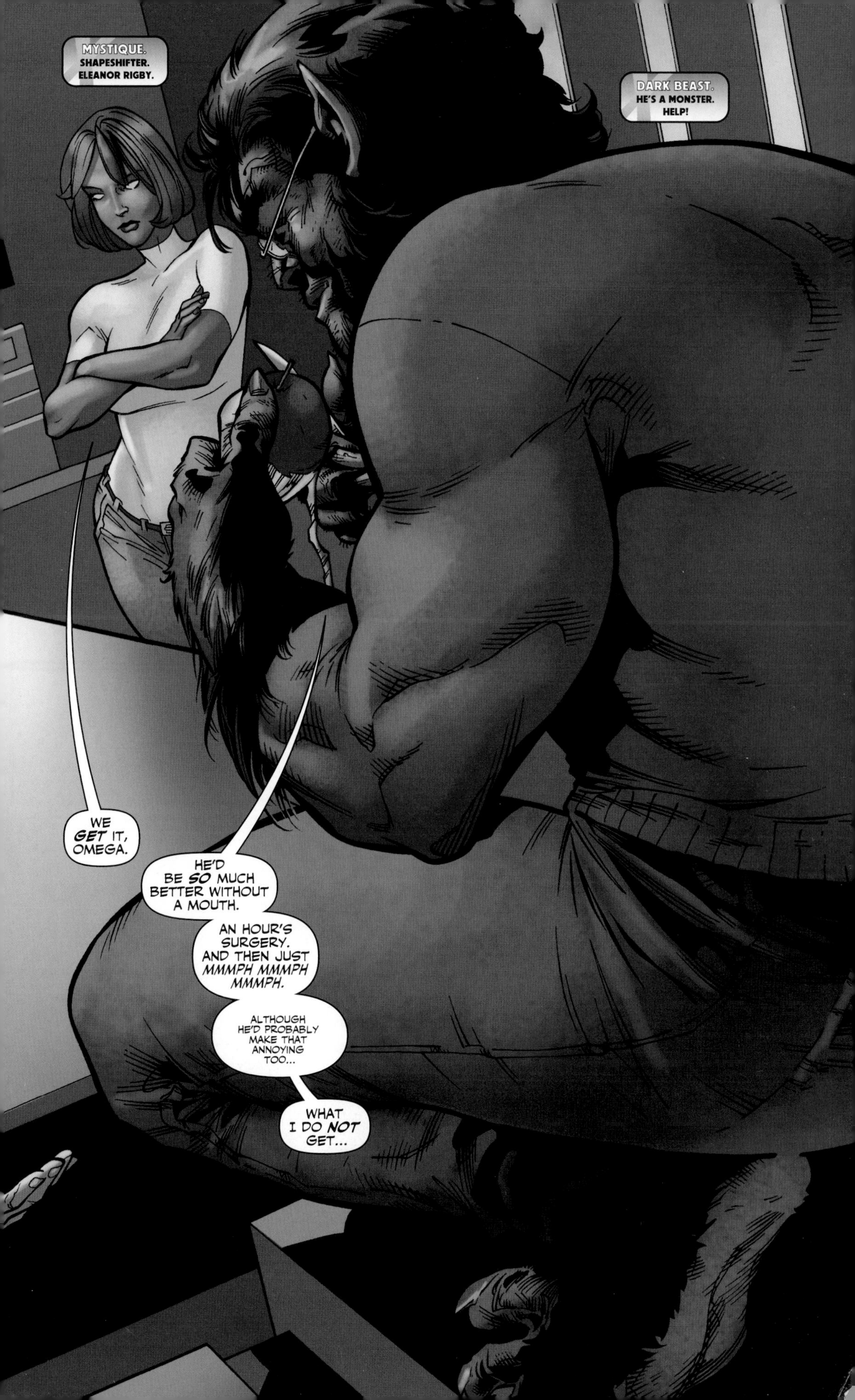

MYSTIQUE.
SHAPESHIFTER.
ELEANOR RIGBY.
DARK BEAST.
HE'S A MONSTER.
HELP!
WE *GET* IT, OMEGA.
HE'D BE *SO* MUCH BETTER WITHOUT A MOUTH.
AN HOUR'S SURGERY. AND THEN JUST *MMMPH MMMPH MMMPH.*
ALTHOUGH HE'D PROBABLY MAKE THAT ANNOYING TOO...
WHAT I DO *NOT* GET...

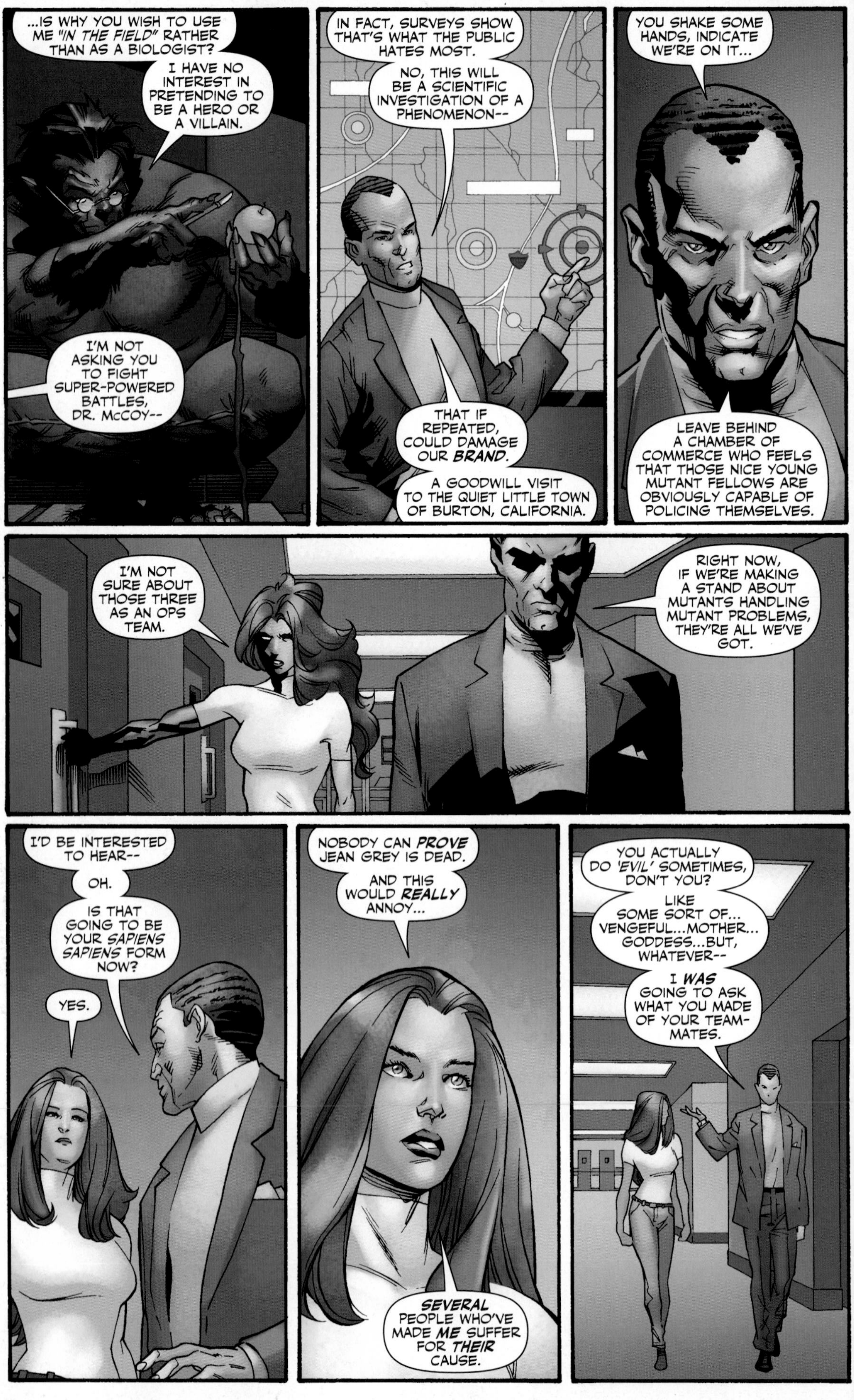
...IS WHY YOU WISH TO USE ME "IN THE FIELD" RATHER THAN AS A BIOLOGIST?
I HAVE NO INTEREST IN PRETENDING TO BE A HERO OR A VILLAIN.
I'M NOT ASKING YOU TO FIGHT SUPER-POWERED BATTLES, DR. McCOY--
IN FACT, SURVEYS SHOW THAT'S WHAT THE PUBLIC HATES MOST.
NO, THIS WILL BE A SCIENTIFIC INVESTIGATION OF A PHENOMENON--
THAT IF REPEATED, COULD DAMAGE OUR BRAND.
A GOODWILL VISIT TO THE QUIET LITTLE TOWN OF BURTON, CALIFORNIA.
YOU SHAKE SOME HANDS, INDICATE WE'RE ON IT...
LEAVE BEHIND A CHAMBER OF COMMERCE WHO FEELS THAT THOSE NICE YOUNG MUTANT FELLOWS ARE OBVIOUSLY CAPABLE OF POLICING THEMSELVES.
I'M NOT SURE ABOUT THOSE THREE AS AN OPS TEAM.
RIGHT NOW, IF WE'RE MAKING A STAND ABOUT MUTANTS HANDLING MUTANT PROBLEMS, THEY'RE ALL WE'VE GOT.
I'D BE INTERESTED TO HEAR--
OH.
IS THAT GOING TO BE YOUR SAPIENS SAPIENS FORM NOW?
YES.
NOBODY CAN PROVE JEAN GREY IS DEAD.
AND THIS WOULD REALLY ANNOY...
SEVERAL PEOPLE WHO'VE MADE ME SUFFER FOR THEIR CAUSE.
YOU ACTUALLY DO 'EVIL' SOMETIMES, DON'T YOU?
LIKE SOME SORT OF... VENGEFUL...MOTHER... GODDESS...BUT, WHATEVER--
I WAS GOING TO ASK WHAT YOU MADE OF YOUR TEAM-MATES.

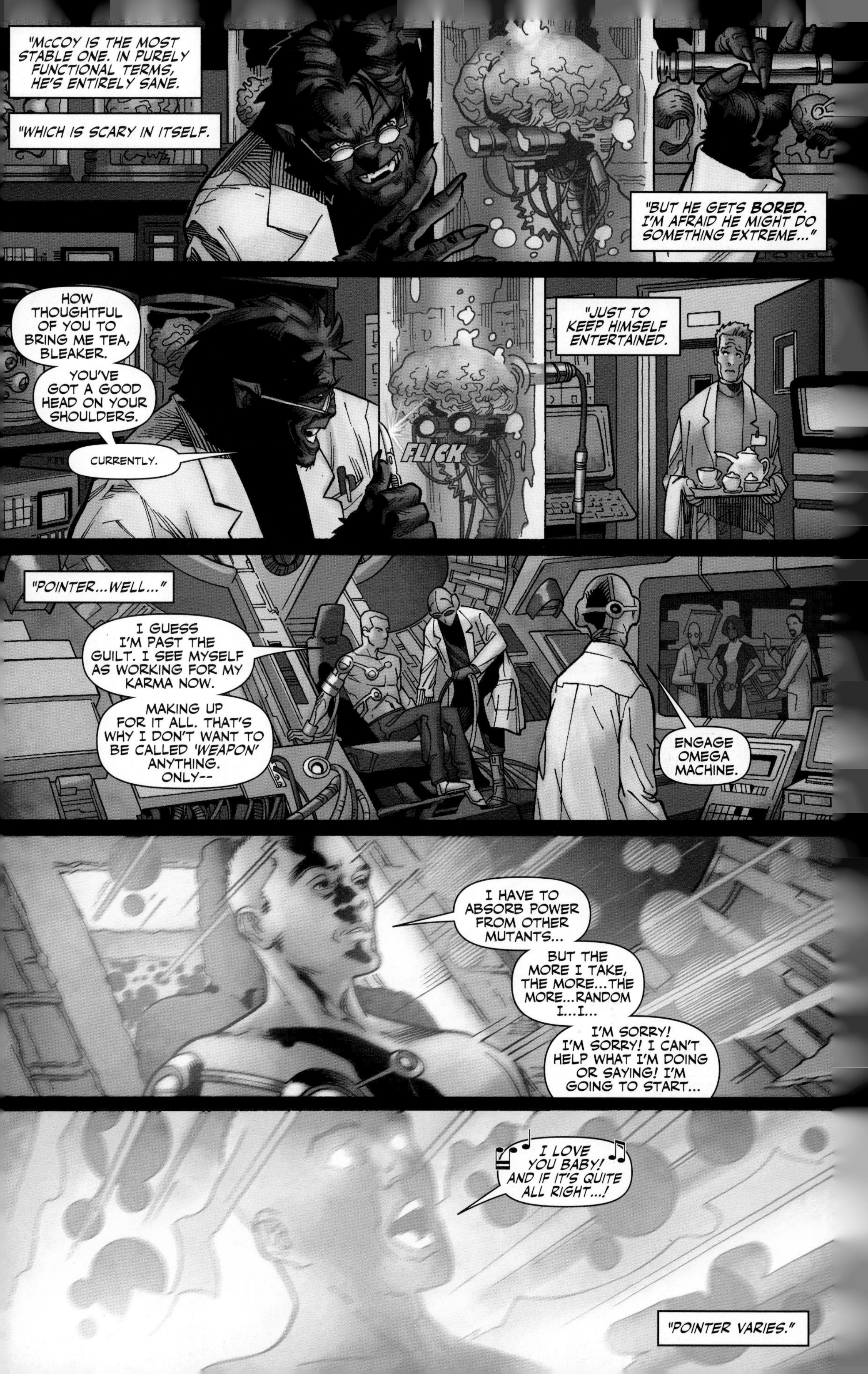
"McCOY IS THE MOST STABLE ONE. IN PURELY FUNCTIONAL TERMS, HE'S ENTIRELY SANE.
"WHICH IS SCARY IN ITSELF.
"BUT HE GETS BORED. I'M AFRAID HE MIGHT DO SOMETHING EXTREME..."
HOW THOUGHTFUL OF YOU TO BRING ME TEA, BLEAKER.
YOU'VE GOT A GOOD HEAD ON YOUR SHOULDERS.
CURRENTLY.
FLICK
"JUST TO KEEP HIMSELF ENTERTAINED.
"POINTER...WELL..."
I GUESS I'M PAST THE GUILT. I SEE MYSELF AS WORKING FOR MY KARMA NOW.
MAKING UP FOR IT ALL. THAT'S WHY I DON'T WANT TO BE CALLED 'WEAPON' ANYTHING. ONLY--
ENGAGE OMEGA MACHINE.
I HAVE TO ABSORB POWER FROM OTHER MUTANTS...
BUT THE MORE I TAKE, THE MORE...THE MORE...RANDOM I...I...
I'M SORRY! I'M SORRY! I CAN'T HELP WHAT I'M DOING OR SAYING! I'M GOING TO START...
I LOVE YOU BABY! AND IF IT'S QUITE ALL RIGHT...!
"POINTER VARIES."

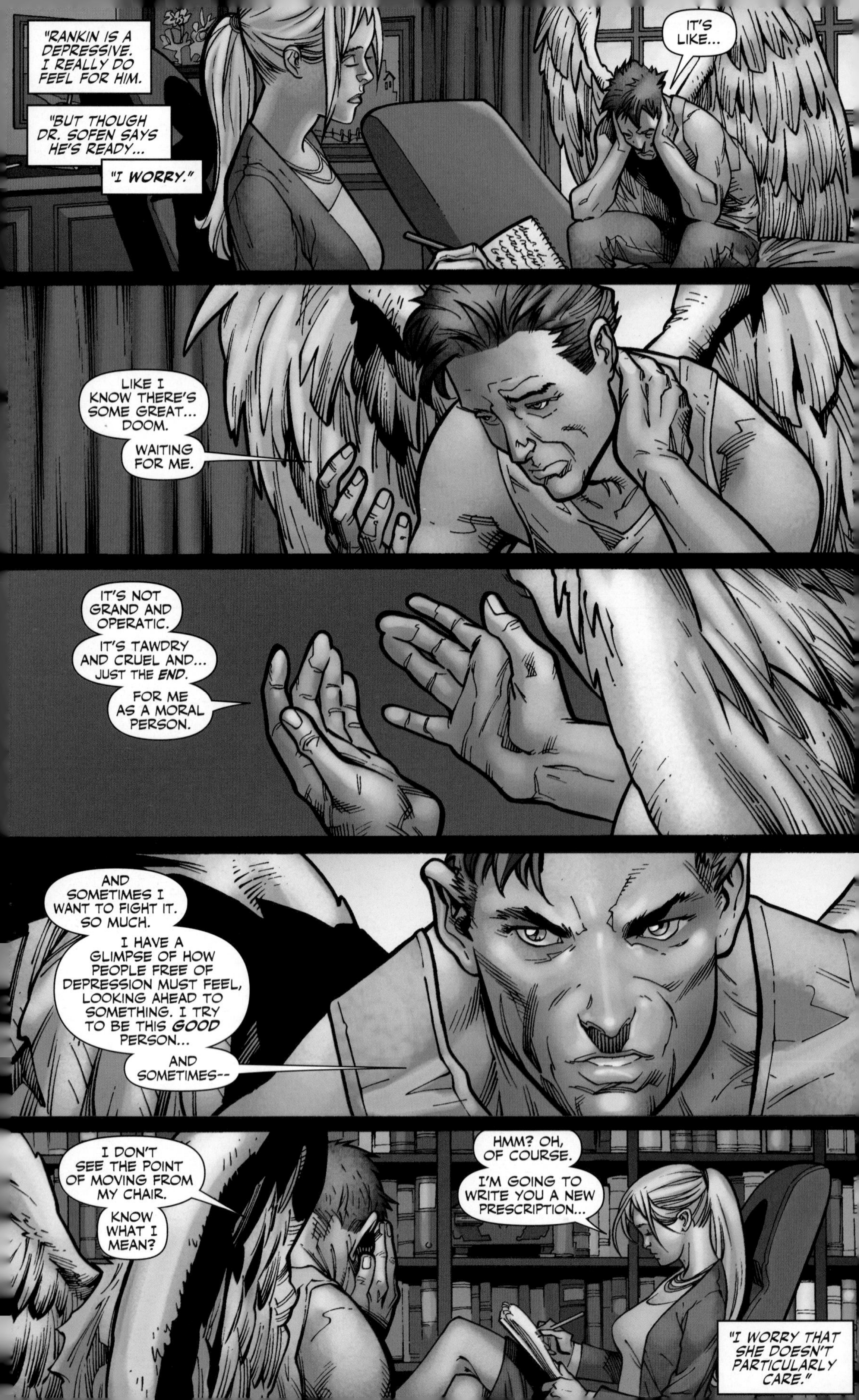

"RANKIN IS A DEPRESSIVE. I REALLY DO FEEL FOR HIM.
"BUT THOUGH DR. SOFEN SAYS HE'S READY...
"I *WORRY*."
IT'S LIKE...
LIKE I KNOW THERE'S SOME GREAT... DOOM.
WAITING FOR ME.
IT'S NOT GRAND AND OPERATIC.
IT'S TAWDRY AND CRUEL AND... JUST THE *END*.
FOR ME AS A MORAL PERSON.
AND SOMETIMES I WANT TO FIGHT IT. SO MUCH.
I HAVE A GLIMPSE OF HOW PEOPLE FREE OF DEPRESSION MUST FEEL, LOOKING AHEAD TO SOMETHING. I TRY TO BE THIS *GOOD* PERSON...
AND SOMETIMES--
I DON'T SEE THE POINT OF MOVING FROM MY CHAIR.
KNOW WHAT I MEAN?
HMM? OH, OF COURSE.
I'M GOING TO WRITE YOU A NEW PRESCRIPTION...
"I WORRY THAT SHE DOESN'T PARTICULARLY CARE."

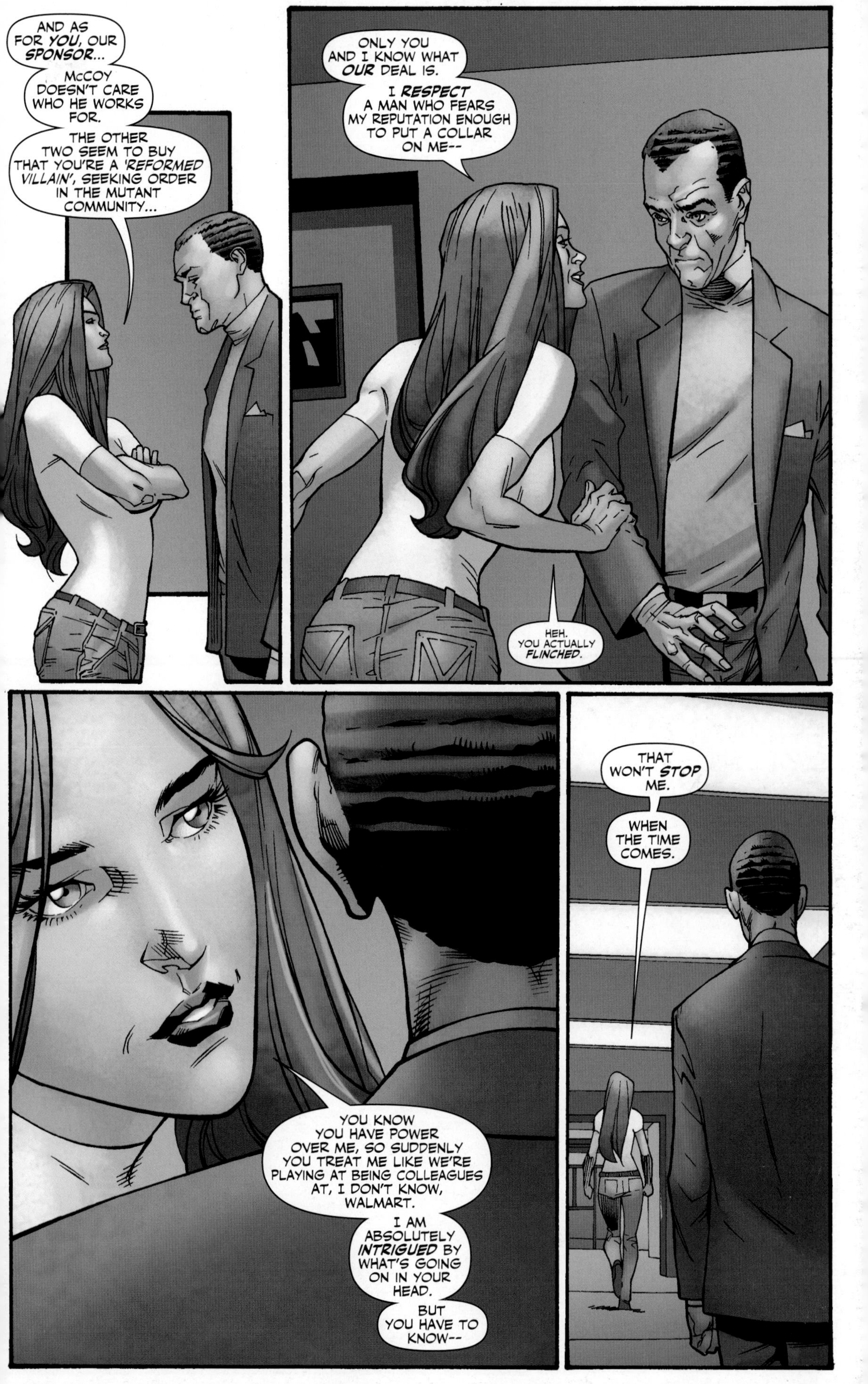
AND AS FOR *YOU*, OUR *SPONSOR*...
McCOY DOESN'T CARE WHO HE WORKS FOR.
THE OTHER TWO SEEM TO BUY THAT YOU'RE A *'REFORMED VILLAIN'*, SEEKING ORDER IN THE MUTANT COMMUNITY...
ONLY YOU AND I KNOW WHAT *OUR* DEAL IS.
I *RESPECT* A MAN WHO FEARS MY REPUTATION ENOUGH TO PUT A COLLAR ON ME--
HEH. YOU ACTUALLY *FLINCHED*.
YOU KNOW YOU HAVE POWER OVER ME, SO SUDDENLY YOU TREAT ME LIKE WE'RE PLAYING AT BEING COLLEAGUES AT, I DON'T KNOW, WALMART.
I AM ABSOLUTELY *INTRIGUED* BY WHAT'S GOING ON IN YOUR HEAD.
BUT YOU HAVE TO KNOW--
THAT WON'T *STOP* ME.
WHEN THE TIME COMES.

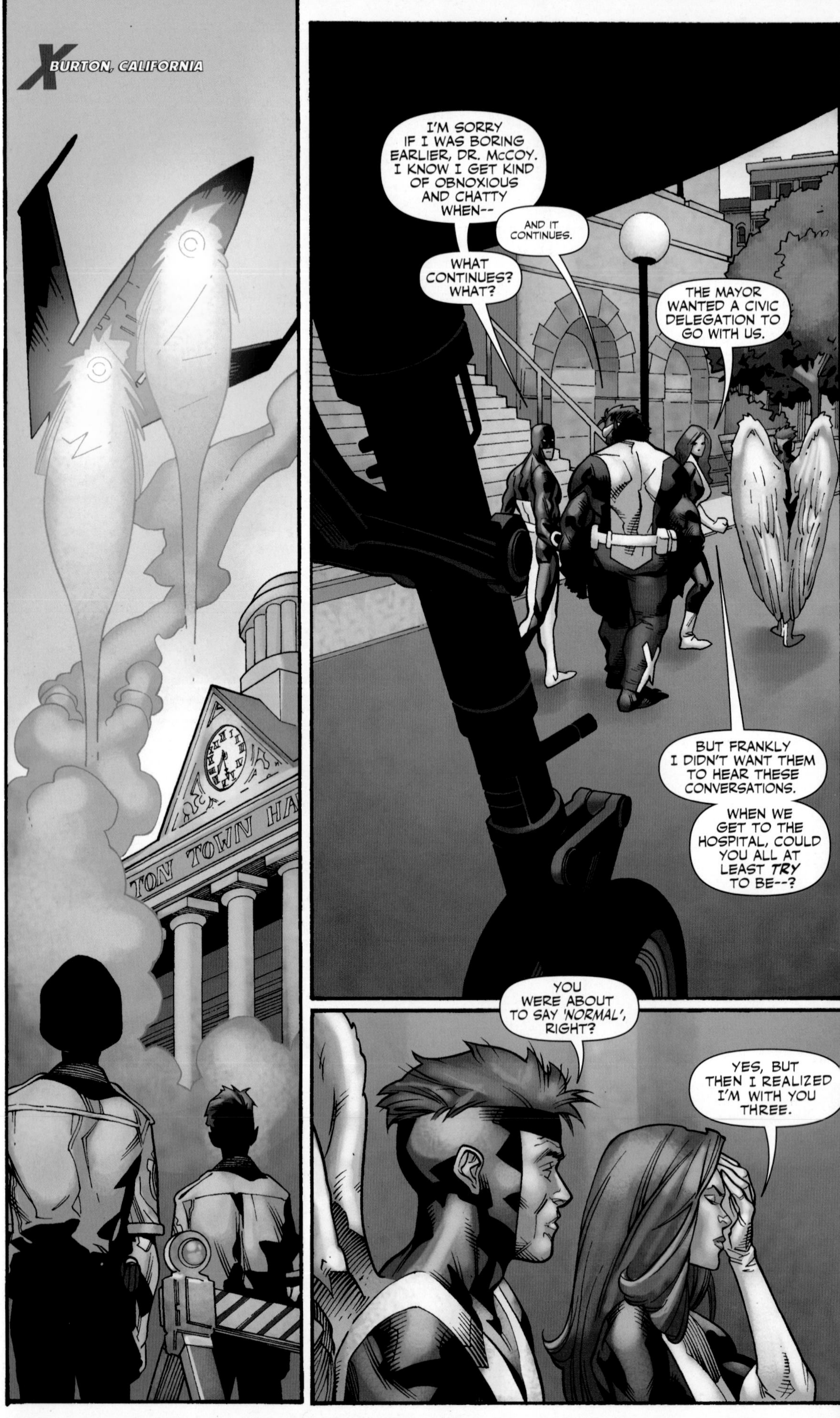
BURTON, CALIFORNIA
TON TOWN HA
I'M SORRY IF I WAS BORING EARLIER, DR. McCOY. I KNOW I GET KIND OF OBNOXIOUS AND CHATTY WHEN--
AND IT CONTINUES.
WHAT CONTINUES? WHAT?
THE MAYOR WANTED A CIVIC DELEGATION TO GO WITH US.
BUT FRANKLY I DIDN'T WANT THEM TO HEAR THESE CONVERSATIONS.
WHEN WE GET TO THE HOSPITAL, COULD YOU ALL AT LEAST *TRY* TO BE--?
YOU WERE ABOUT TO SAY *'NORMAL'*, RIGHT?
YES, BUT THEN I REALIZED I'M WITH YOU THREE.

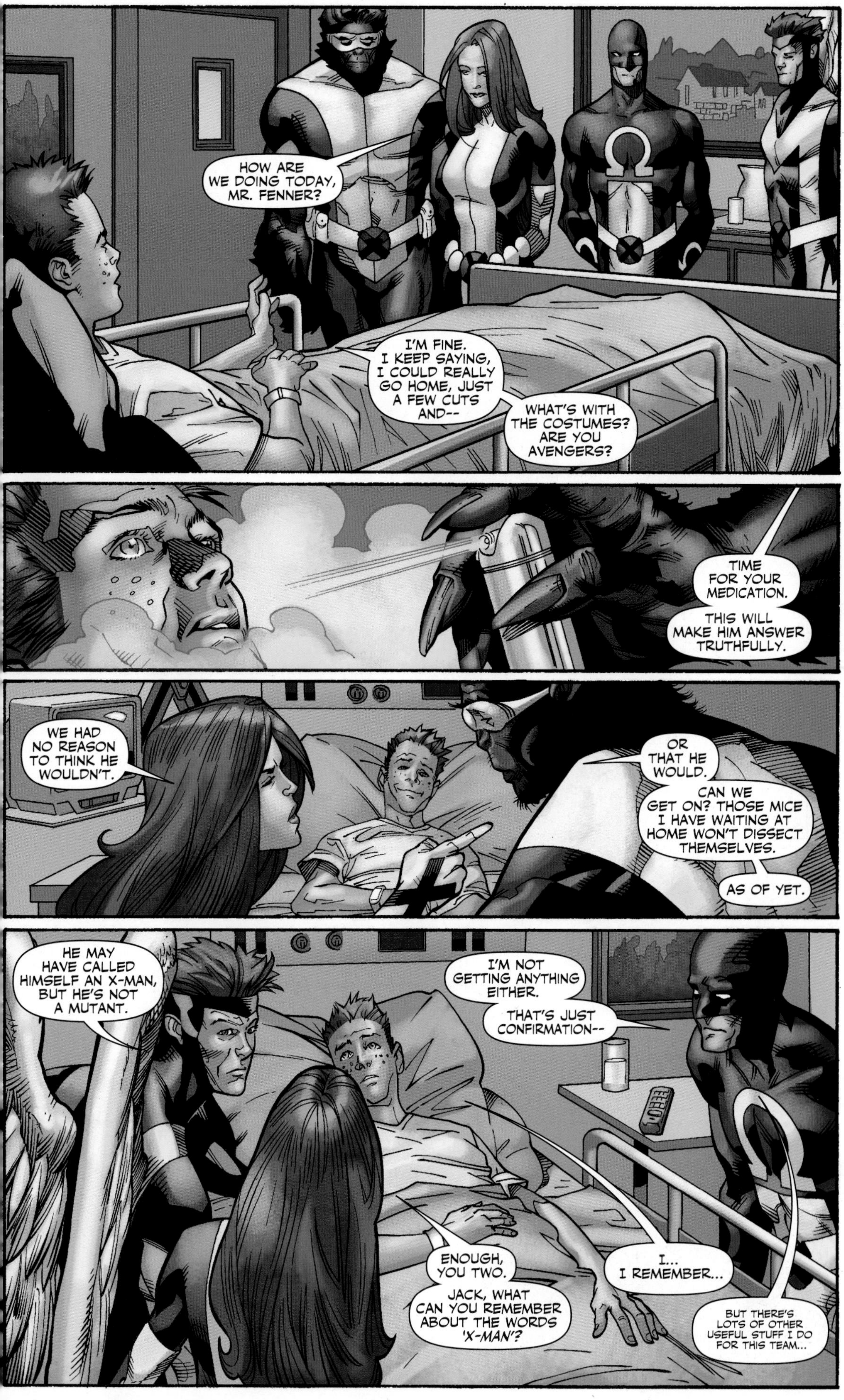
HOW ARE WE DOING TODAY, MR. FENNER?
I'M FINE. I KEEP SAYING, I COULD REALLY GO HOME, JUST A FEW CUTS AND--
WHAT'S WITH THE COSTUMES? ARE YOU AVENGERS?
TIME FOR YOUR MEDICATION.
THIS WILL MAKE HIM ANSWER TRUTHFULLY.
WE HAD NO REASON TO THINK HE WOULDN'T.
OR THAT HE WOULD.
CAN WE GET ON? THOSE MICE I HAVE WAITING AT HOME WON'T DISSECT THEMSELVES.
AS OF YET.
HE MAY HAVE CALLED HIMSELF AN X-MAN, BUT HE'S NOT A MUTANT.
I'M NOT GETTING ANYTHING EITHER.
THAT'S JUST CONFIRMATION--
ENOUGH, YOU TWO.
JACK, WHAT CAN YOU REMEMBER ABOUT THE WORDS 'X-MAN'?
I... I REMEMBER...
BUT THERE'S LOTS OF OTHER USEFUL STUFF I DO FOR THIS TEAM...

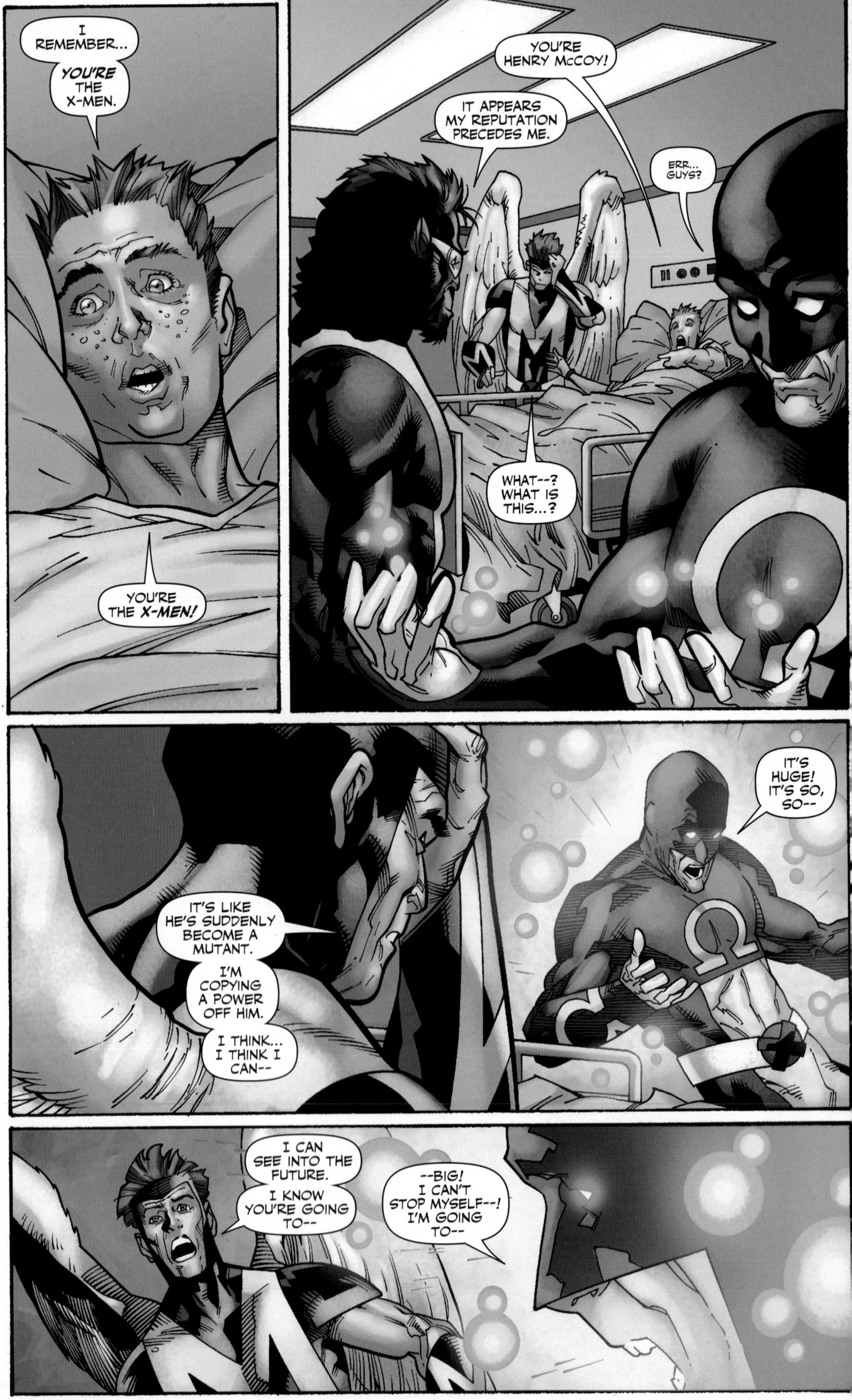

I REMEMBER...
YOU'RE THE X-MEN.
YOU'RE THE X-MEN!
YOU'RE HENRY McCOY!
IT APPEARS MY REPUTATION PRECEDES ME.
ERR... GUYS?
WHAT--? WHAT IS THIS...?
IT'S LIKE HE'S SUDDENLY BECOME A MUTANT.
I'M COPYING A POWER OFF HIM.
I THINK... I THINK I CAN--
IT'S HUGE! IT'S SO, SO--
I CAN SEE INTO THE FUTURE.
I KNOW YOU'RE GOING TO--
--BIG! I CAN'T STOP MYSELF--! I'M GOING TO--

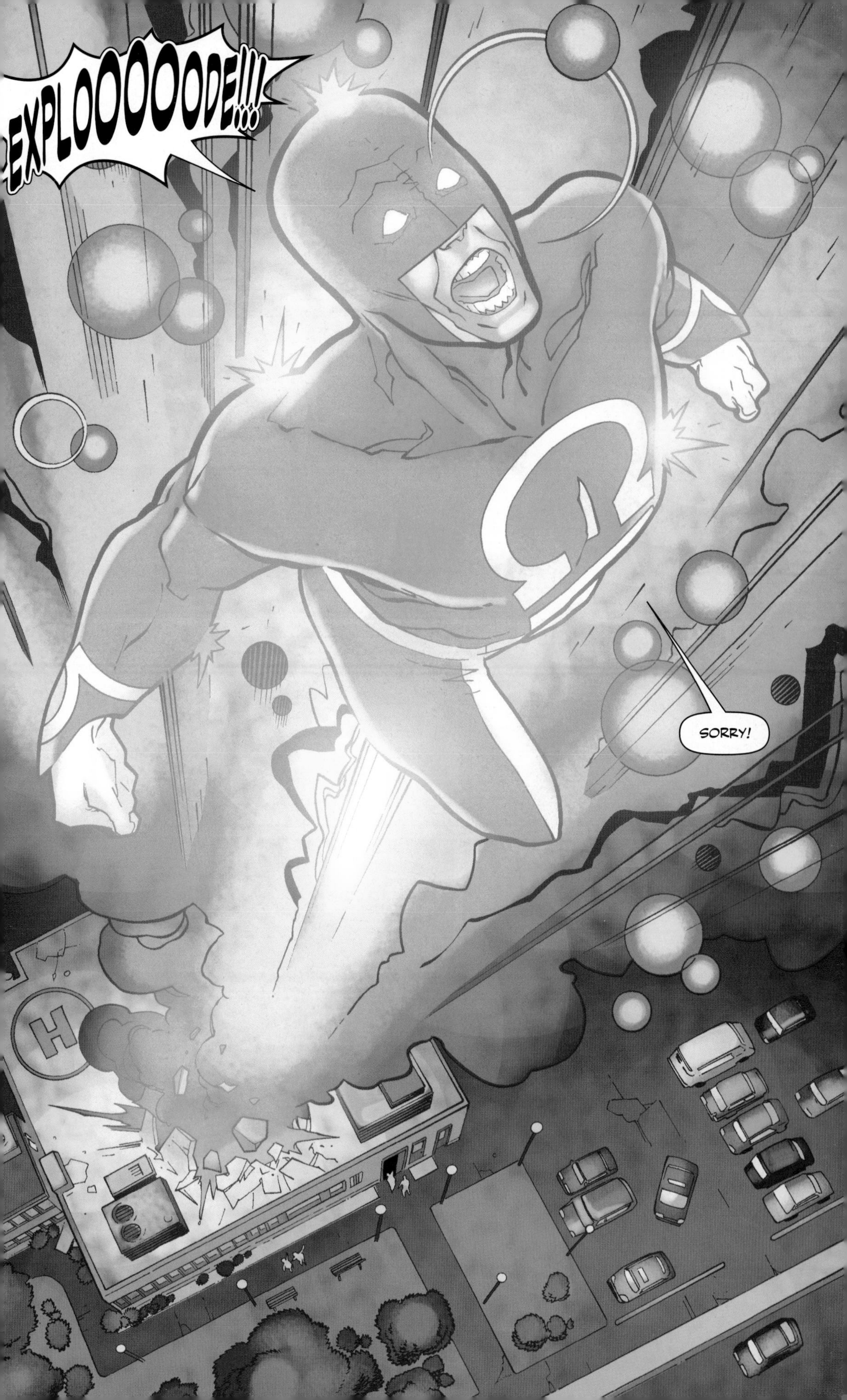
EXPLOOOOODE!!!
SORRY!

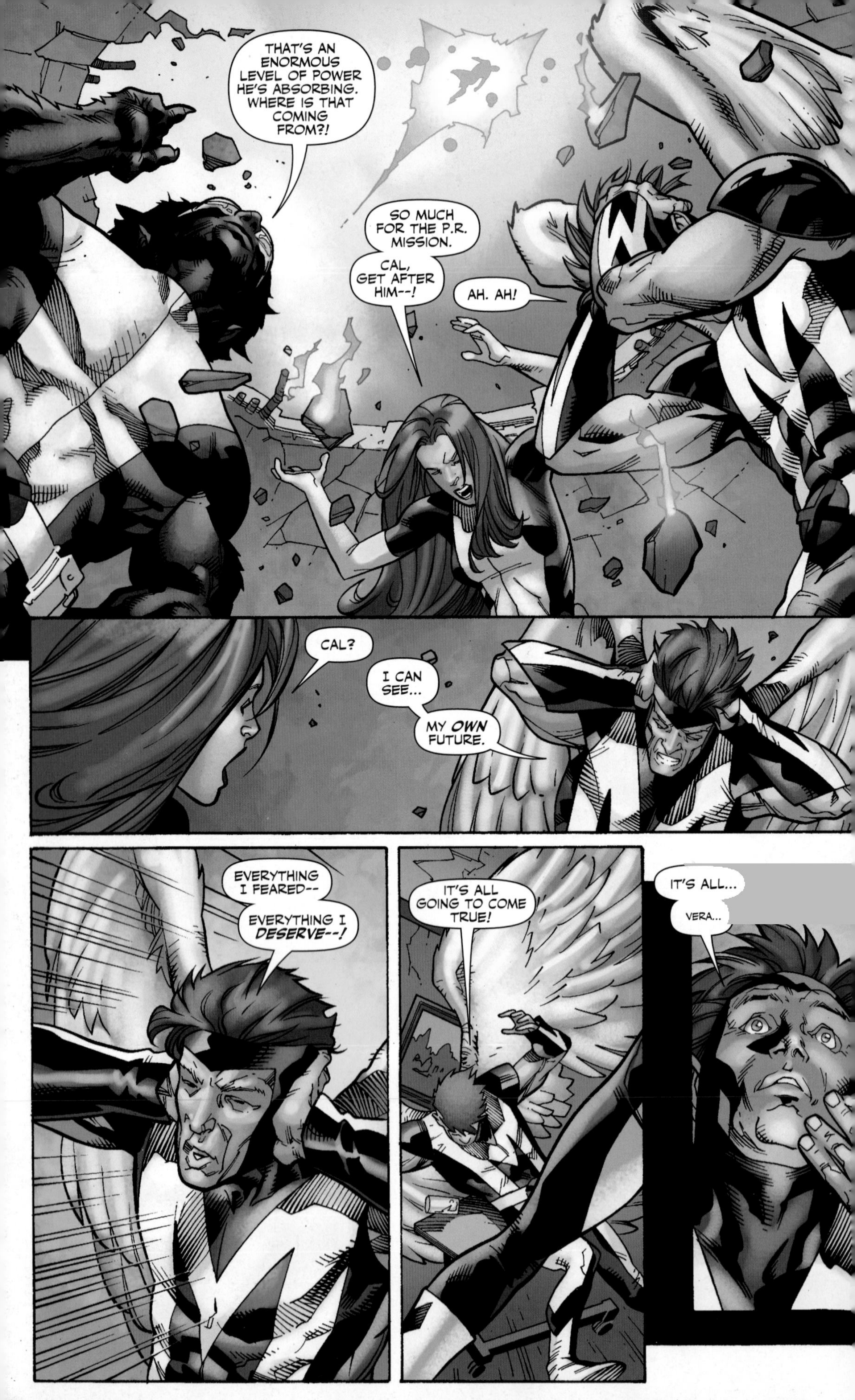
THAT'S AN ENORMOUS LEVEL OF POWER HE'S ABSORBING. WHERE IS THAT COMING FROM?!
SO MUCH FOR THE P.R. MISSION.
CAL, GET AFTER HIM--!
AH. AH!
CAL?
I CAN SEE...
MY OWN FUTURE.
EVERYTHING I FEARED--
EVERYTHING I DESERVE--!
IT'S ALL GOING TO COME TRUE!
IT'S ALL...
VERA...

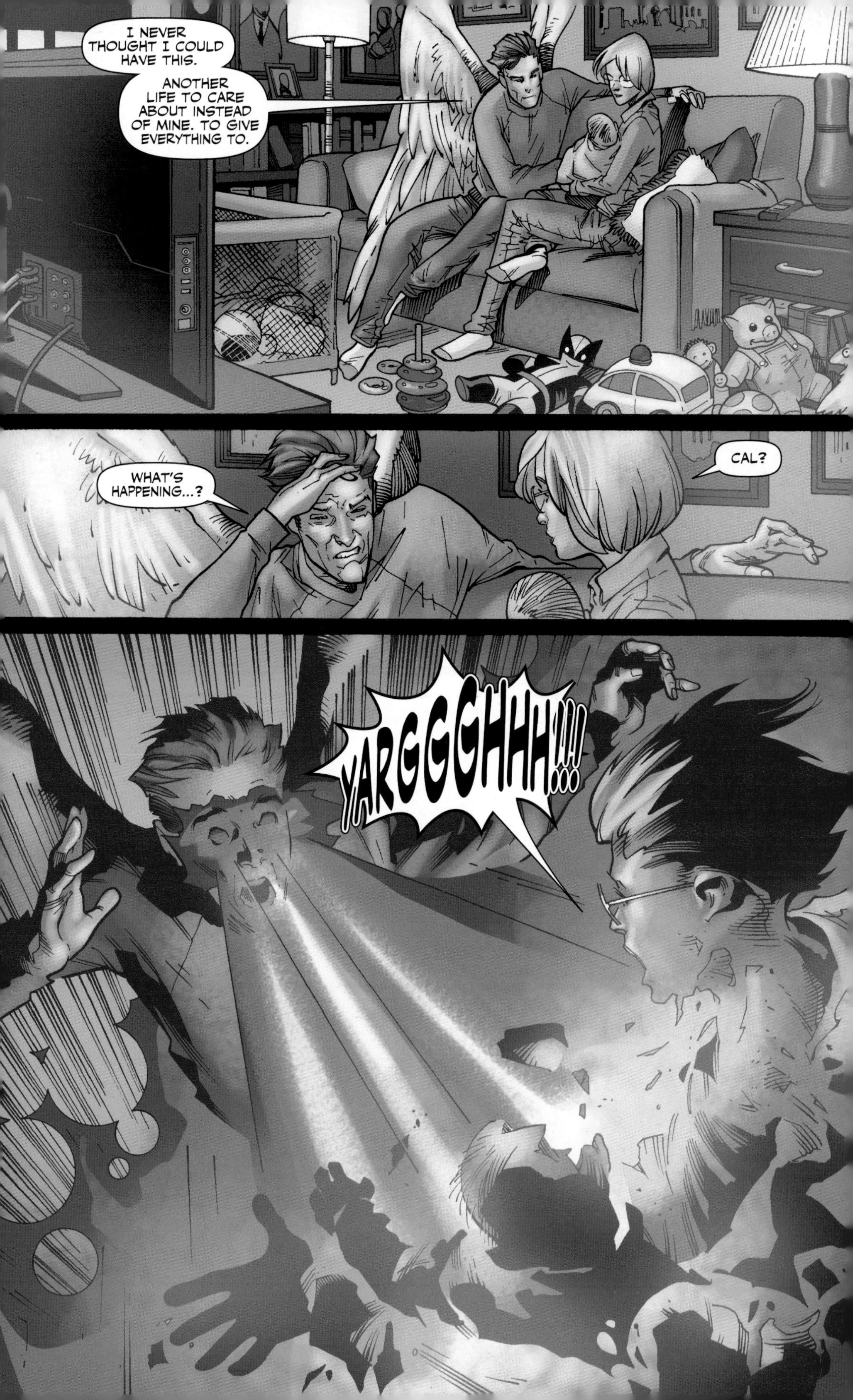
I NEVER THOUGHT I COULD HAVE THIS.
ANOTHER LIFE TO CARE ABOUT INSTEAD OF MINE. TO GIVE EVERYTHING TO.
WHAT'S HAPPENING...?
CAL?
YARGGGHHH!!!

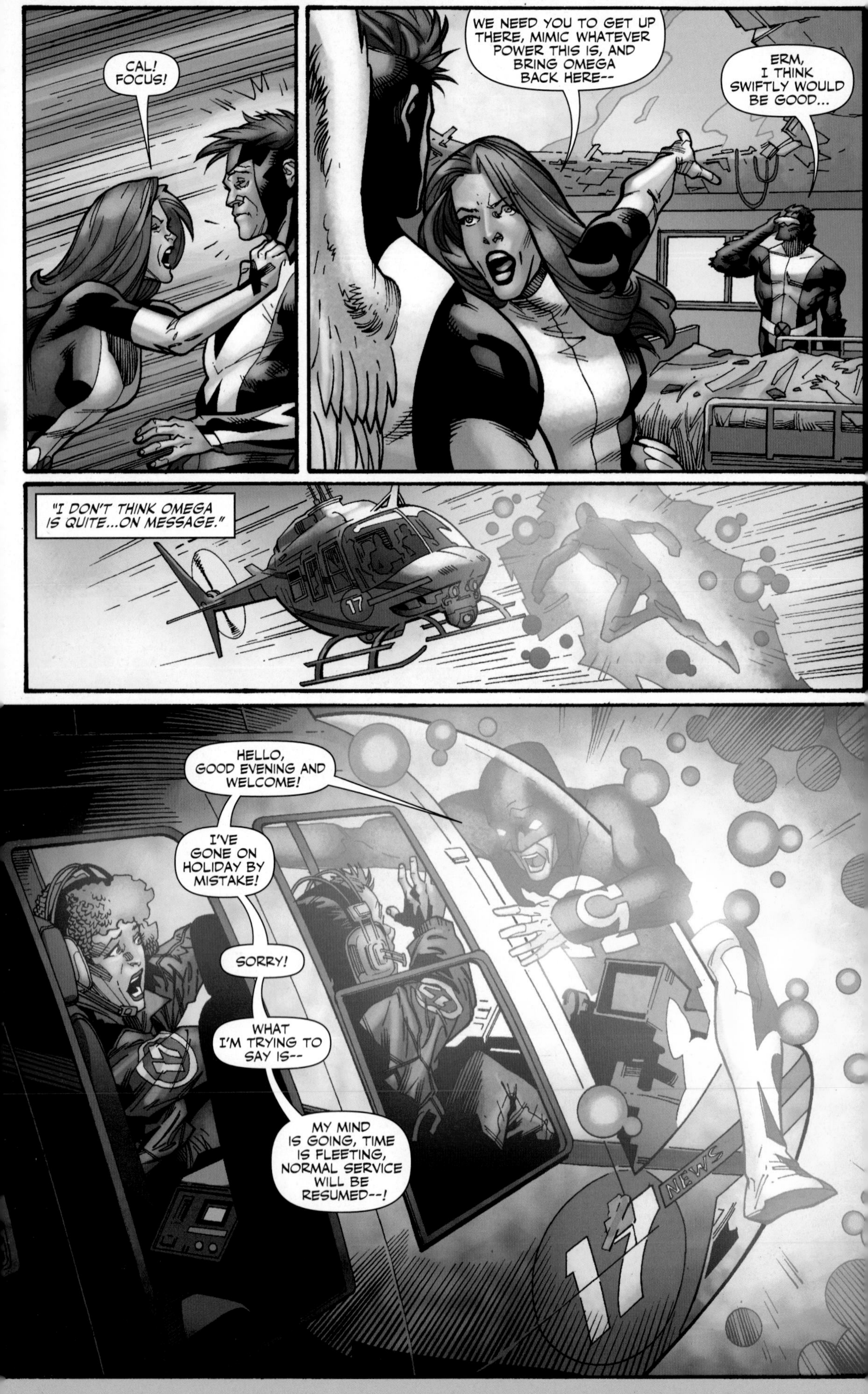
CAL! FOCUS!
WE NEED YOU TO GET UP THERE, MIMIC WHATEVER POWER THIS IS, AND BRING OMEGA BACK HERE--
ERM, I THINK SWIFTLY WOULD BE GOOD...
"I DON'T THINK OMEGA IS QUITE...ON MESSAGE."
17
HELLO, GOOD EVENING AND WELCOME!
I'VE GONE ON HOLIDAY BY MISTAKE!
SORRY!
WHAT I'M TRYING TO SAY IS--
MY MIND IS GOING, TIME IS FLEETING, NORMAL SERVICE WILL BE RESUMED--!
NEWS
17

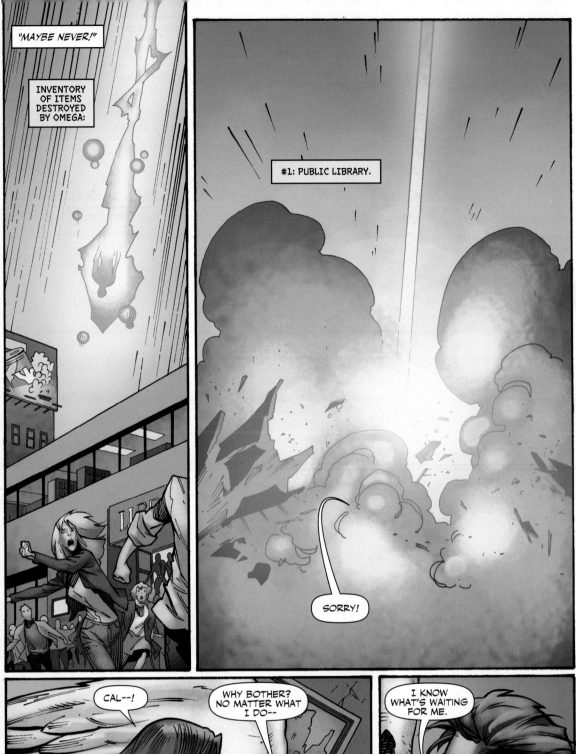

"MAYBE NEVER!"

INVENTORY OF ITEMS DESTROYED BY OMEGA:

#1: PUBLIC LIBRARY.

SORRY!

CAL--!

WHY BOTHER? NO MATTER WHAT I DO--

I KNOW WHAT'S WAITING FOR ME.

LET'S CUT TO THE CHASE, SHALL WE?

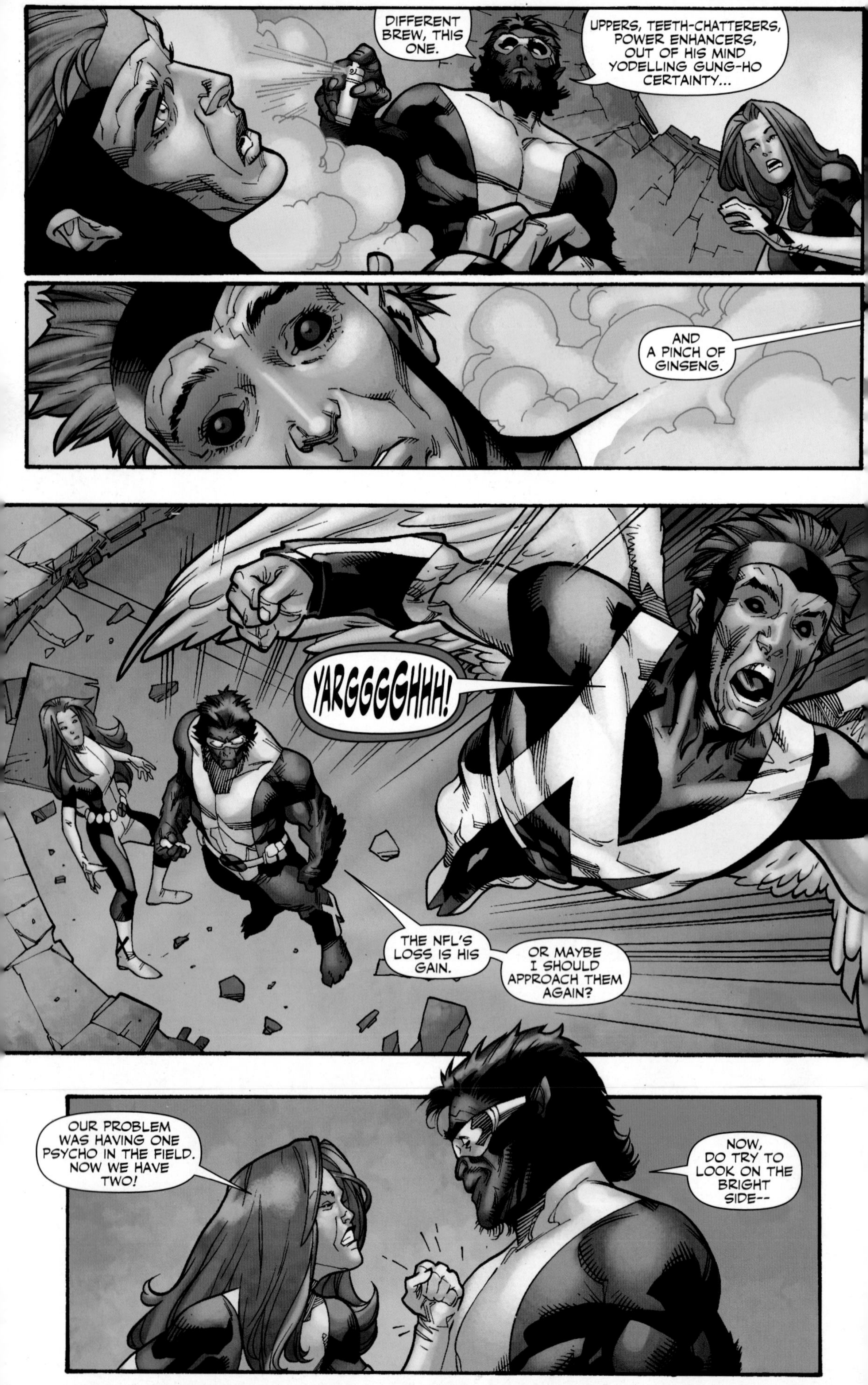

DIFFERENT BREW, THIS ONE.
UPPERS, TEETH-CHATTERERS, POWER ENHANCERS, OUT OF HIS MIND YODELLING GUNG-HO CERTAINTY...
AND A PINCH OF GINSENG.
YARGGGGHHH!
THE NFL'S LOSS IS HIS GAIN.
OR MAYBE I SHOULD APPROACH THEM AGAIN?
OUR PROBLEM WAS HAVING ONE PSYCHO IN THE FIELD. NOW WE HAVE TWO!
NOW, DO TRY TO LOOK ON THE BRIGHT SIDE--

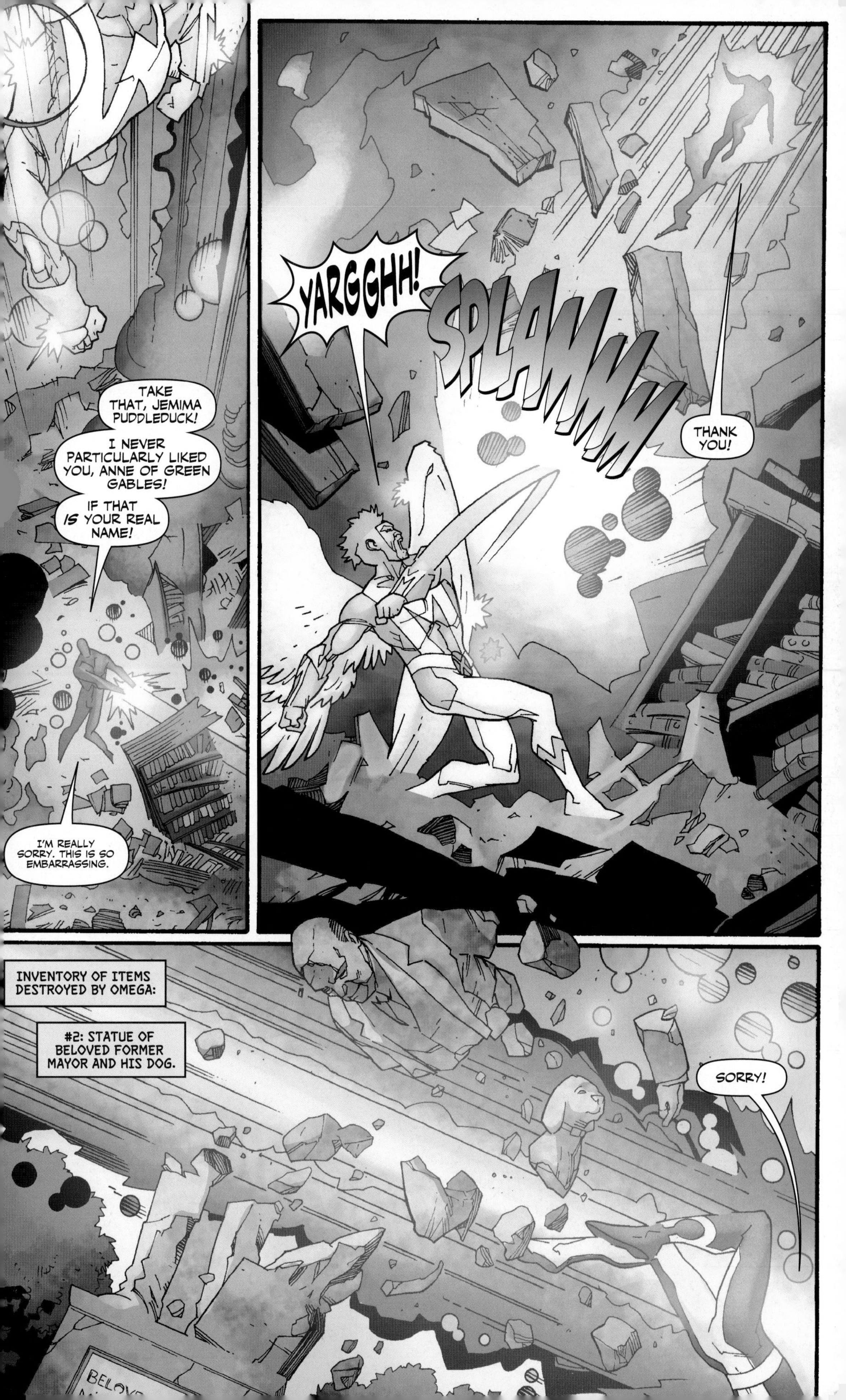

TAKE THAT, JEMIMA PUDDLEDUCK!
I NEVER PARTICULARLY LIKED YOU, ANNE OF GREEN GABLES!
IF THAT *IS* YOUR REAL NAME!
I'M REALLY SORRY. THIS IS SO EMBARRASSING.
YARGGHH!
SPLAMMM
THANK YOU!
INVENTORY OF ITEMS DESTROYED BY OMEGA:
#2: STATUE OF BELOVED FORMER MAYOR AND HIS DOG.
SORRY!

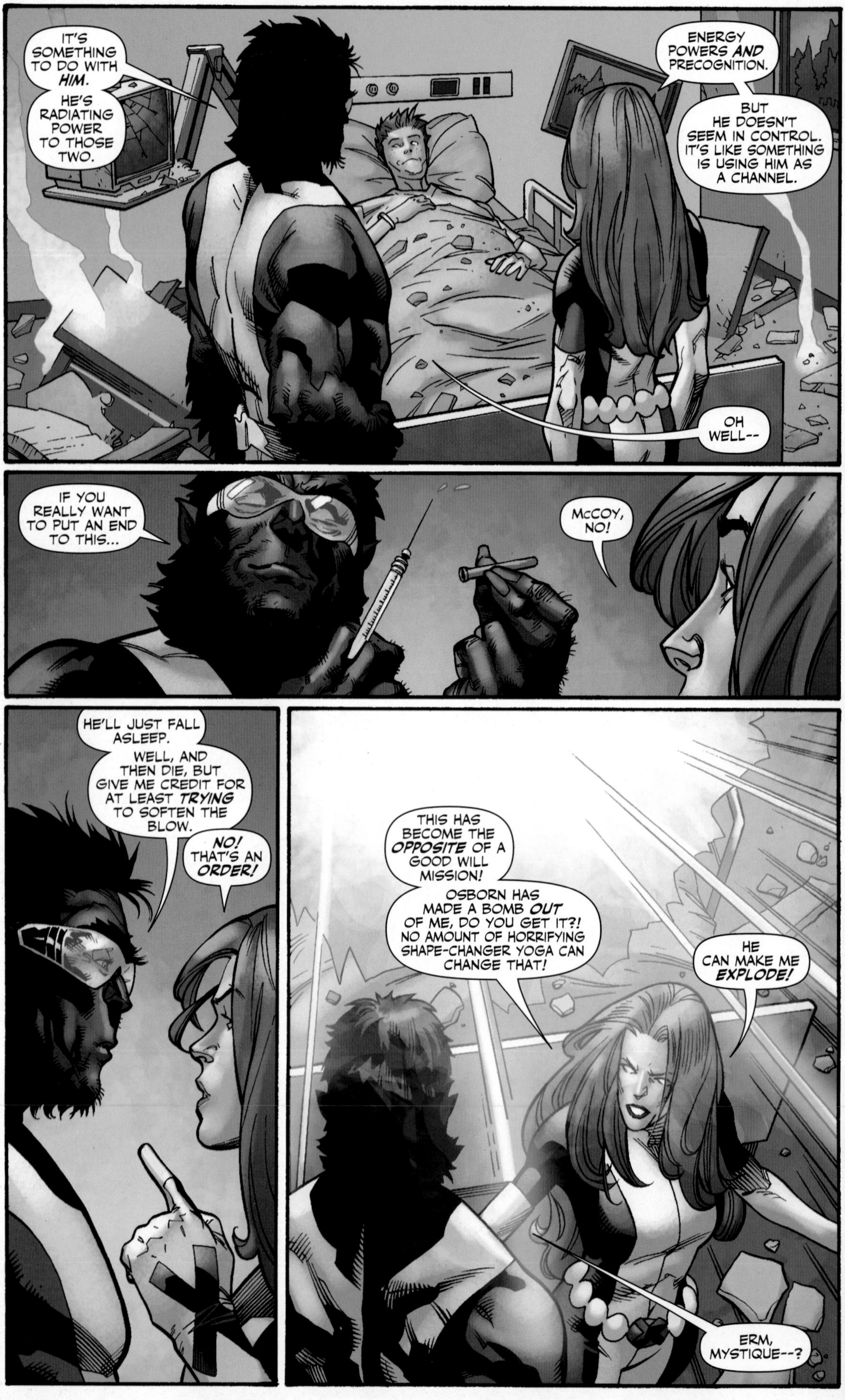
IT'S SOMETHING TO DO WITH *HIM*.
HE'S RADIATING POWER TO THOSE TWO.
ENERGY POWERS *AND* PRECOGNITION.
BUT HE DOESN'T SEEM IN CONTROL. IT'S LIKE SOMETHING IS USING HIM AS A CHANNEL.
OH WELL--
IF YOU REALLY WANT TO PUT AN END TO THIS...
McCOY, NO!
HE'LL JUST FALL ASLEEP.
WELL, AND THEN DIE, BUT GIVE ME CREDIT FOR AT LEAST *TRYING* TO SOFTEN THE BLOW.
NO! THAT'S AN *ORDER!*
THIS HAS BECOME THE *OPPOSITE* OF A GOOD WILL MISSION!
OSBORN HAS MADE A BOMB *OUT* OF ME, DO YOU GET IT?! NO AMOUNT OF HORRIFYING SHAPE-CHANGER YOGA CAN CHANGE THAT!
HE CAN MAKE ME *EXPLODE!*
ERM, MYSTIQUE--?

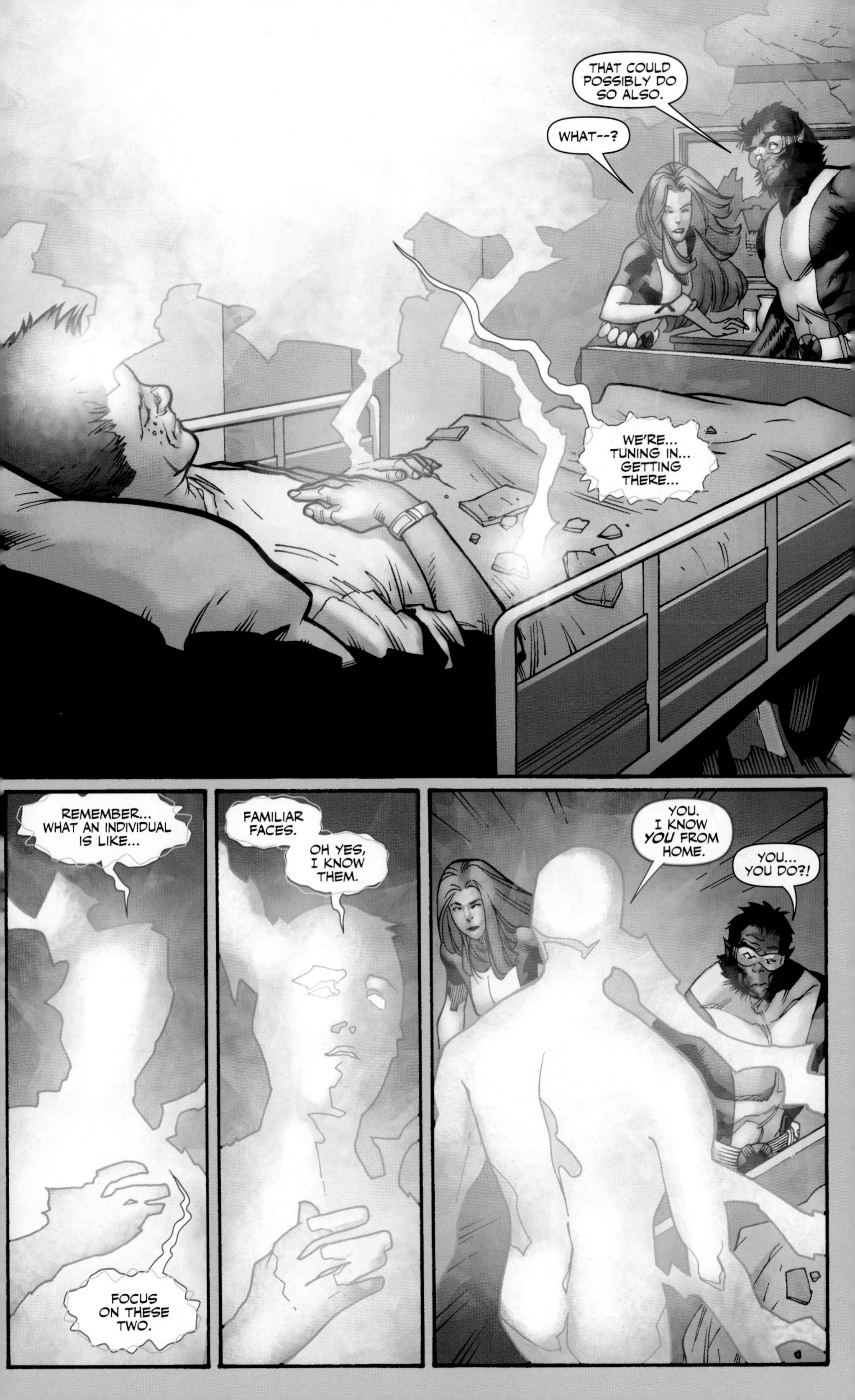
THAT COULD POSSIBLY DO SO ALSO.
WHAT--?
WE'RE... TUNING IN... GETTING THERE...
REMEMBER... WHAT AN INDIVIDUAL IS LIKE...
FOCUS ON THESE TWO.
FAMILIAR FACES.
OH YES, I KNOW THEM.
YOU. I KNOW *YOU* FROM HOME.
YOU... YOU DO?!

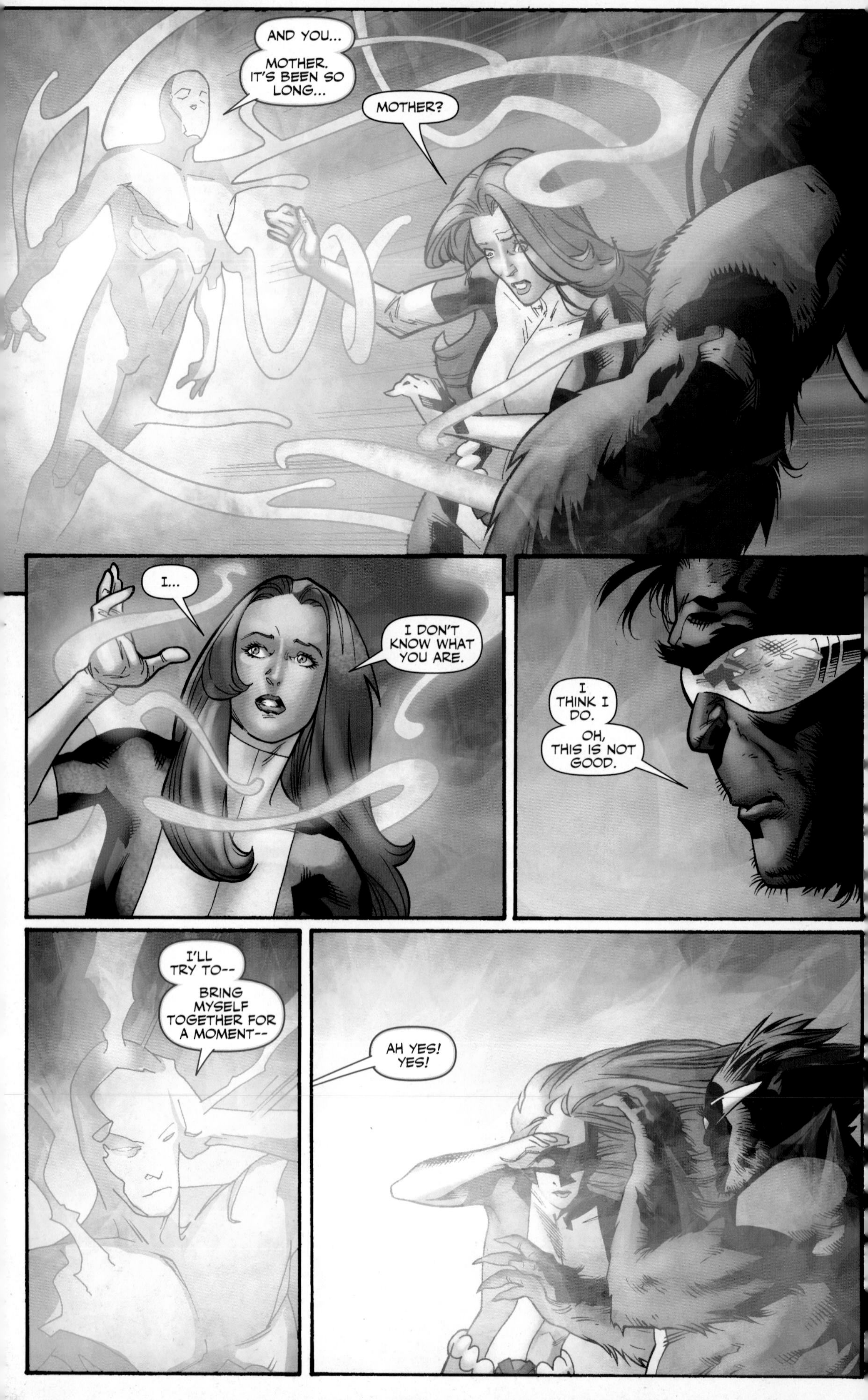
AND YOU...
MOTHER. IT'S BEEN SO LONG...
MOTHER?
I...
I DON'T KNOW WHAT YOU ARE.
I THINK I DO.
OH, THIS IS NOT GOOD.
I'LL TRY TO--
BRING MYSELF TOGETHER FOR A MOMENT--
AH YES! YES!

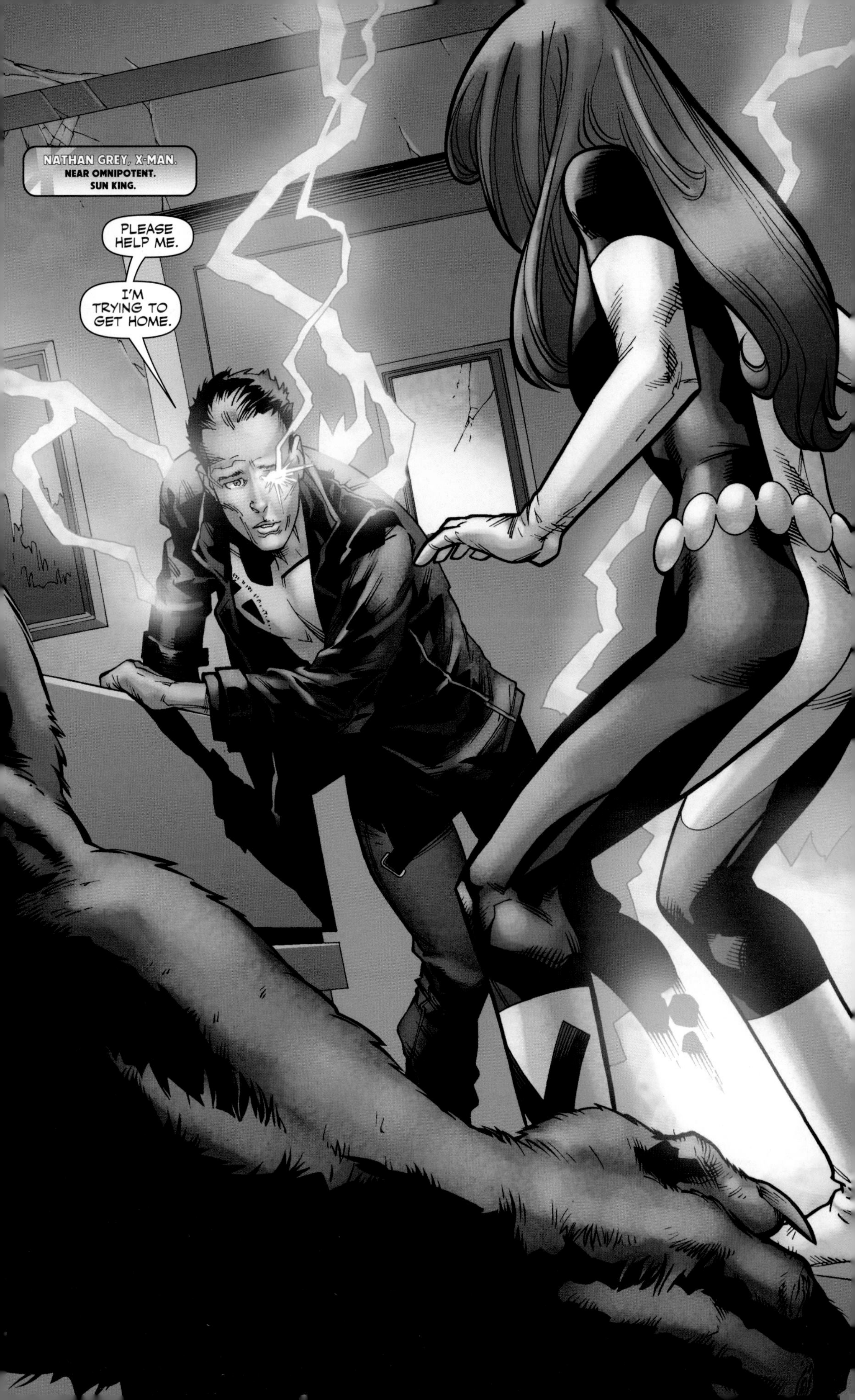
NATHAN GREY, X-MAN.
NEAR OMNIPOTENT.
SUN KING.
PLEASE HELP ME.
I'M TRYING TO GET HOME.

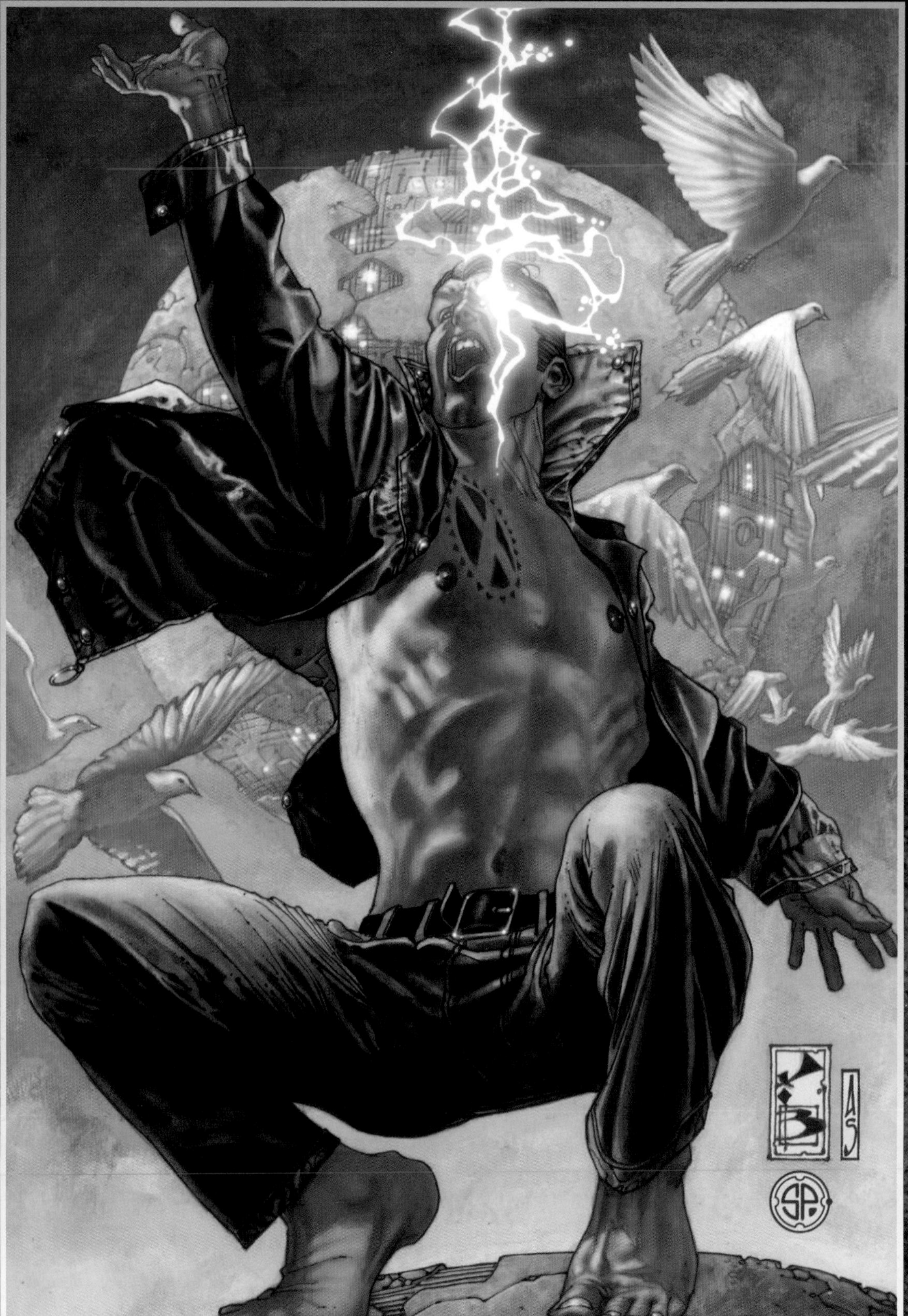

2

MOM? CAN YOU HEAR ME?
IT'S ME, NATE!
I'M TRYING TO GET HOME.
YOU HAVE TO KNOW...THAT MAN STANDING THERE--
THAT'S NOT THE REAL HENRY McCOY!
MYSTIQUE. SHAPESHIFTER. RUBY TUESDAY.
DARK BEAST. BESTIAL BIOLOGIST. THE MIDNIGHT RAMBLER.
NATHAN GREY, X-MAN. NEAR OMNIPOTENT. JUMPING JACK FLASH.
JOURNEY TO THE CENTER OF THE GOBLIN
Part Two

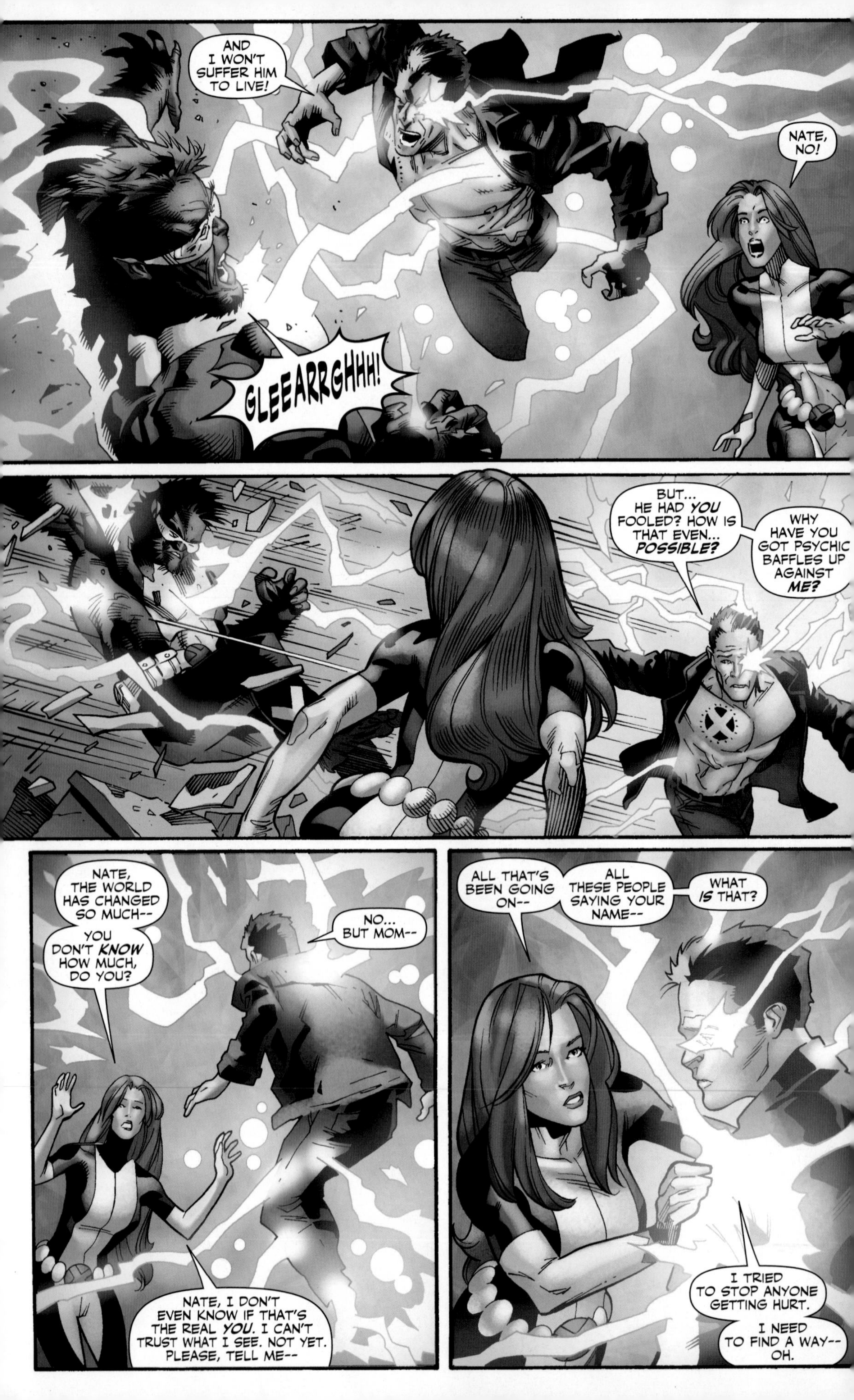
AND I WON'T SUFFER HIM TO LIVE!
NATE, NO!
GLEEARRGHHH!
BUT... HE HAD *YOU* FOOLED? HOW IS THAT EVEN... *POSSIBLE?*
WHY HAVE YOU GOT PSYCHIC BAFFLES UP AGAINST *ME?*
NATE, THE WORLD HAS CHANGED SO MUCH--
YOU DON'T *KNOW* HOW MUCH, DO YOU?
NO... BUT MOM--
NATE, I DON'T EVEN KNOW IF THAT'S THE REAL *YOU*. I CAN'T TRUST WHAT I SEE. NOT YET. PLEASE, TELL ME--
ALL THAT'S BEEN GOING ON--
ALL THESE PEOPLE SAYING YOUR NAME--
WHAT *IS* THAT?
I TRIED TO STOP ANYONE GETTING HURT.
I NEED TO FIND A WAY-- OH.

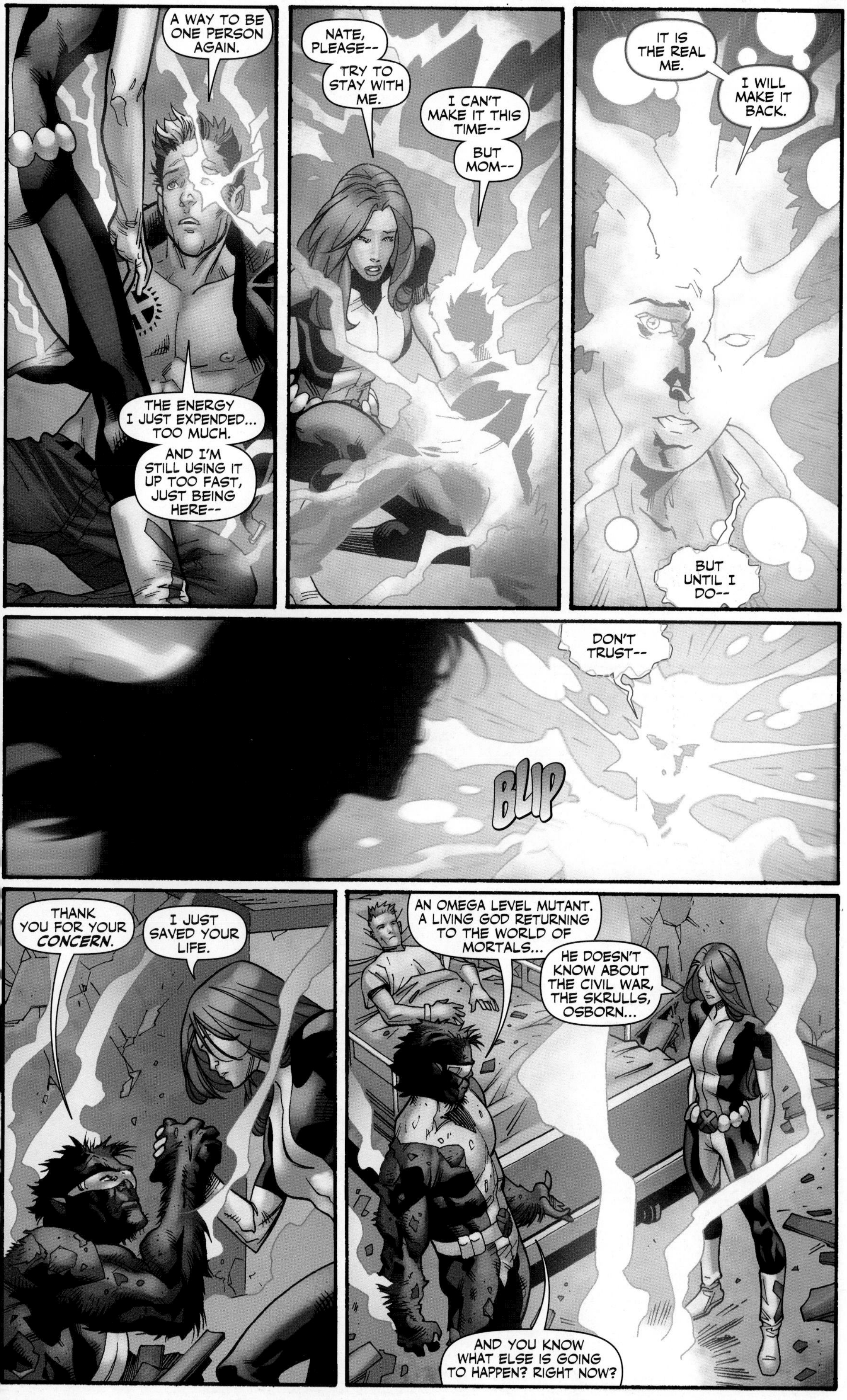
A WAY TO BE ONE PERSON AGAIN.
THE ENERGY I JUST EXPENDED... TOO MUCH.
AND I'M STILL USING IT UP TOO FAST, JUST BEING HERE--
NATE, PLEASE--
TRY TO STAY WITH ME.
I CAN'T MAKE IT THIS TIME--
BUT MOM--
IT IS THE REAL ME.
I WILL MAKE IT BACK.
BUT UNTIL I DO--
DON'T TRUST--
BLIP
THANK YOU FOR YOUR CONCERN.
I JUST SAVED YOUR LIFE.
AN OMEGA LEVEL MUTANT. A LIVING GOD RETURNING TO THE WORLD OF MORTALS...
HE DOESN'T KNOW ABOUT THE CIVIL WAR, THE SKRULLS, OSBORN...
AND YOU KNOW WHAT ELSE IS GOING TO HAPPEN? RIGHT NOW?

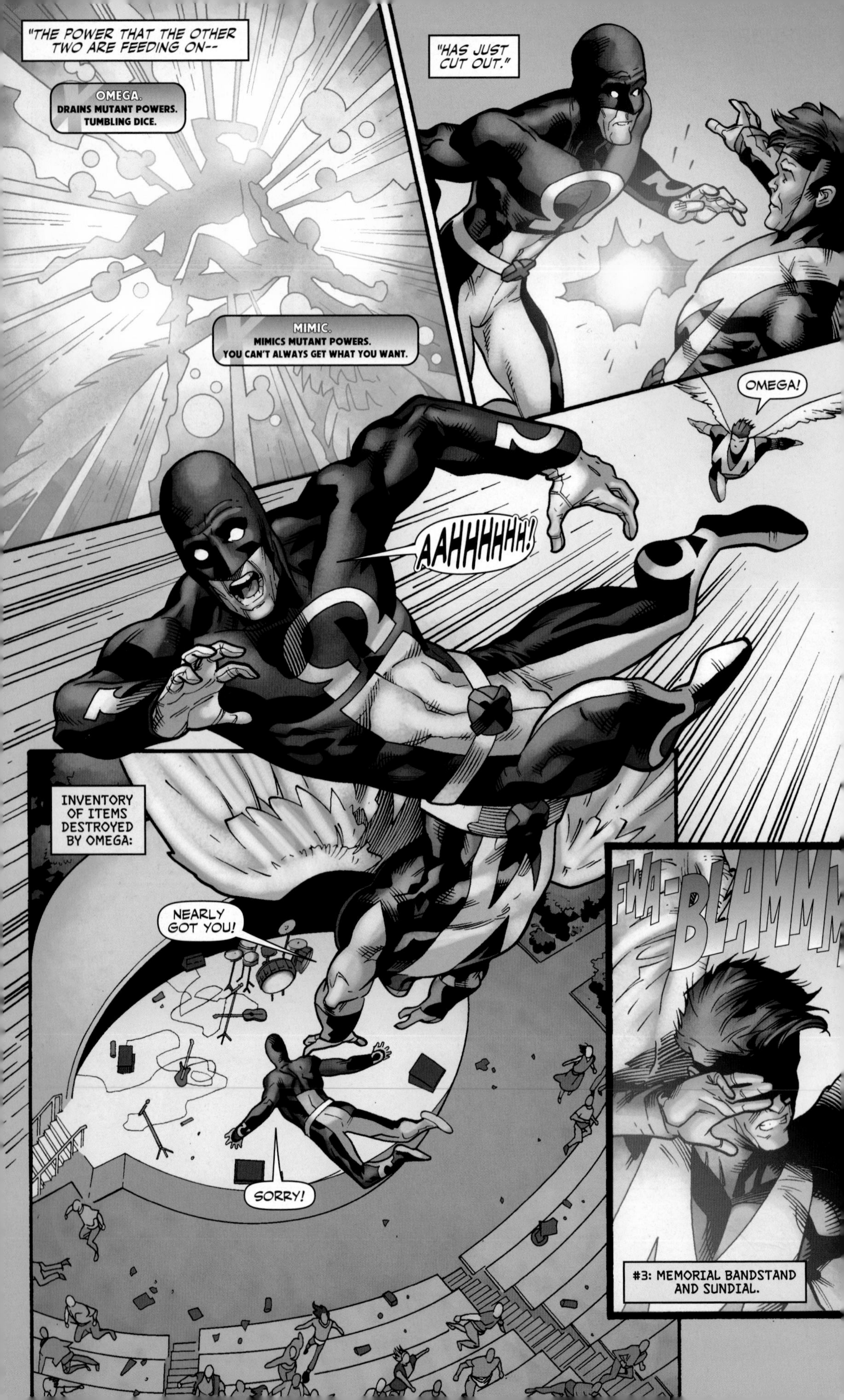
"THE POWER THAT THE OTHER TWO ARE FEEDING ON--
OMEGA.
DRAINS MUTANT POWERS.
TUMBLING DICE.
MIMIC.
MIMICS MUTANT POWERS.
YOU CAN'T ALWAYS GET WHAT YOU WANT.
"HAS JUST CUT OUT."
OMEGA!
AAHHHHHH!
INVENTORY OF ITEMS DESTROYED BY OMEGA:
NEARLY GOT YOU!
SORRY!
FWA-BLAMMM
#3: MEMORIAL BANDSTAND AND SUNDIAL.

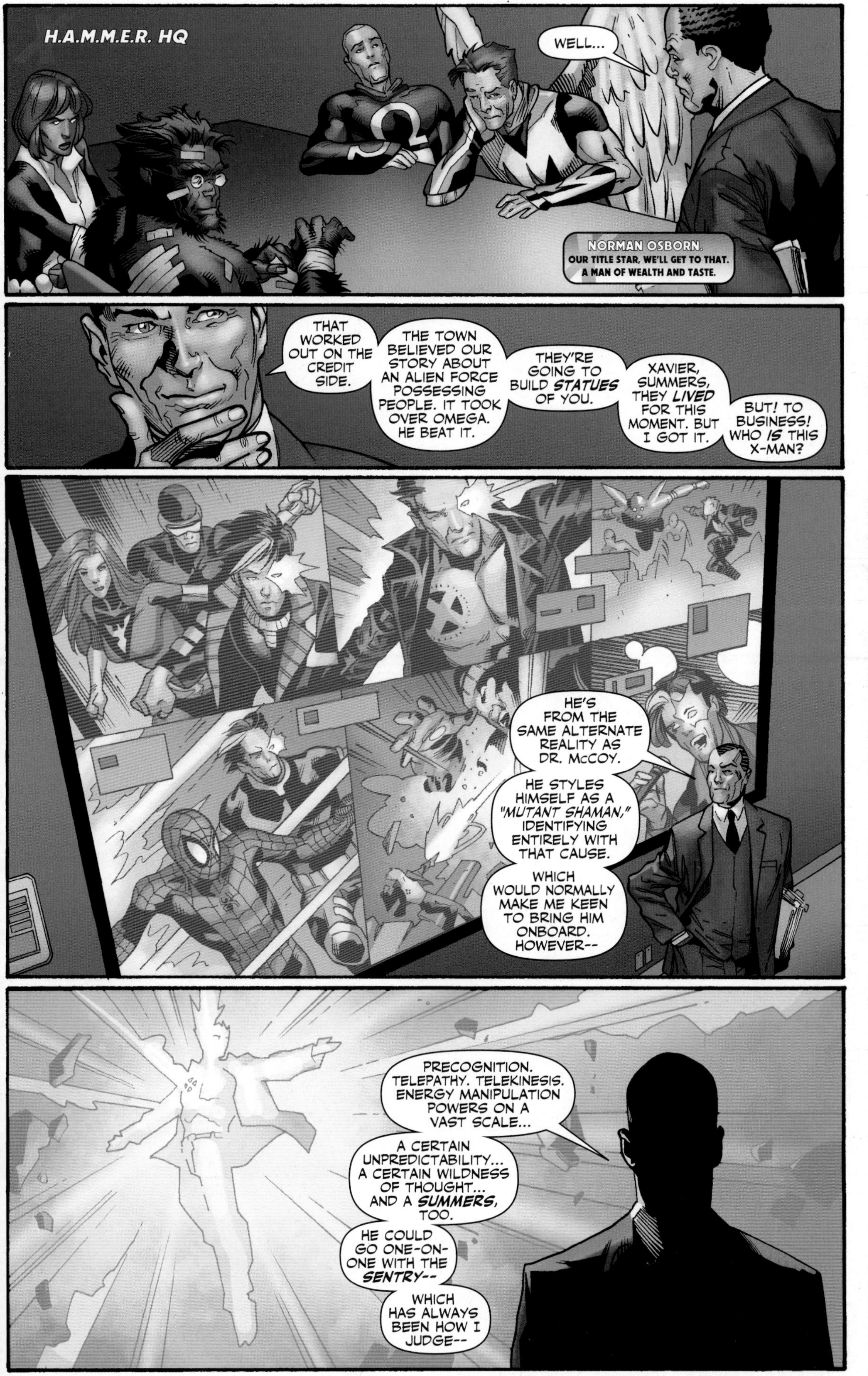
H.A.M.M.E.R. HQ
WELL...
NORMAN OSBORN. OUR TITLE STAR, WE'LL GET TO THAT. A MAN OF WEALTH AND TASTE.
THAT WORKED OUT ON THE CREDIT SIDE.
THE TOWN BELIEVED OUR STORY ABOUT AN ALIEN FORCE POSSESSING PEOPLE. IT TOOK OVER OMEGA. HE BEAT IT.
THEY'RE GOING TO BUILD STATUES OF YOU.
XAVIER, SUMMERS, THEY LIVED FOR THIS MOMENT. BUT I GOT IT.
BUT! TO BUSINESS! WHO IS THIS X-MAN?
HE'S FROM THE SAME ALTERNATE REALITY AS DR. McCOY.
HE STYLES HIMSELF AS A "MUTANT SHAMAN," IDENTIFYING ENTIRELY WITH THAT CAUSE.
WHICH WOULD NORMALLY MAKE ME KEEN TO BRING HIM ONBOARD. HOWEVER--
PRECOGNITION. TELEPATHY. TELEKINESIS. ENERGY MANIPULATION POWERS ON A VAST SCALE...
A CERTAIN UNPREDICTABILITY... A CERTAIN WILDNESS OF THOUGHT... AND A SUMMERS, TOO.
HE COULD GO ONE-ON-ONE WITH THE SENTRY--
WHICH HAS ALWAYS BEEN HOW I JUDGE--

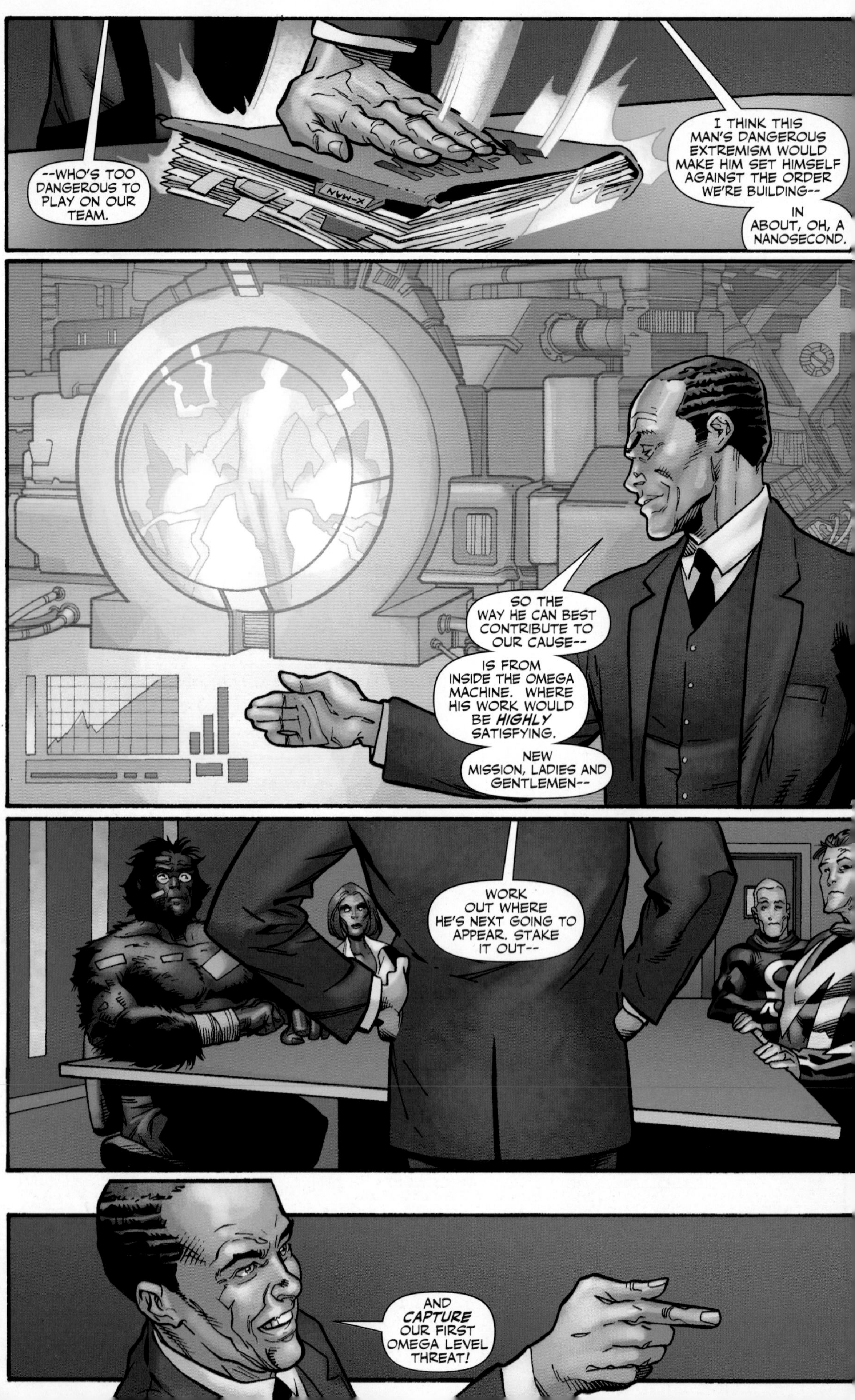
--WHO'S TOO DANGEROUS TO PLAY ON OUR TEAM.
X-MAN
I THINK THIS MAN'S DANGEROUS EXTREMISM WOULD MAKE HIM SET HIMSELF AGAINST THE ORDER WE'RE BUILDING--
IN ABOUT, OH, A NANOSECOND.
SO THE WAY HE CAN BEST CONTRIBUTE TO OUR CAUSE--
IS FROM INSIDE THE OMEGA MACHINE. WHERE HIS WORK WOULD BE HIGHLY SATISFYING.
NEW MISSION, LADIES AND GENTLEMEN--
WORK OUT WHERE HE'S NEXT GOING TO APPEAR. STAKE IT OUT--
AND CAPTURE OUR FIRST OMEGA LEVEL THREAT!

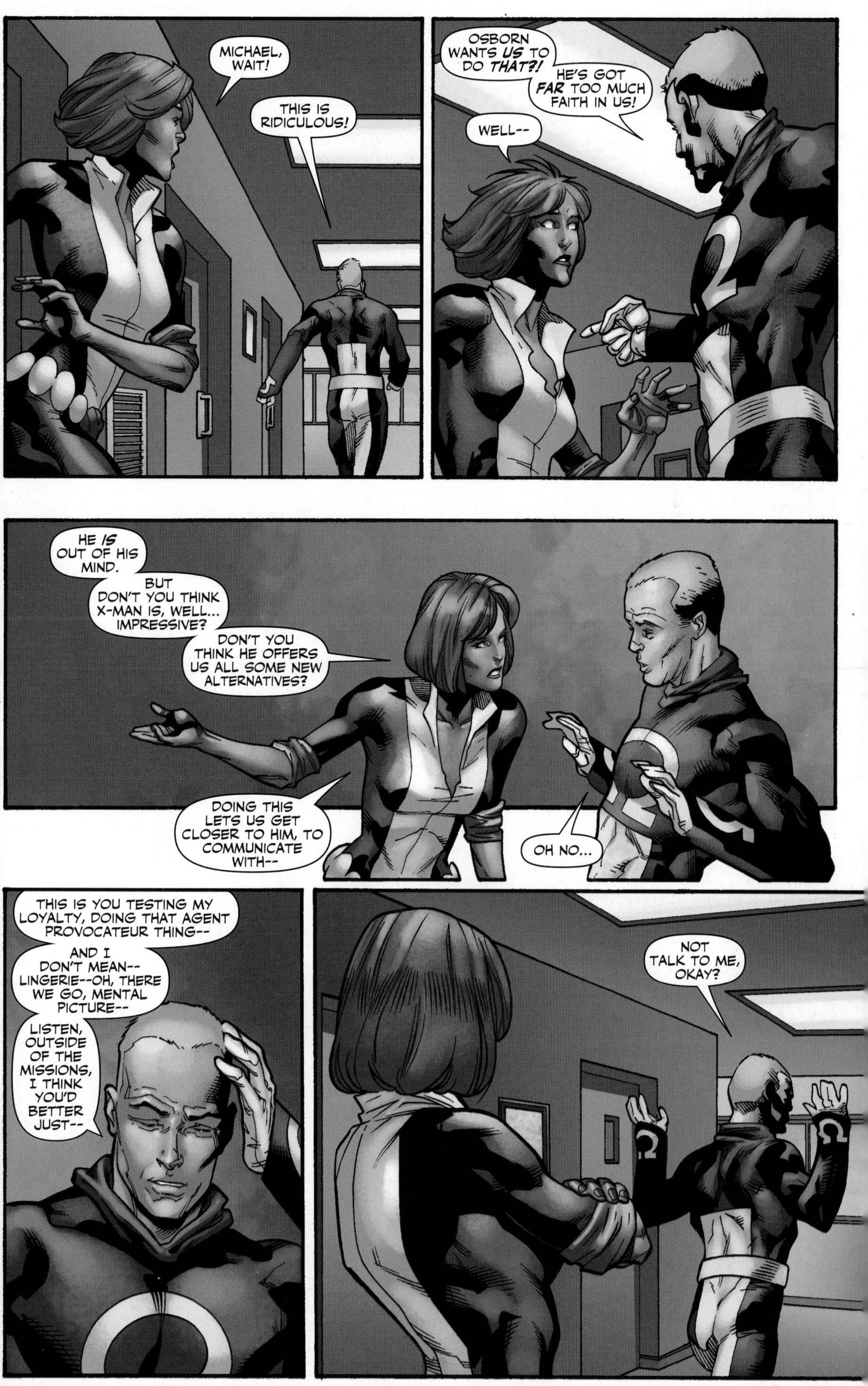
MICHAEL, WAIT!
THIS IS RIDICULOUS!
OSBORN WANTS US TO DO THAT?!
HE'S GOT FAR TOO MUCH FAITH IN US!
WELL--
HE IS OUT OF HIS MIND.
BUT DON'T YOU THINK X-MAN IS, WELL... IMPRESSIVE?
DON'T YOU THINK HE OFFERS US ALL SOME NEW ALTERNATIVES?
DOING THIS LETS US GET CLOSER TO HIM, TO COMMUNICATE WITH--
OH NO...
THIS IS YOU TESTING MY LOYALTY, DOING THAT AGENT PROVOCATEUR THING--
AND I DON'T MEAN-- LINGERIE--OH, THERE WE GO, MENTAL PICTURE--
LISTEN, OUTSIDE OF THE MISSIONS, I THINK YOU'D BETTER JUST--
NOT TALK TO ME, OKAY?

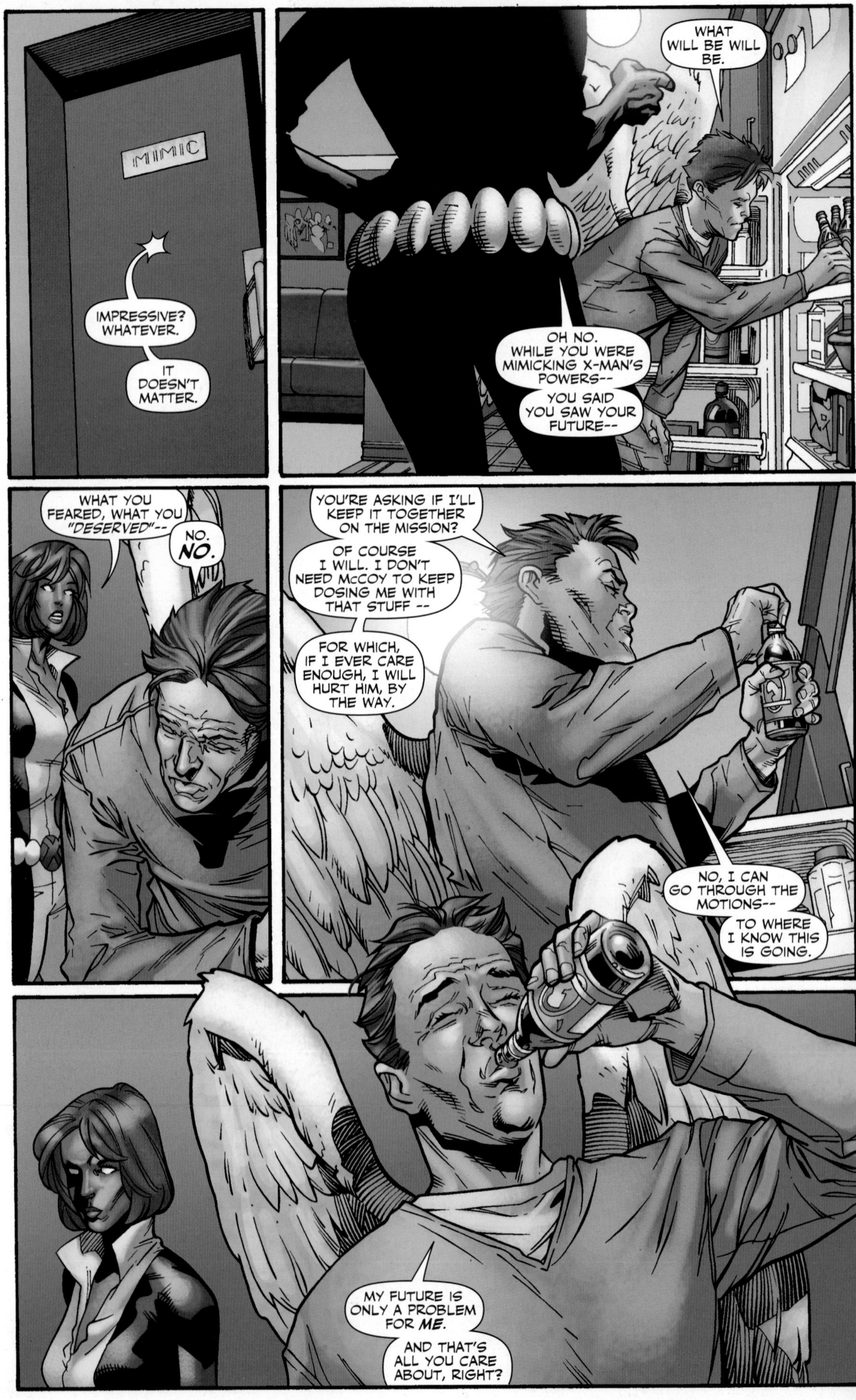
MIMIC
IMPRESSIVE? WHATEVER.
IT DOESN'T MATTER.
WHAT WILL BE WILL BE.
OH NO. WHILE YOU WERE MIMICKING X-MAN'S POWERS--
YOU SAID YOU SAW YOUR FUTURE--
WHAT YOU FEARED, WHAT YOU "DESERVED"--
NO. NO.
YOU'RE ASKING IF I'LL KEEP IT TOGETHER ON THE MISSION?
OF COURSE I WILL. I DON'T NEED McCOY TO KEEP DOSING ME WITH THAT STUFF --
FOR WHICH, IF I EVER CARE ENOUGH, I WILL HURT HIM, BY THE WAY.
NO, I CAN GO THROUGH THE MOTIONS--
TO WHERE I KNOW THIS IS GOING.
MY FUTURE IS ONLY A PROBLEM FOR ME.
AND THAT'S ALL YOU CARE ABOUT, RIGHT?

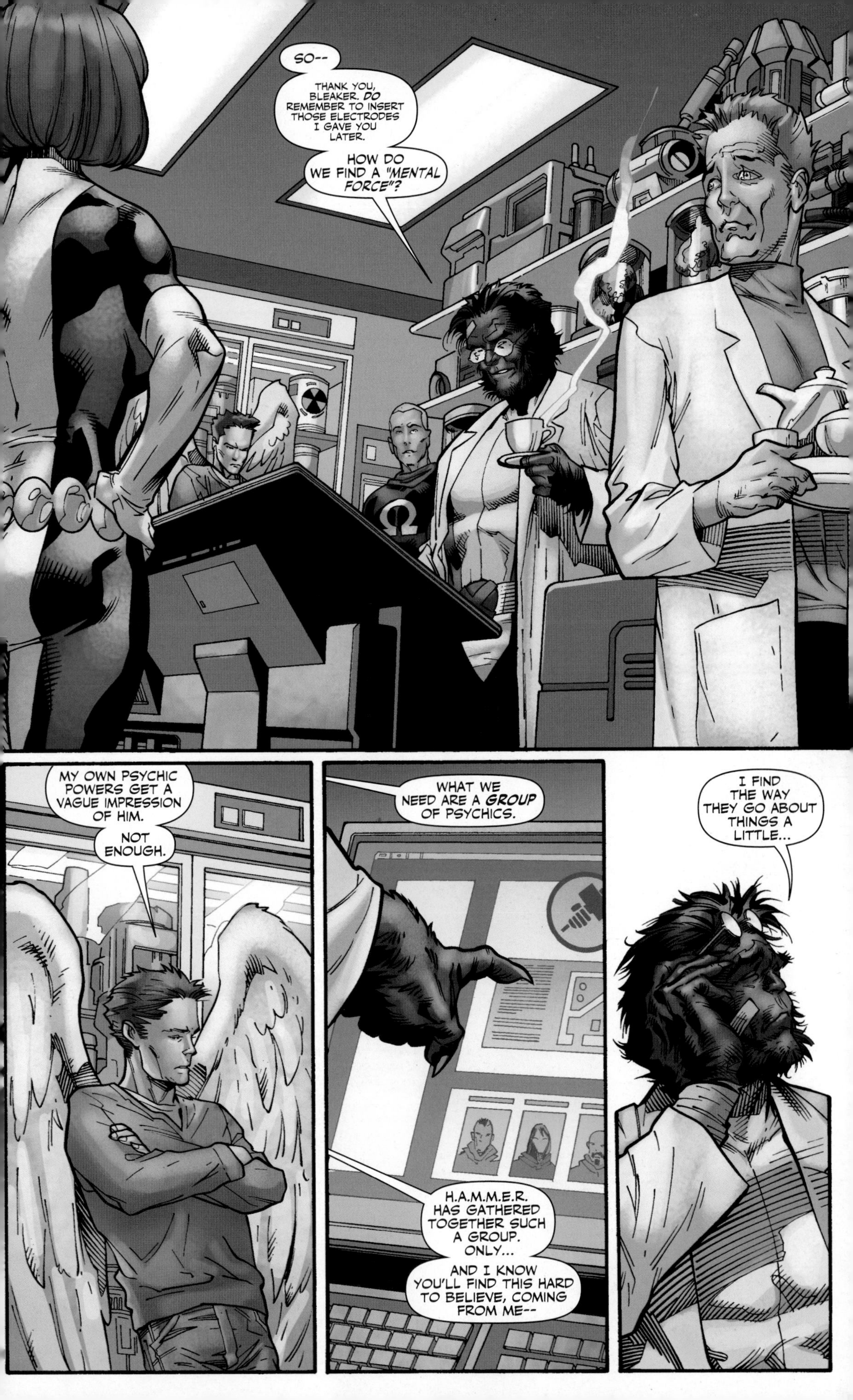
SO--
THANK YOU, BLEAKER. *DO* REMEMBER TO INSERT THOSE ELECTRODES I GAVE YOU LATER.
HOW DO WE FIND A *"MENTAL FORCE"*?
MY OWN PSYCHIC POWERS GET A VAGUE IMPRESSION OF HIM.
NOT ENOUGH.
WHAT WE NEED ARE A *GROUP* OF PSYCHICS.
H.A.M.M.E.R. HAS GATHERED TOGETHER SUCH A GROUP. ONLY...
AND I KNOW YOU'LL FIND THIS HARD TO BELIEVE, COMING FROM ME--
I FIND THE WAY THEY GO ABOUT THINGS A LITTLE...

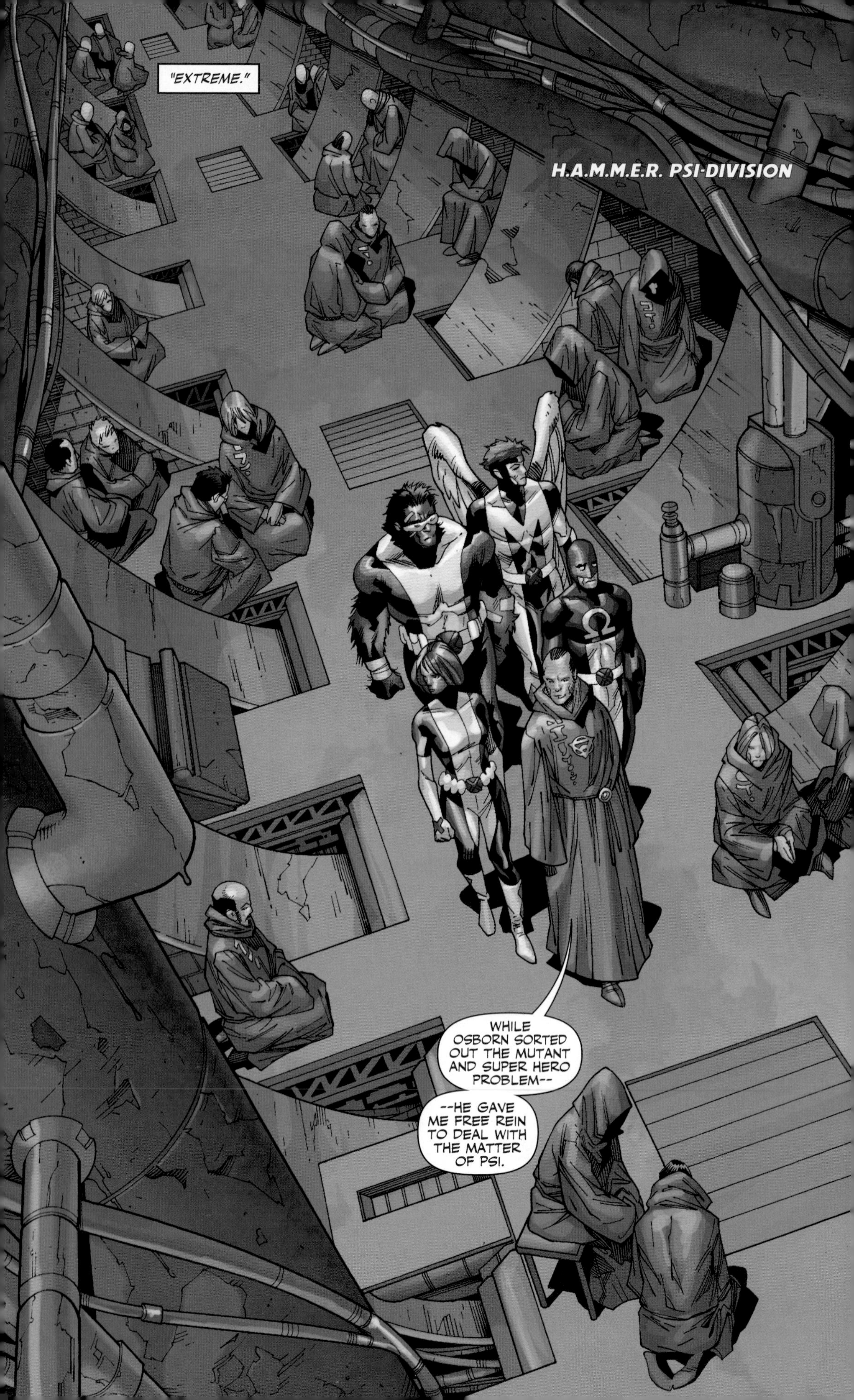
"EXTREME."
H.A.M.M.E.R. PSI-DIVISION
WHILE OSBORN SORTED OUT THE MUTANT AND SUPER HERO PROBLEM--
--HE GAVE ME FREE REIN TO DEAL WITH THE MATTER OF PSI.

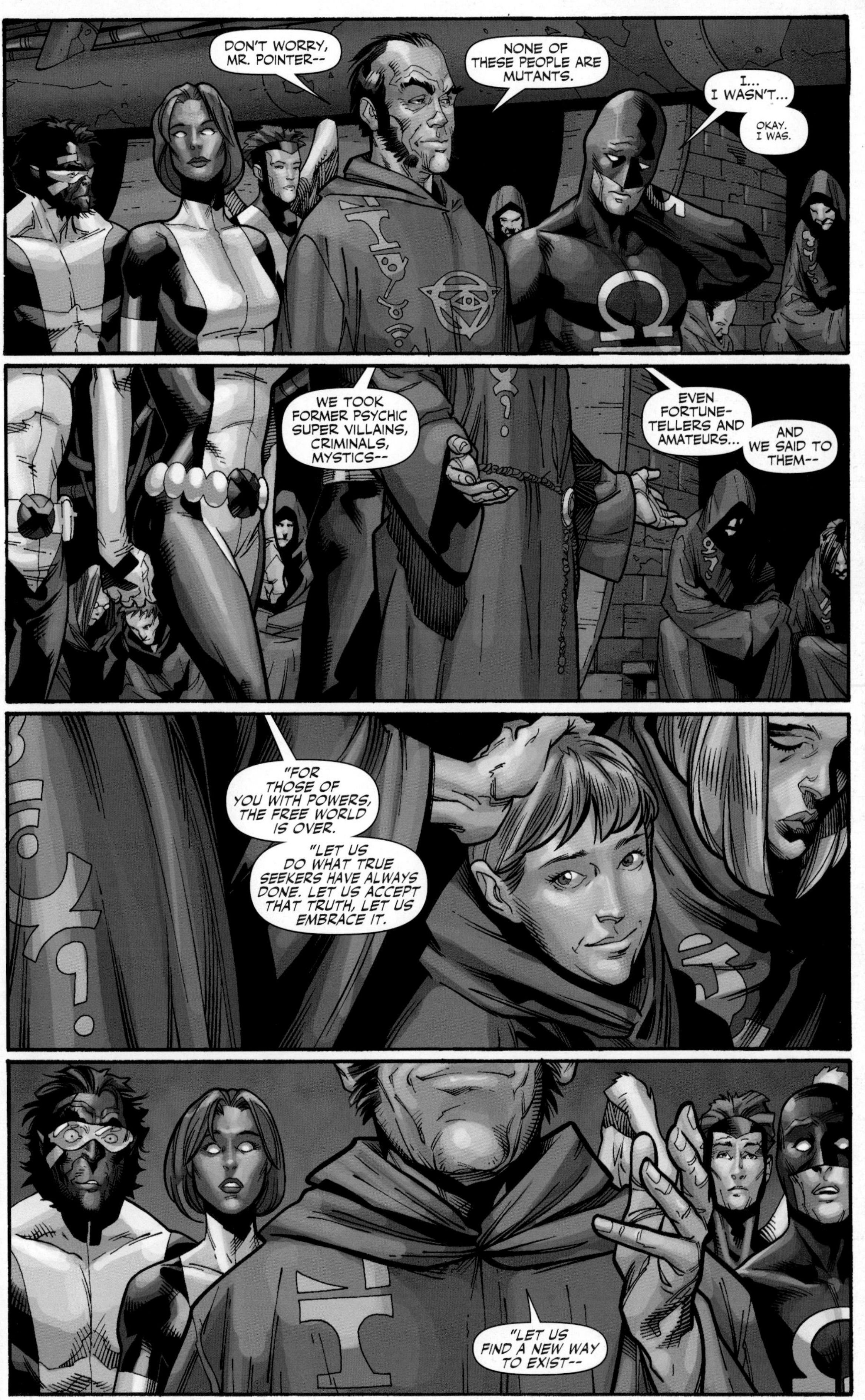
DON'T WORRY, MR. POINTER--
NONE OF THESE PEOPLE ARE MUTANTS.
I... I WASN'T...
OKAY. I WAS.
WE TOOK FORMER PSYCHIC SUPER VILLAINS, CRIMINALS, MYSTICS--
EVEN FORTUNE-TELLERS AND AMATEURS...
AND WE SAID TO THEM--
"FOR THOSE OF YOU WITH POWERS, THE FREE WORLD IS OVER.
"LET US DO WHAT TRUE SEEKERS HAVE ALWAYS DONE. LET US ACCEPT THAT TRUTH, LET US EMBRACE IT.
"LET US FIND A NEW WAY TO EXIST--

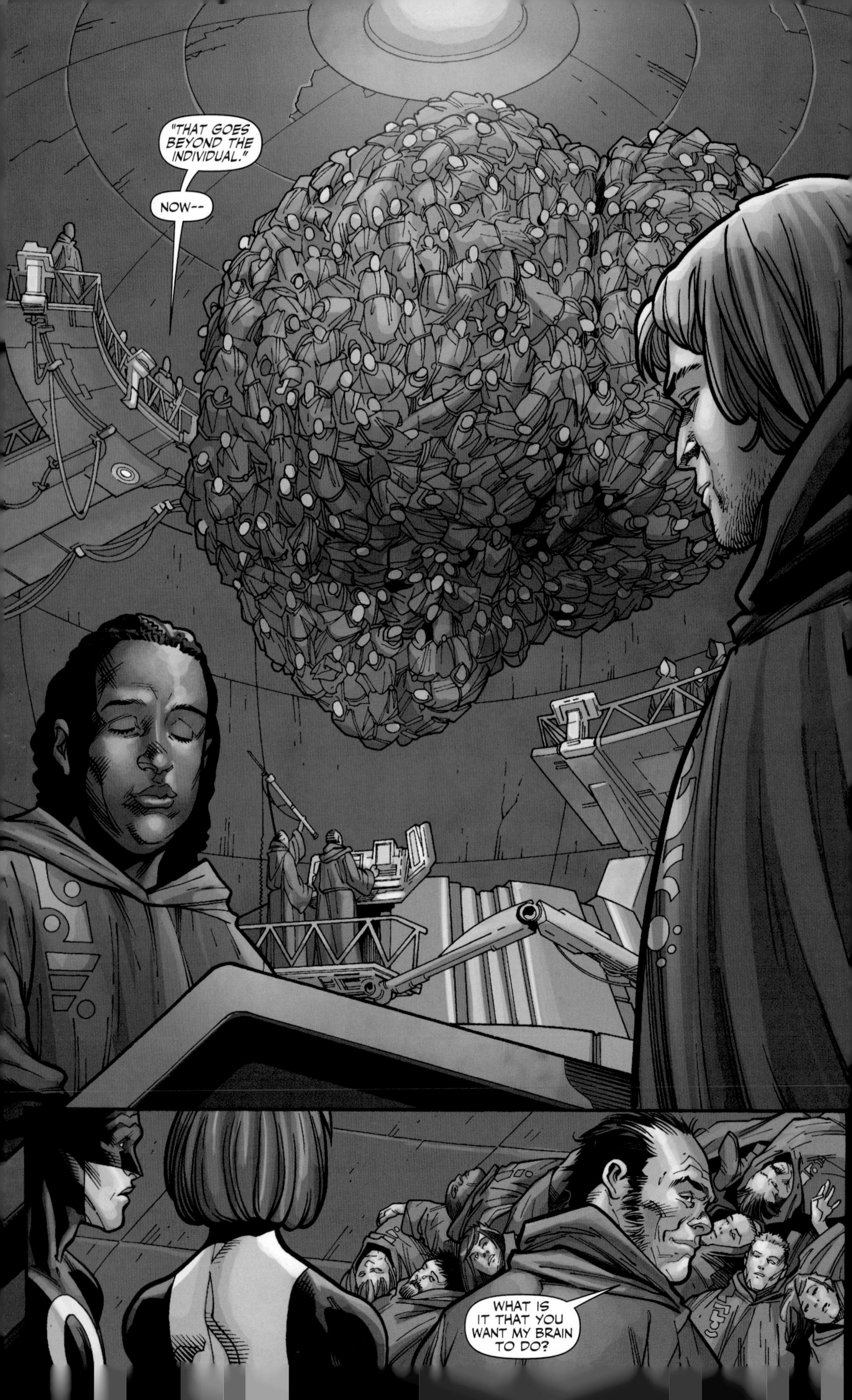
"THAT GOES BEYOND THE INDIVIDUAL."
NOW--
WHAT IS IT THAT YOU WANT MY BRAIN TO DO?

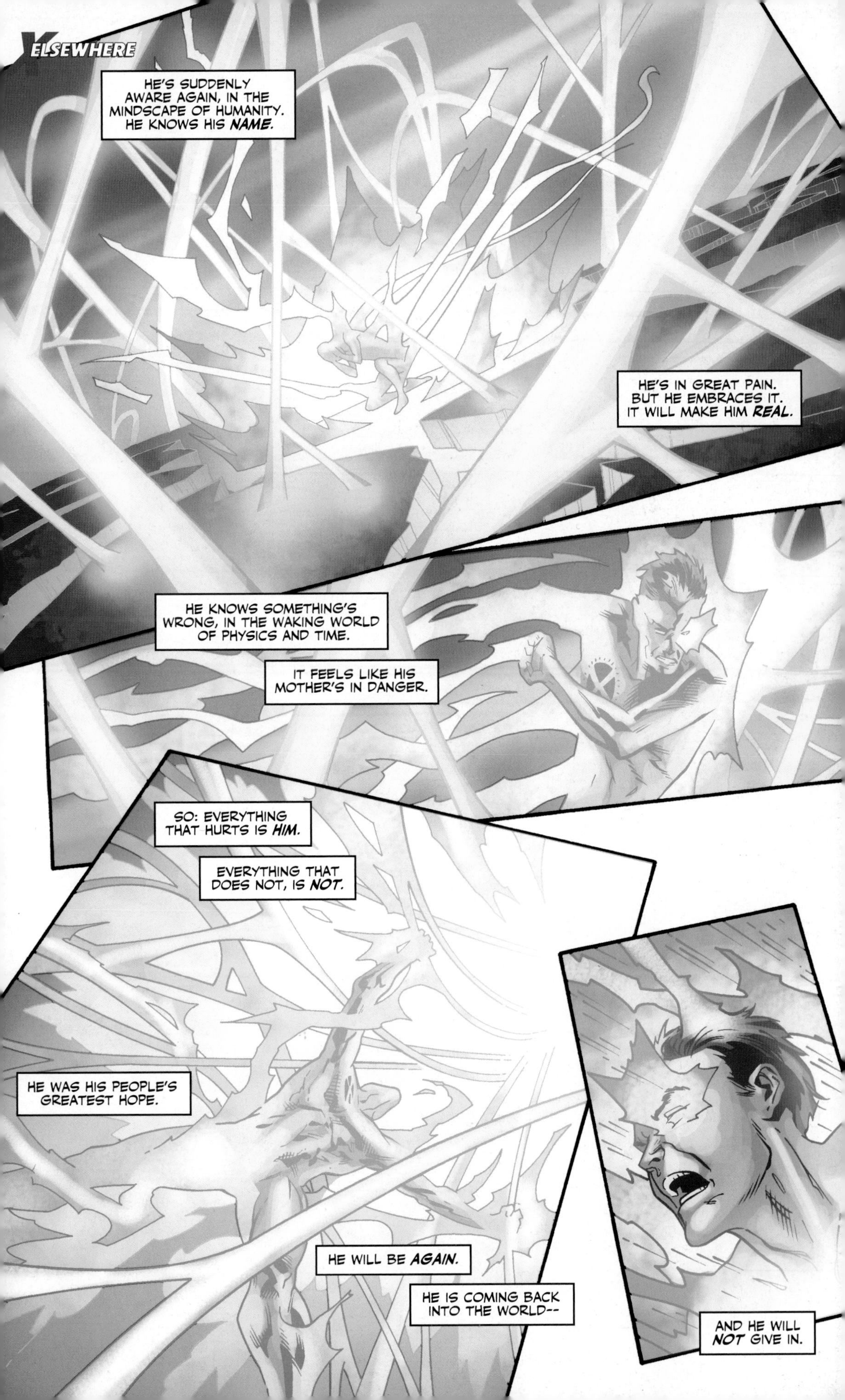
ELSEWHERE
HE'S SUDDENLY AWARE AGAIN, IN THE MINDSCAPE OF HUMANITY. HE KNOWS HIS NAME.
HE'S IN GREAT PAIN. BUT HE EMBRACES IT. IT WILL MAKE HIM REAL.
HE KNOWS SOMETHING'S WRONG, IN THE WAKING WORLD OF PHYSICS AND TIME.
IT FEELS LIKE HIS MOTHER'S IN DANGER.
SO: EVERYTHING THAT HURTS IS HIM.
EVERYTHING THAT DOES NOT, IS NOT.
HE WAS HIS PEOPLE'S GREATEST HOPE.
HE WILL BE AGAIN.
HE IS COMING BACK INTO THE WORLD--
AND HE WILL NOT GIVE IN.

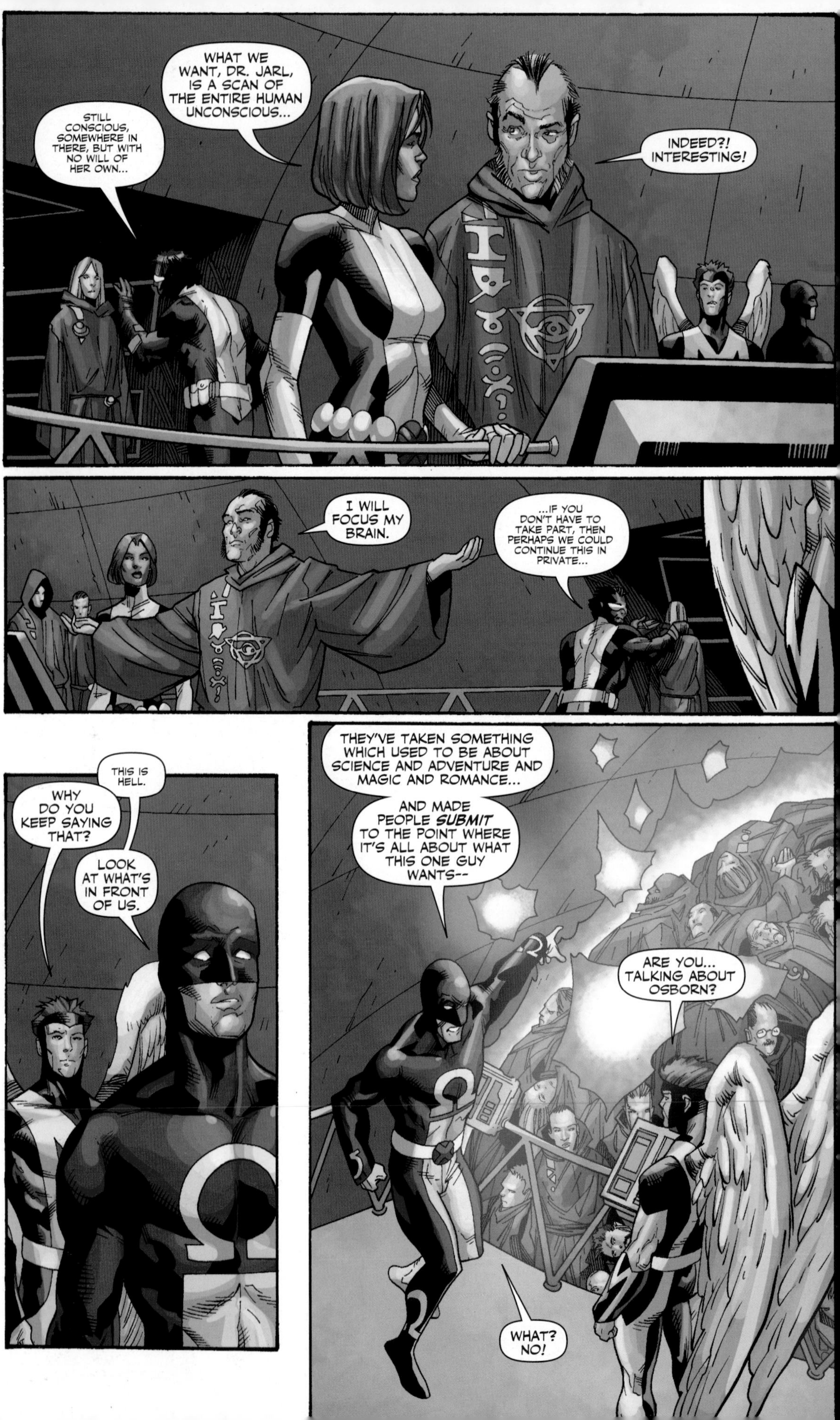
WHAT WE WANT, DR. JARL, IS A SCAN OF THE ENTIRE HUMAN UNCONSCIOUS...
STILL CONSCIOUS, SOMEWHERE IN THERE, BUT WITH NO WILL OF HER OWN...
INDEED?! INTERESTING!
I WILL FOCUS MY BRAIN.
...IF YOU DON'T HAVE TO TAKE PART, THEN PERHAPS WE COULD CONTINUE THIS IN PRIVATE...
THIS IS HELL.
WHY DO YOU KEEP SAYING THAT?
LOOK AT WHAT'S IN FRONT OF US.
THEY'VE TAKEN SOMETHING WHICH USED TO BE ABOUT SCIENCE AND ADVENTURE AND MAGIC AND ROMANCE...
AND MADE PEOPLE SUBMIT TO THE POINT WHERE IT'S ALL ABOUT WHAT THIS ONE GUY WANTS--
ARE YOU... TALKING ABOUT OSBORN?
WHAT? NO!

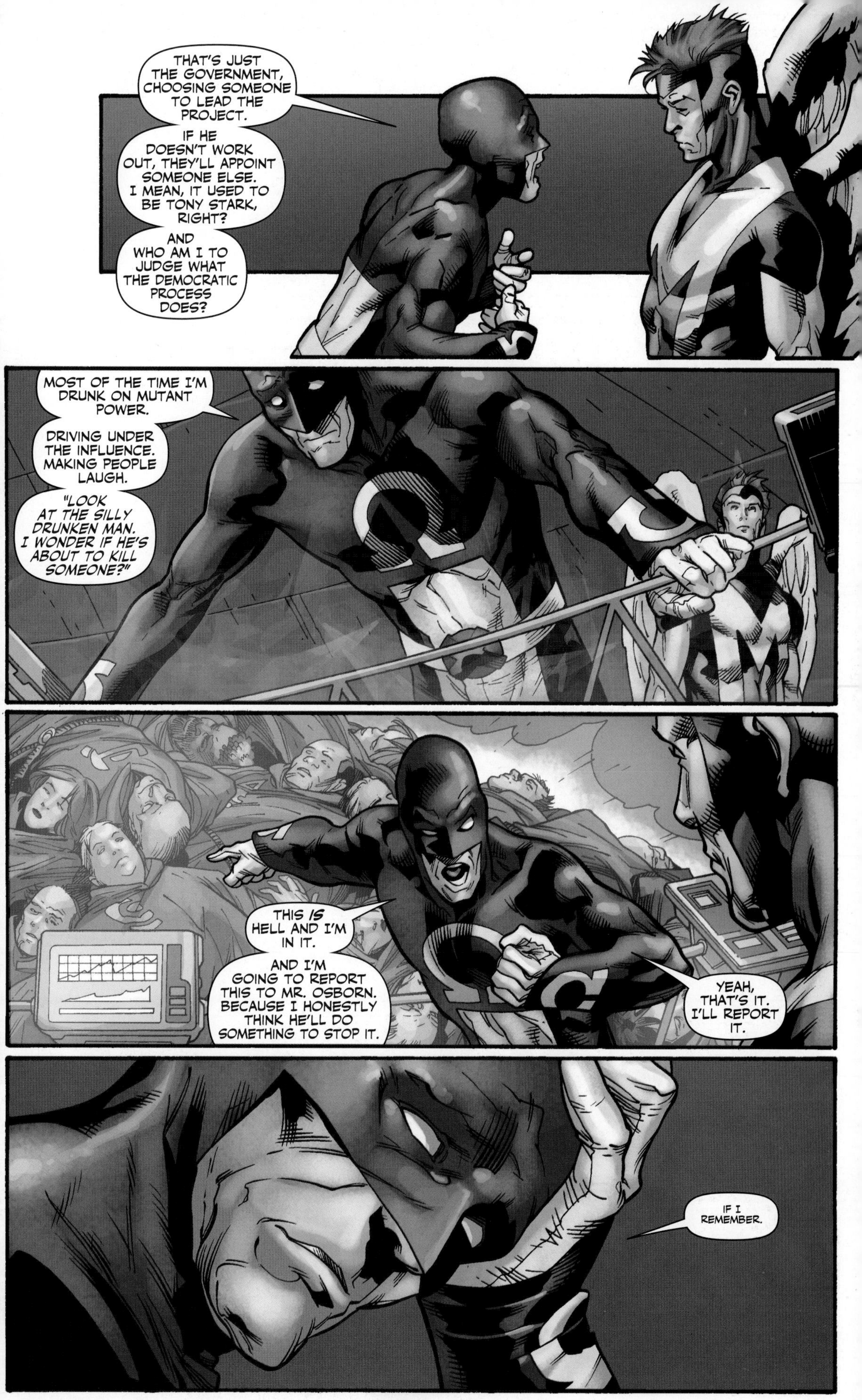
THAT'S JUST THE GOVERNMENT, CHOOSING SOMEONE TO LEAD THE PROJECT.
IF HE DOESN'T WORK OUT, THEY'LL APPOINT SOMEONE ELSE. I MEAN, IT USED TO BE TONY STARK, RIGHT?
AND WHO AM I TO JUDGE WHAT THE DEMOCRATIC PROCESS DOES?
MOST OF THE TIME I'M DRUNK ON MUTANT POWER.
DRIVING UNDER THE INFLUENCE. MAKING PEOPLE LAUGH.
"LOOK AT THE SILLY DRUNKEN MAN. I WONDER IF HE'S ABOUT TO KILL SOMEONE?"
THIS *IS* HELL AND I'M IN IT.
AND I'M GOING TO REPORT THIS TO MR. OSBORN. BECAUSE I HONESTLY THINK HE'LL DO SOMETHING TO STOP IT.
YEAH, THAT'S IT. I'LL REPORT IT.
IF I REMEMBER.

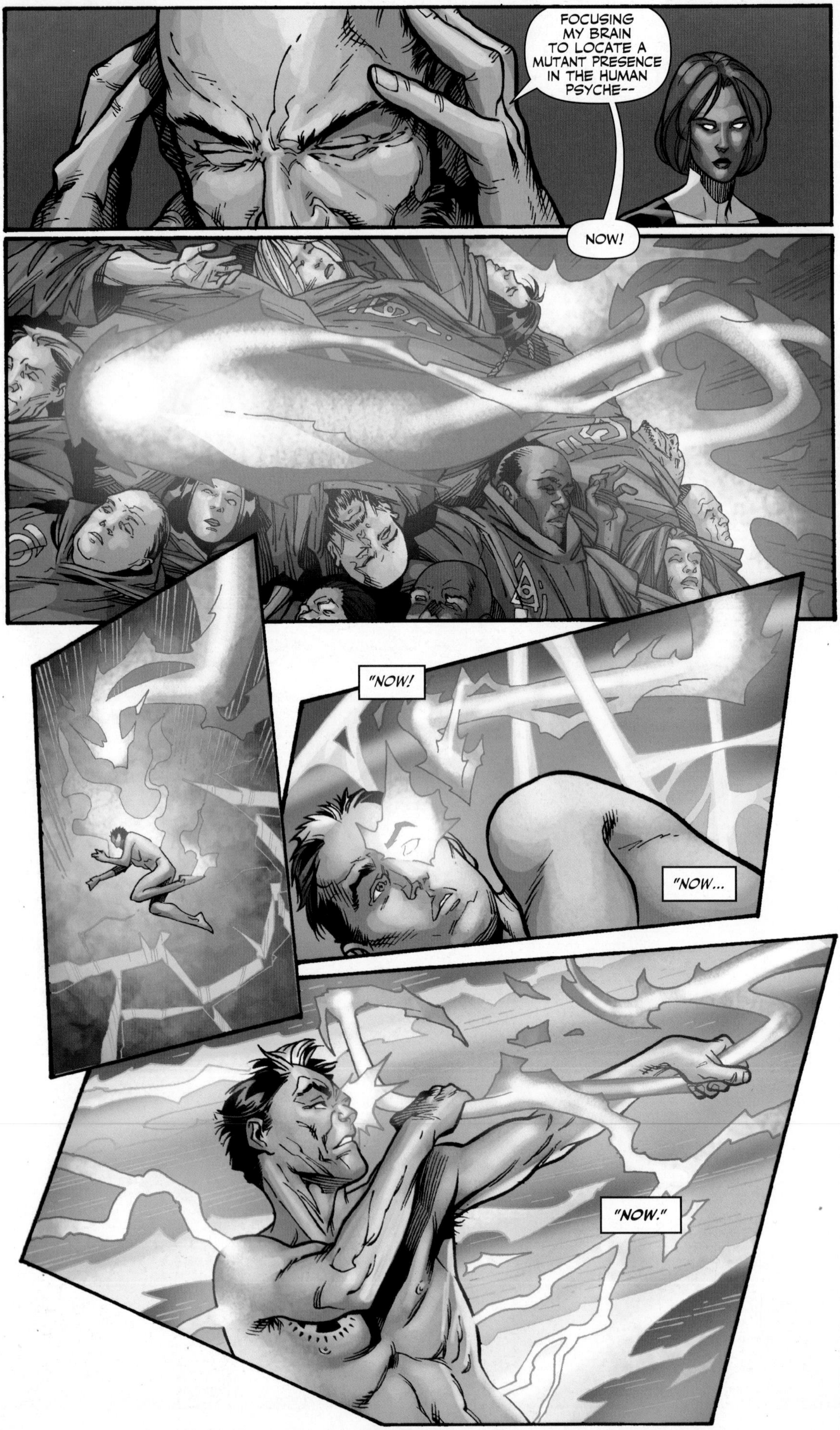
FOCUSING MY BRAIN TO LOCATE A MUTANT PRESENCE IN THE HUMAN PSYCHE--
NOW!
"NOW!
"NOW...
"NOW."

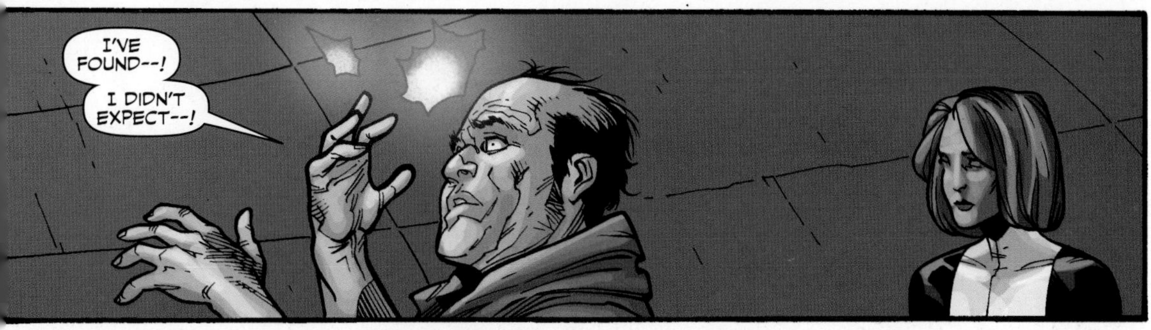
I'VE FOUND--!
I DIDN'T EXPECT--!

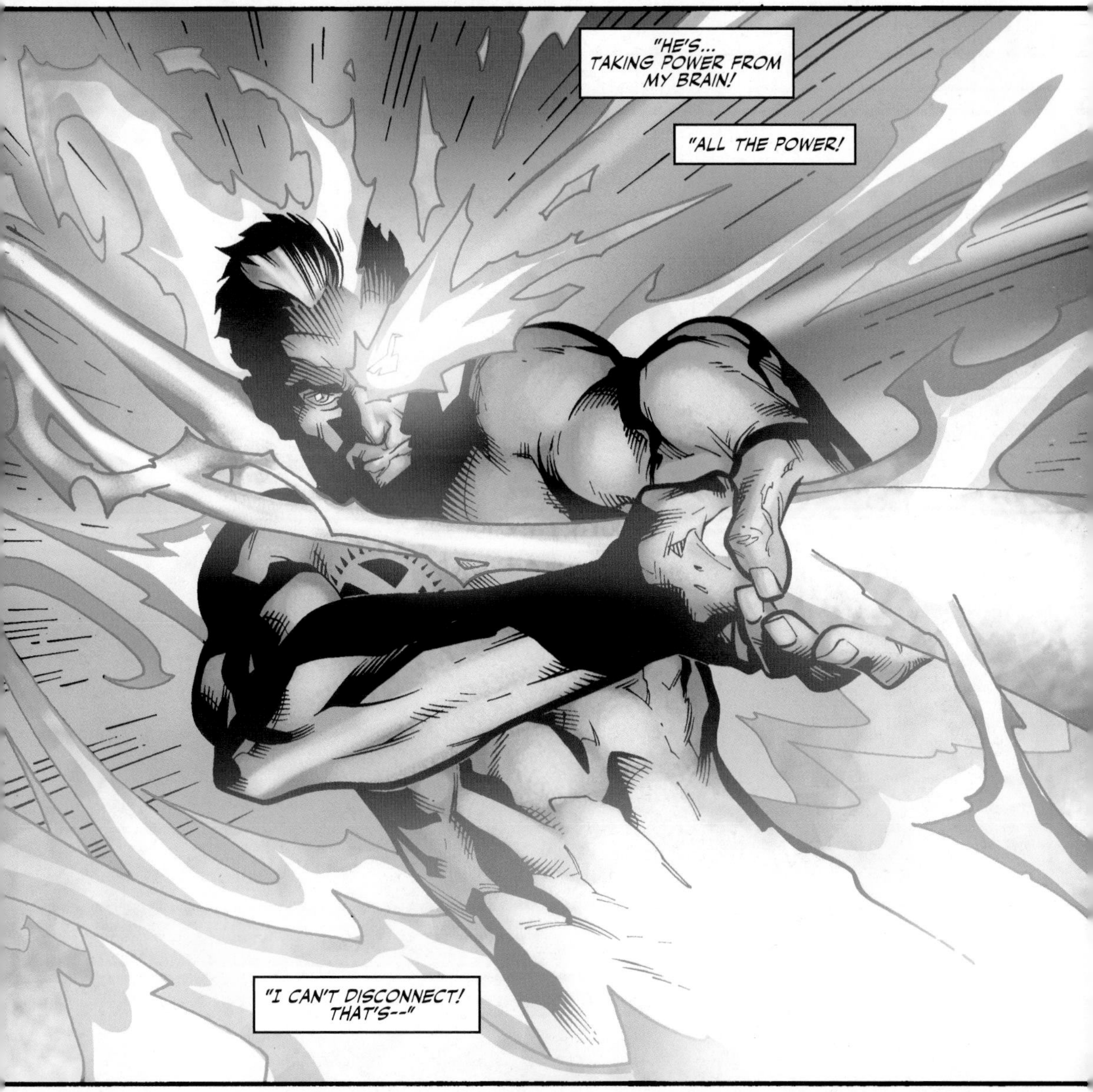
"HE'S... TAKING POWER FROM MY BRAIN!
"ALL THE POWER!
"I CAN'T DISCONNECT! THAT'S--"

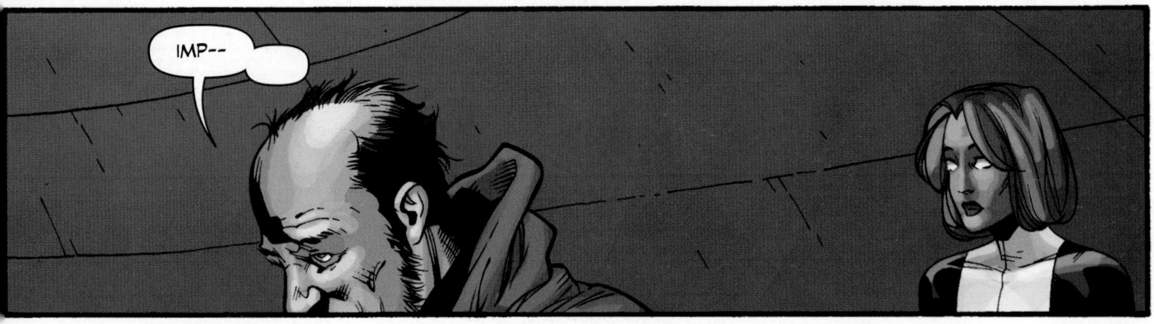
IMP--

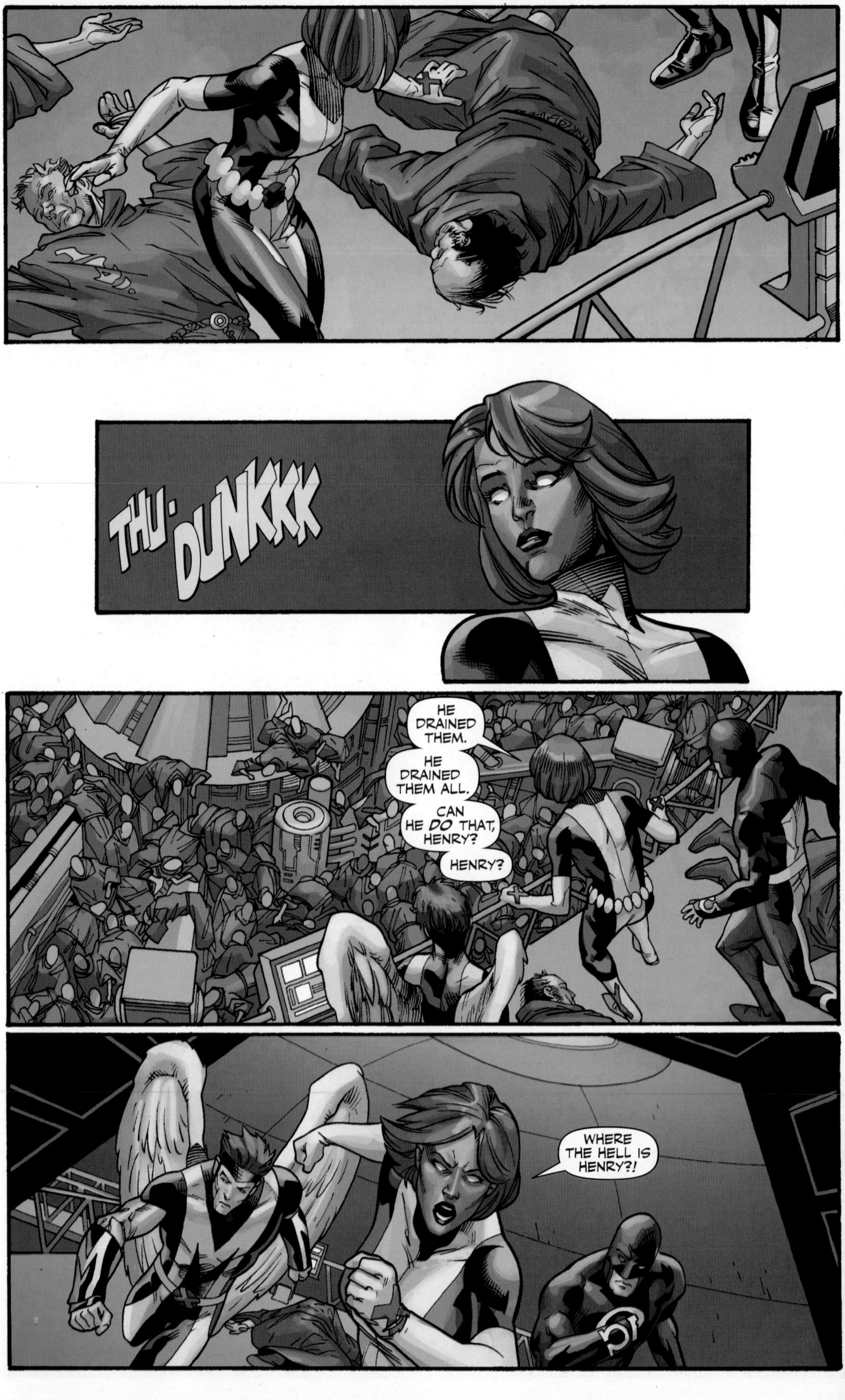
THU-DUNKKK
HE DRAINED THEM.
HE DRAINED THEM ALL.
CAN HE *DO* THAT, HENRY?
HENRY?
WHERE THE HELL IS HENRY?!

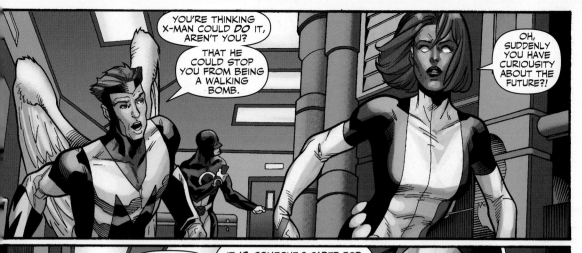

YOU'RE THINKING X-MAN COULD *DO* IT, AREN'T YOU?

THAT HE COULD STOP YOU FROM BEING A WALKING BOMB.

OH, SUDDENLY YOU HAVE CURIOUSITY ABOUT THE FUTURE?!

YES! AND ISN'T THAT GREAT?!

IT *IS*. SOMEONE I CARED FOR VERY MUCH USED TO LIVE UNDER EXACTLY THE BURDEN YOU DO NOW.

I WISH SHE WAS HERE TO GIVE YOU LESSONS!

ERM, GUYS? THIS IS THE RIGHT ROOM...

BUT... WHAT'S THAT SMELL?

LIKE... A BUTCHER'S SHOP?

EITHER STAND THERE AND CONTINUE YOUR SOAP OPERA OR COME IN.

DON'T TELL ME WHAT'S BEEN GOING ON. I KNOW BETTER THAN YOU DO. THAT'S WHY I CAME HERE.

MIND THE...

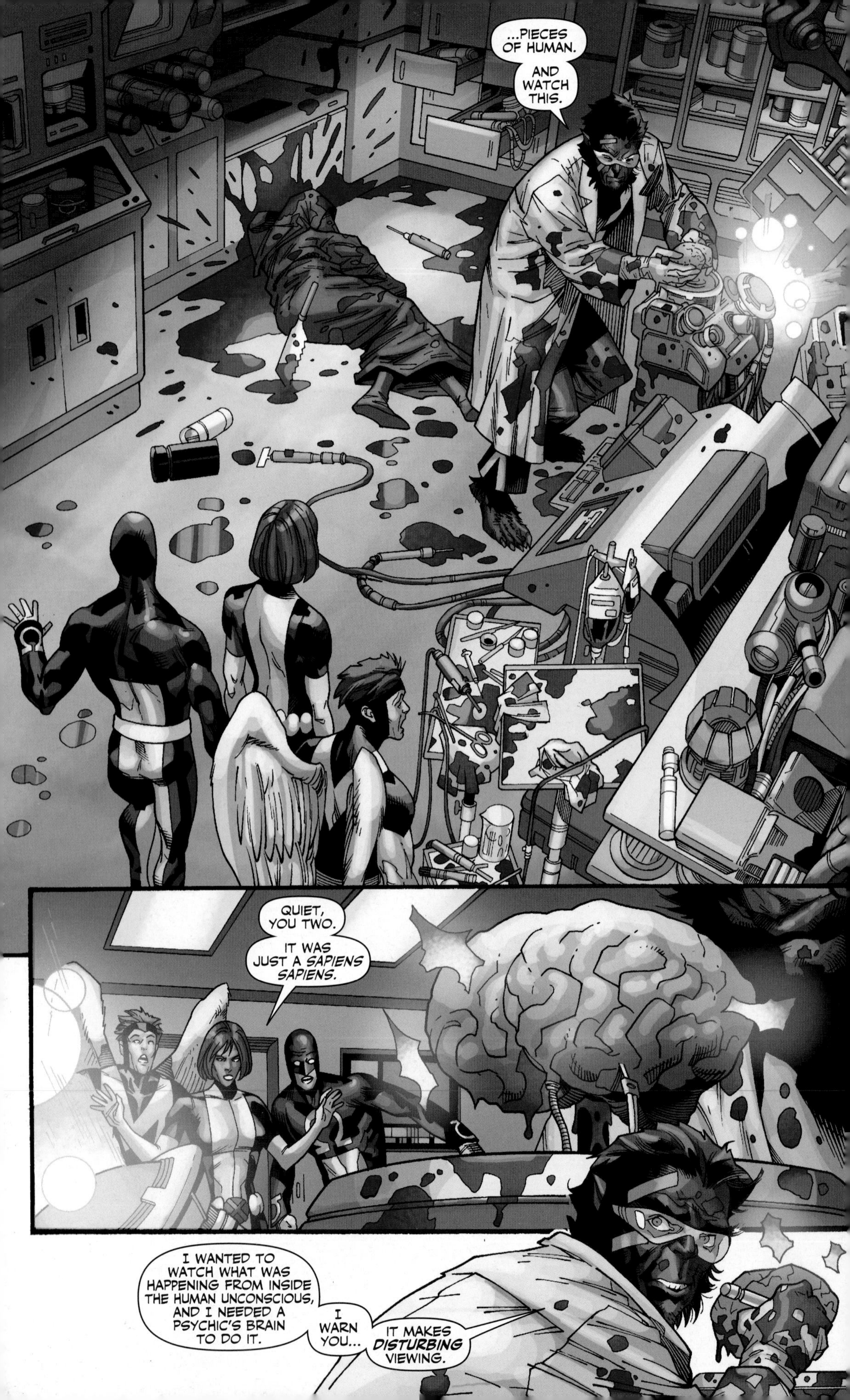

...PIECES OF HUMAN.
AND WATCH THIS.
QUIET, YOU TWO.
IT WAS JUST A SAPIENS SAPIENS.
I WANTED TO WATCH WHAT WAS HAPPENING FROM INSIDE THE HUMAN UNCONSCIOUS, AND I NEEDED A PSYCHIC'S BRAIN TO DO IT.
I WARN YOU...
IT MAKES DISTURBING VIEWING.

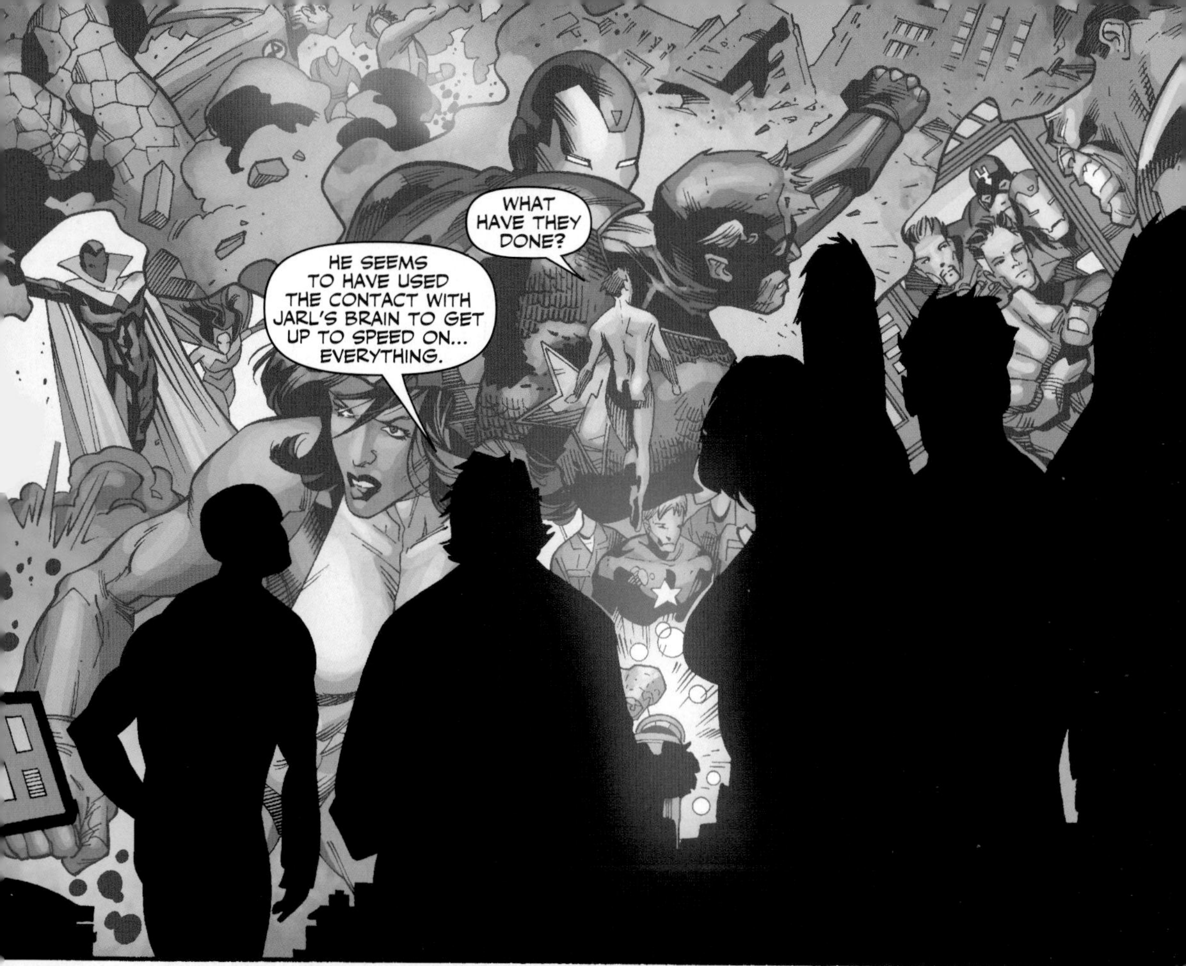
WHAT HAVE THEY DONE?
HE SEEMS TO HAVE USED THE CONTACT WITH JARL'S BRAIN TO GET UP TO SPEED ON... EVERYTHING.

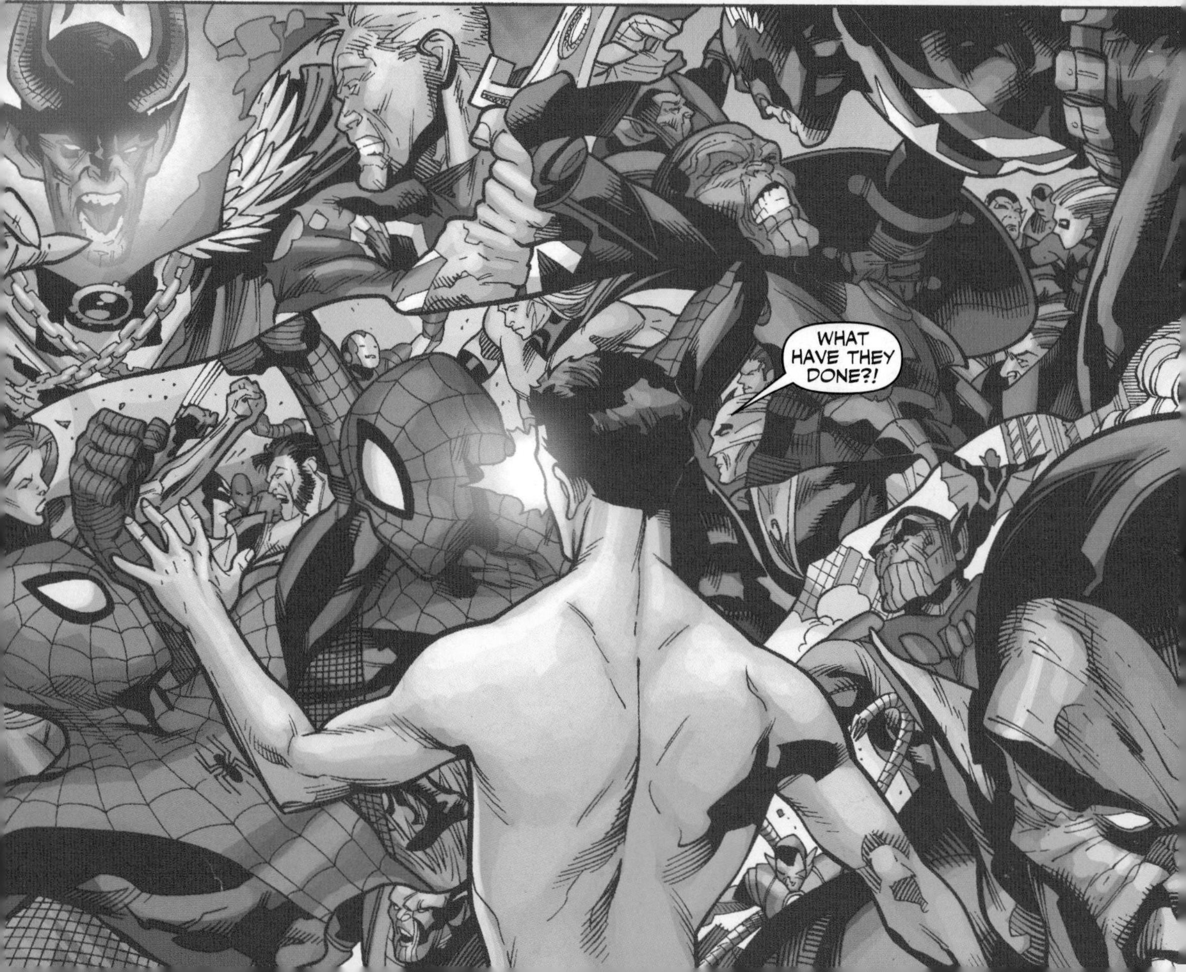
WHAT HAVE THEY DONE?!

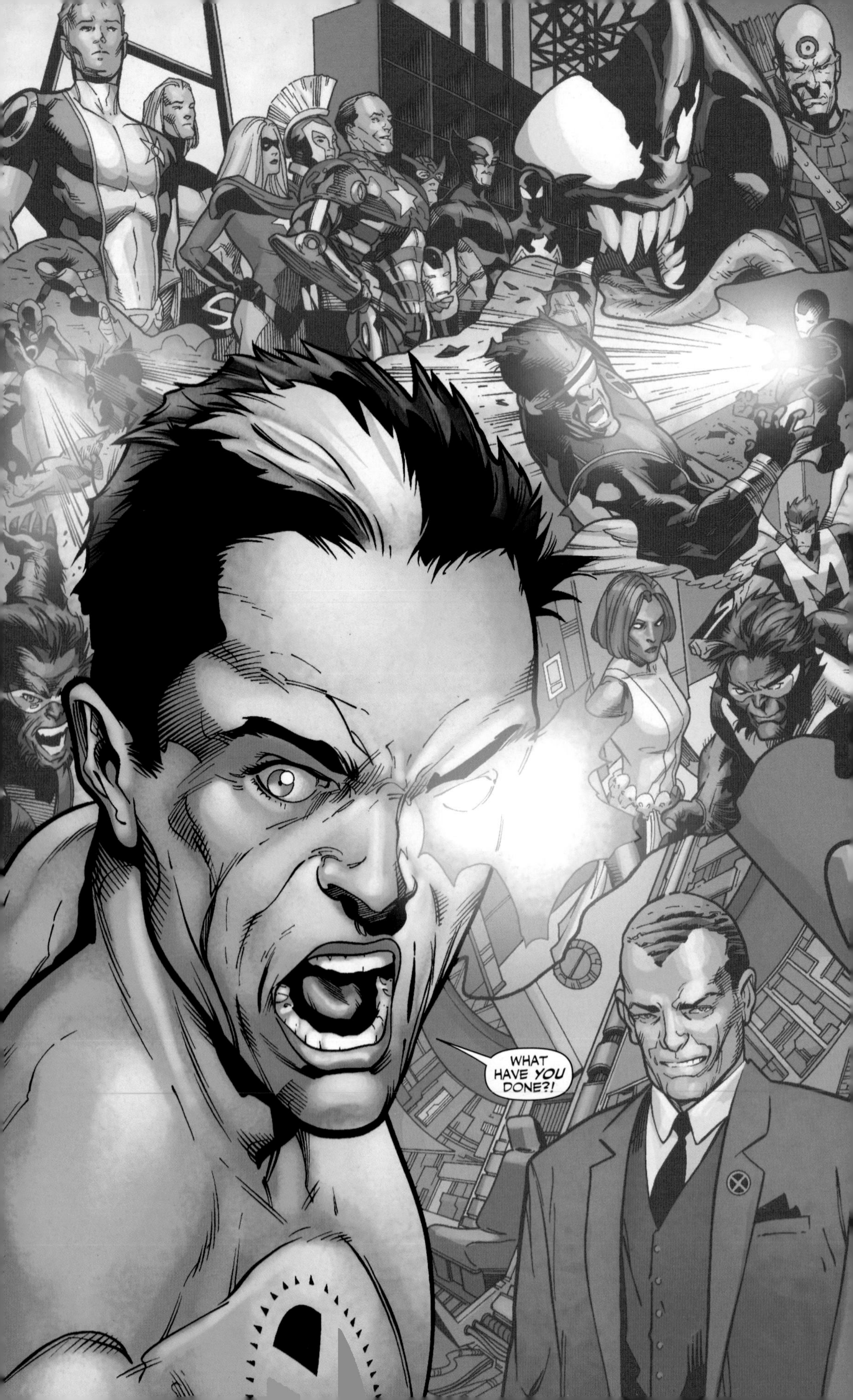
WHAT HAVE YOU DONE?!

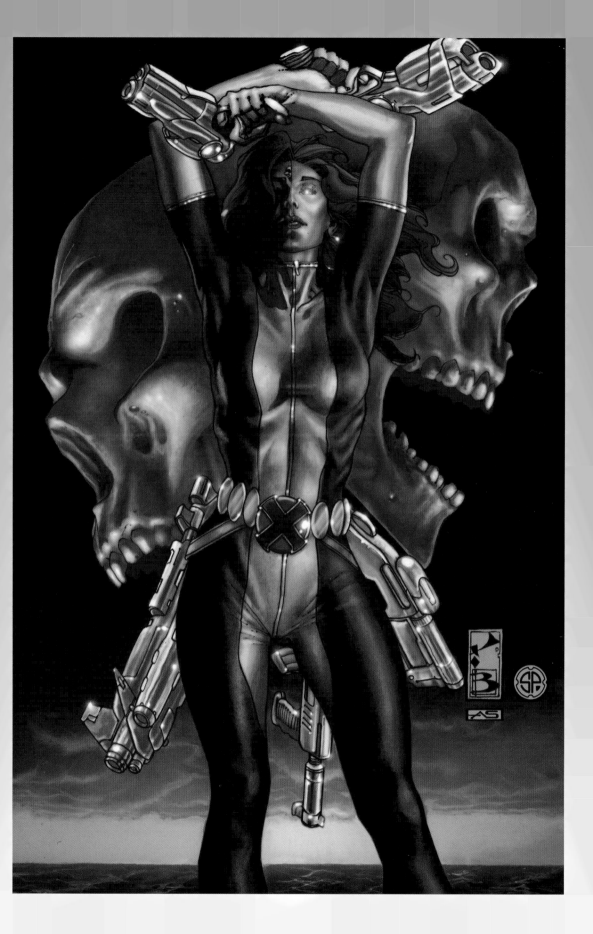

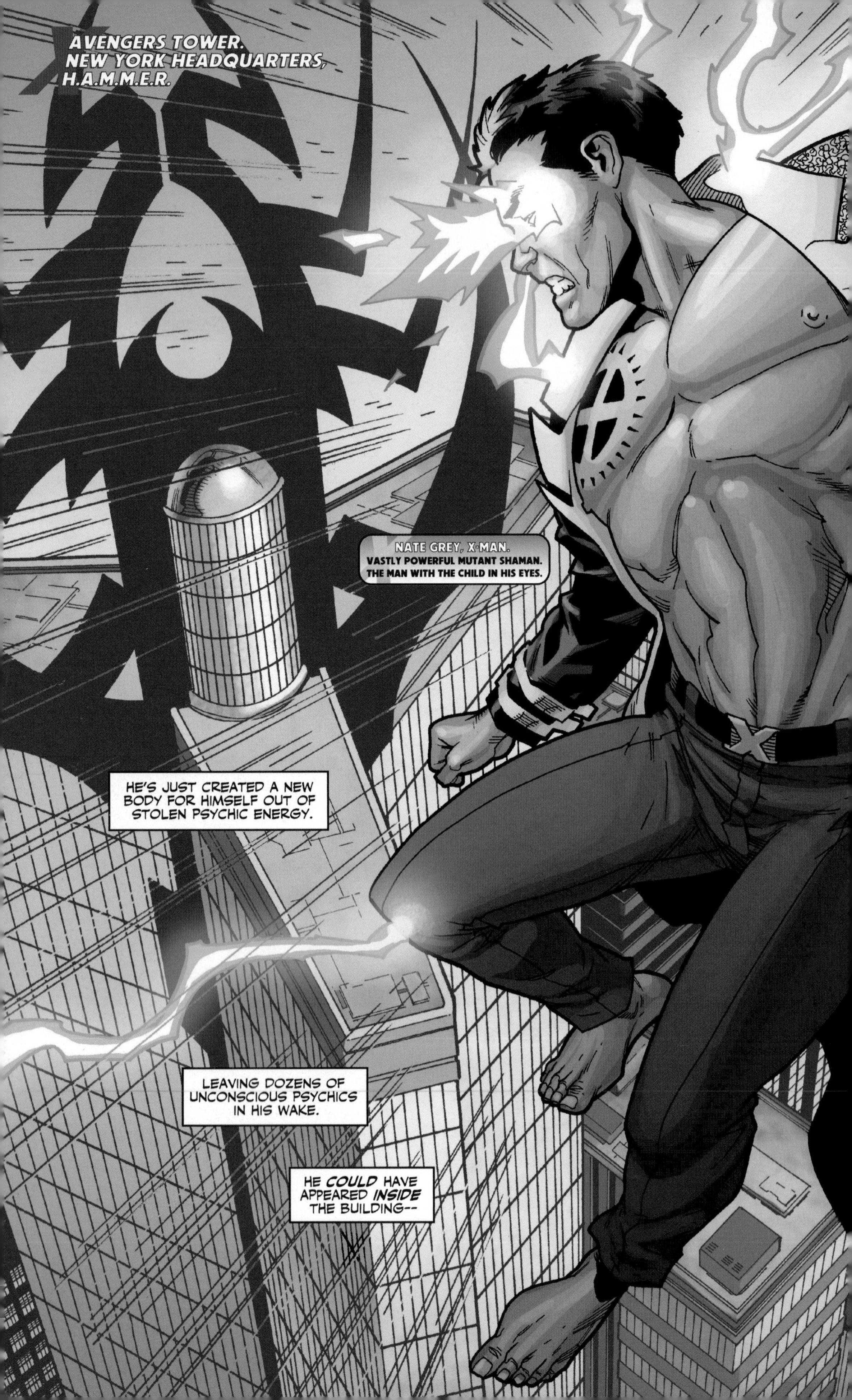
AVENGERS TOWER.
NEW YORK HEADQUARTERS,
H.A.M.M.E.R.
NATE GREY, X-MAN.
VASTLY POWERFUL MUTANT SHAMAN.
THE MAN WITH THE CHILD IN HIS EYES.
HE'S JUST CREATED A NEW BODY FOR HIMSELF OUT OF STOLEN PSYCHIC ENERGY.
LEAVING DOZENS OF UNCONSCIOUS PSYCHICS IN HIS WAKE.
HE COULD HAVE APPEARED INSIDE THE BUILDING--

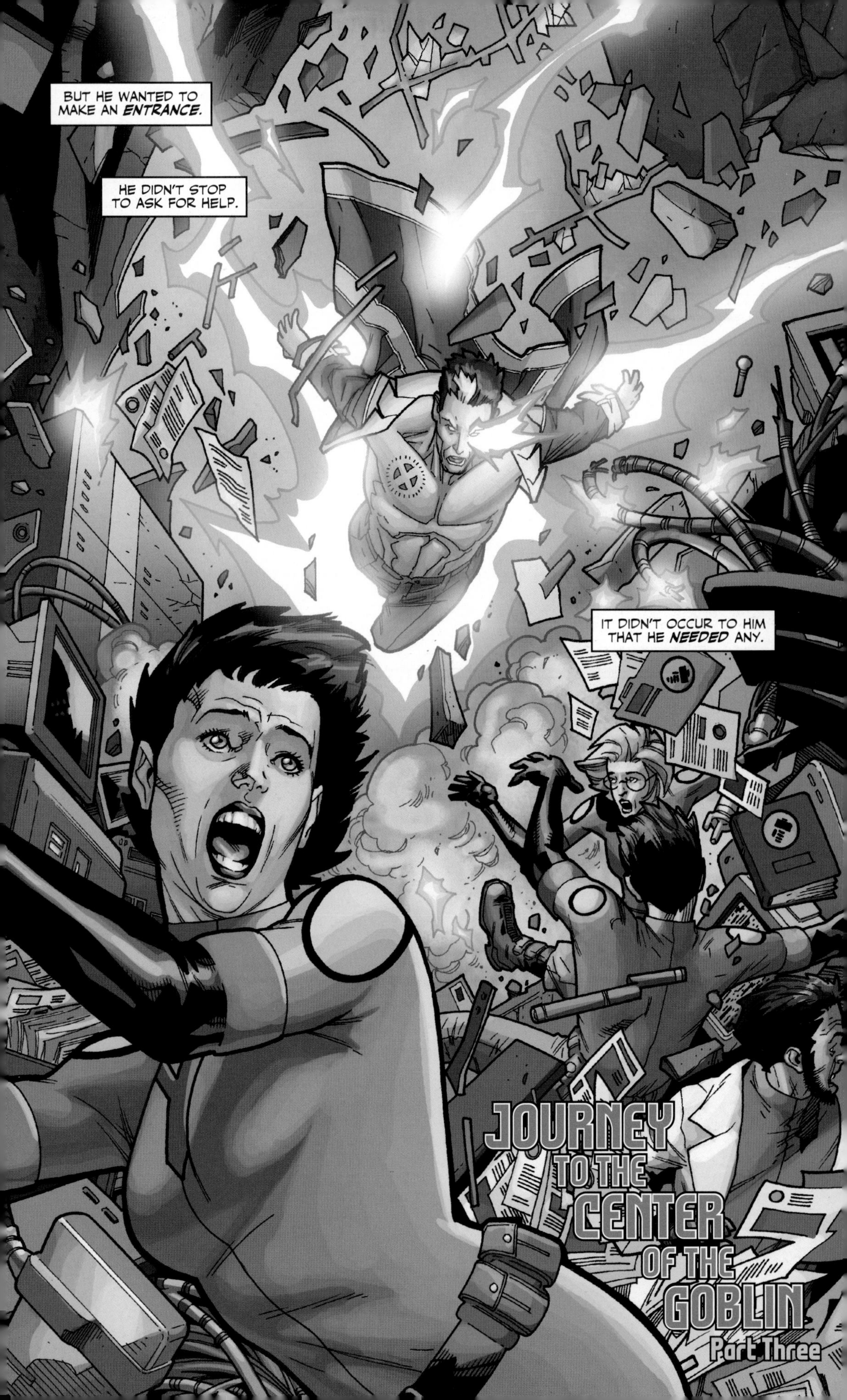
BUT HE WANTED TO MAKE AN ENTRANCE.
HE DIDN'T STOP TO ASK FOR HELP.
IT DIDN'T OCCUR TO HIM THAT HE NEEDED ANY.
JOURNEY TO THE CENTER OF THE GOBLIN
Part Three

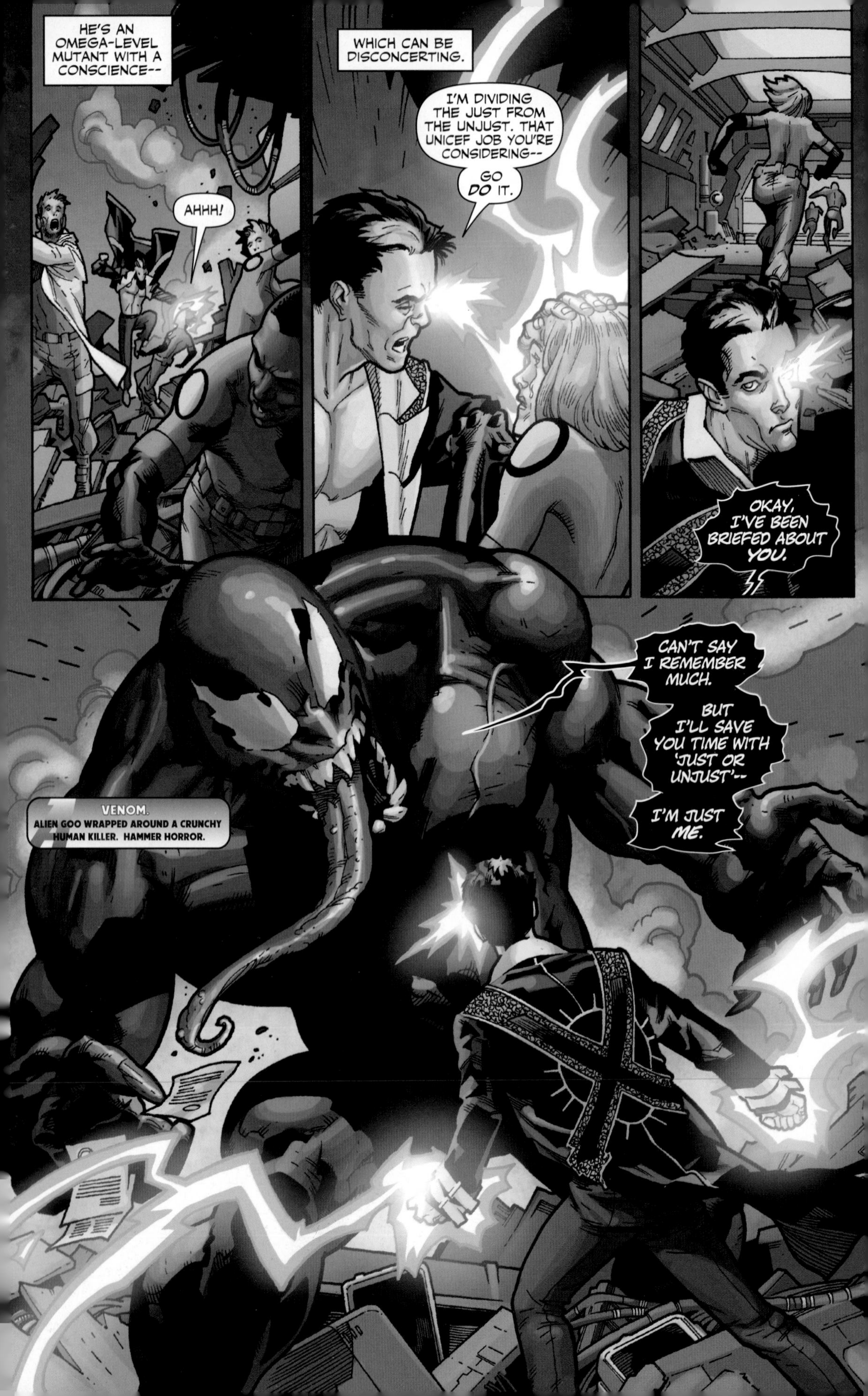

HE'S AN OMEGA-LEVEL MUTANT WITH A CONSCIENCE--
AHHH!
WHICH CAN BE DISCONCERTING.
I'M DIVIDING THE JUST FROM THE UNJUST. THAT UNICEF JOB YOU'RE CONSIDERING--
GO DO IT.
OKAY, I'VE BEEN BRIEFED ABOUT YOU.
CAN'T SAY I REMEMBER MUCH.
BUT I'LL SAVE YOU TIME WITH 'JUST OR UNJUST'--
I'M JUST ME.
VENOM.
ALIEN GOO WRAPPED AROUND A CRUNCHY HUMAN KILLER. HAMMER HORROR.

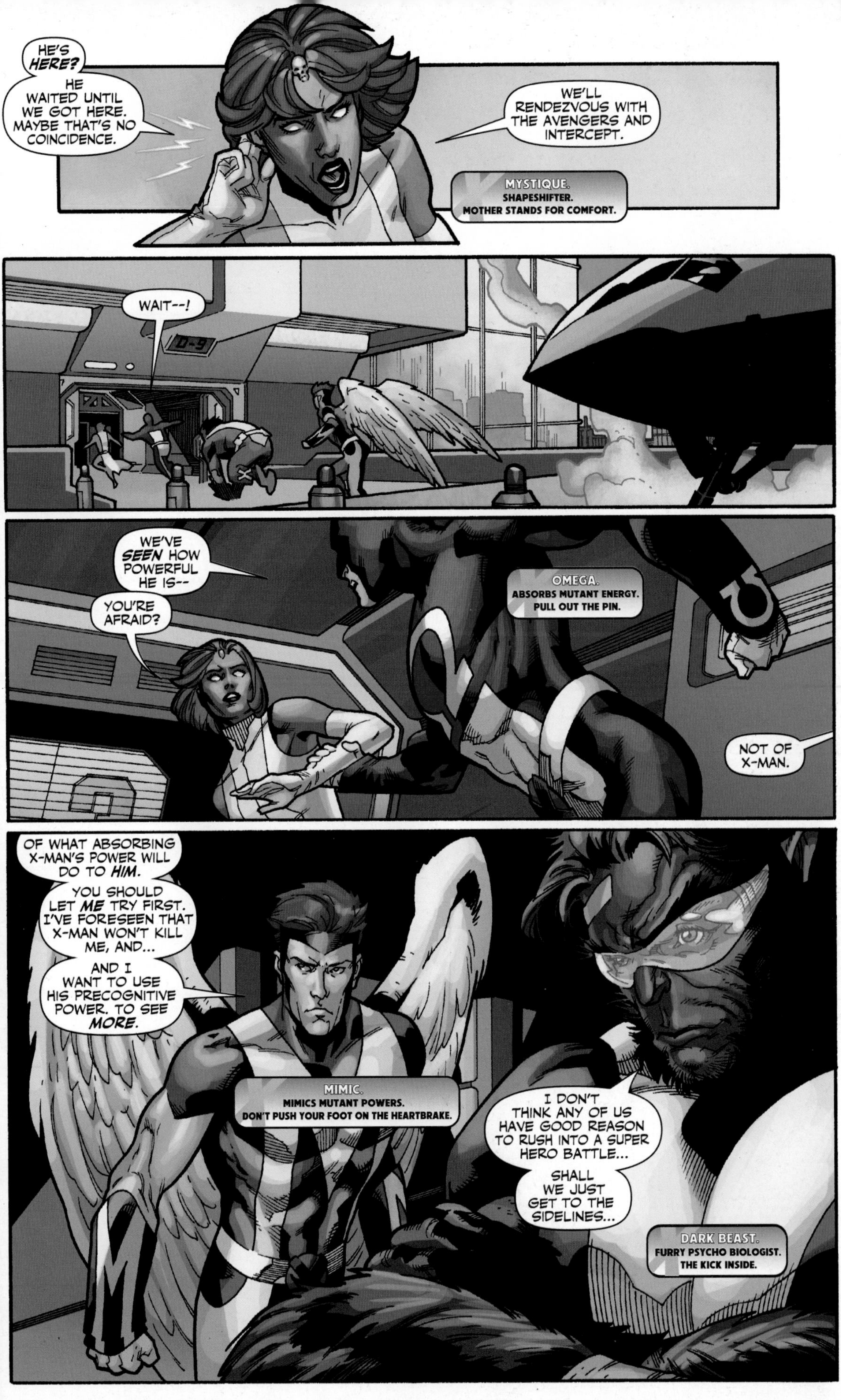
HE'S HERE?
HE WAITED UNTIL WE GOT HERE. MAYBE THAT'S NO COINCIDENCE.
WE'LL RENDEZVOUS WITH THE AVENGERS AND INTERCEPT.
MYSTIQUE. SHAPESHIFTER. MOTHER STANDS FOR COMFORT.
WAIT--!
D-9
WE'VE SEEN HOW POWERFUL HE IS--
YOU'RE AFRAID?
OMEGA. ABSORBS MUTANT ENERGY. PULL OUT THE PIN.
NOT OF X-MAN.
OF WHAT ABSORBING X-MAN'S POWER WILL DO TO HIM.
YOU SHOULD LET ME TRY FIRST. I'VE FORESEEN THAT X-MAN WON'T KILL ME, AND...
AND I WANT TO USE HIS PRECOGNITIVE POWER. TO SEE MORE.
MIMIC. MIMICS MUTANT POWERS. DON'T PUSH YOUR FOOT ON THE HEARTBRAKE.
I DON'T THINK ANY OF US HAVE GOOD REASON TO RUSH INTO A SUPER HERO BATTLE...
SHALL WE JUST GET TO THE SIDELINES...
DARK BEAST. FURRY PSYCHO BIOLOGIST. THE KICK INSIDE.

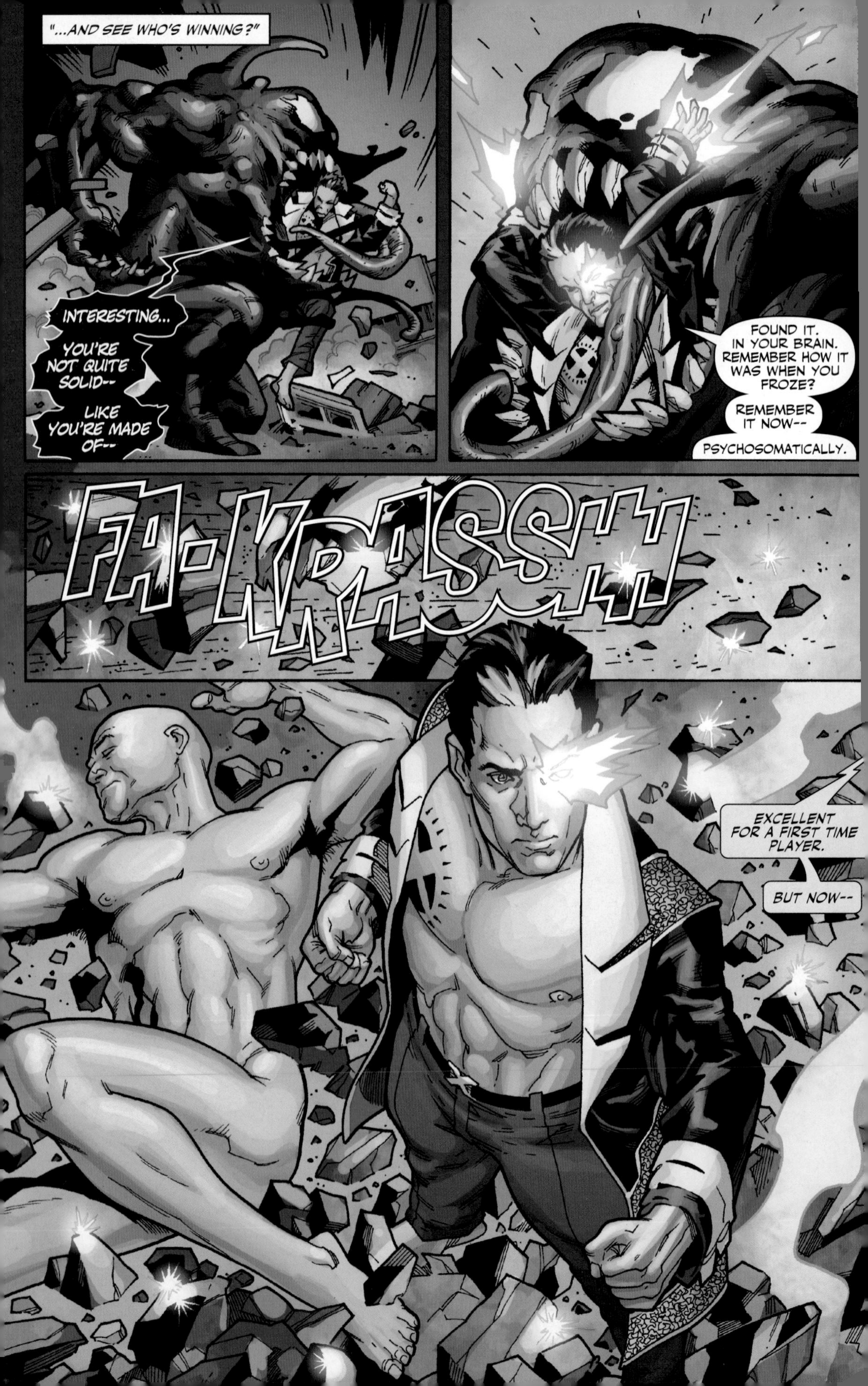
"...AND SEE WHO'S WINNING?"
INTERESTING...
YOU'RE NOT QUITE SOLID--
LIKE YOU'RE MADE OF--
FOUND IT. IN YOUR BRAIN. REMEMBER HOW IT WAS WHEN YOU FROZE?
REMEMBER IT NOW--
PSYCHOSOMATICALLY.
FA-KRASSH
EXCELLENT FOR A FIRST TIME PLAYER.
BUT NOW--

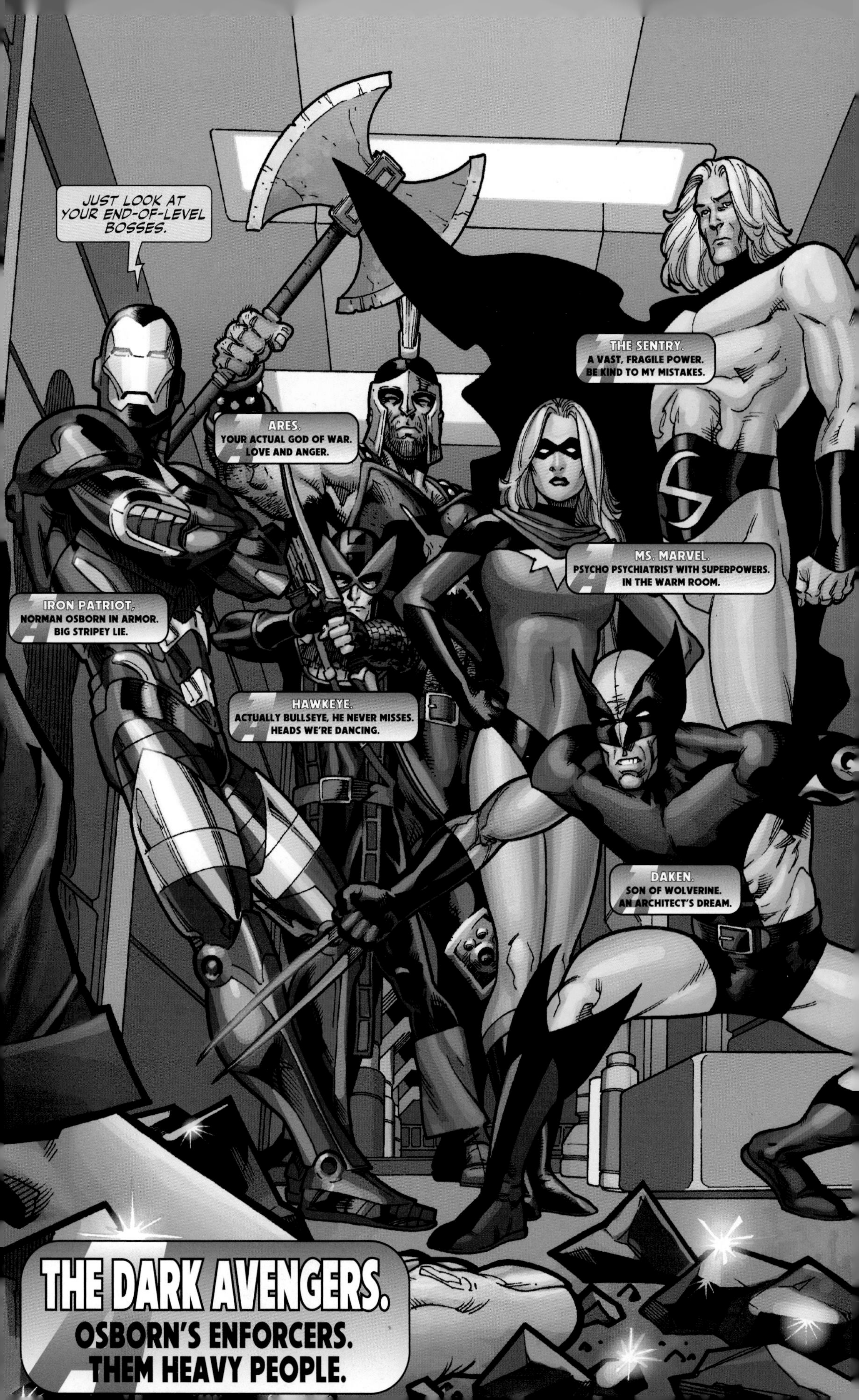
JUST LOOK AT YOUR END-OF-LEVEL BOSSES.
THE SENTRY. A VAST, FRAGILE POWER. BE KIND TO MY MISTAKES.
ARES. YOUR ACTUAL GOD OF WAR. LOVE AND ANGER.
MS. MARVEL. PSYCHO PSYCHIATRIST WITH SUPERPOWERS. IN THE WARM ROOM.
IRON PATRIOT, NORMAN OSBORN IN ARMOR. BIG STRIPEY LIE.
HAWKEYE. ACTUALLY BULLSEYE, HE NEVER MISSES. HEADS WE'RE DANCING.
DAKEN. SON OF WOLVERINE. AN ARCHITECT'S DREAM.
THE DARK AVENGERS. OSBORN'S ENFORCERS. THEM HEAVY PEOPLE.

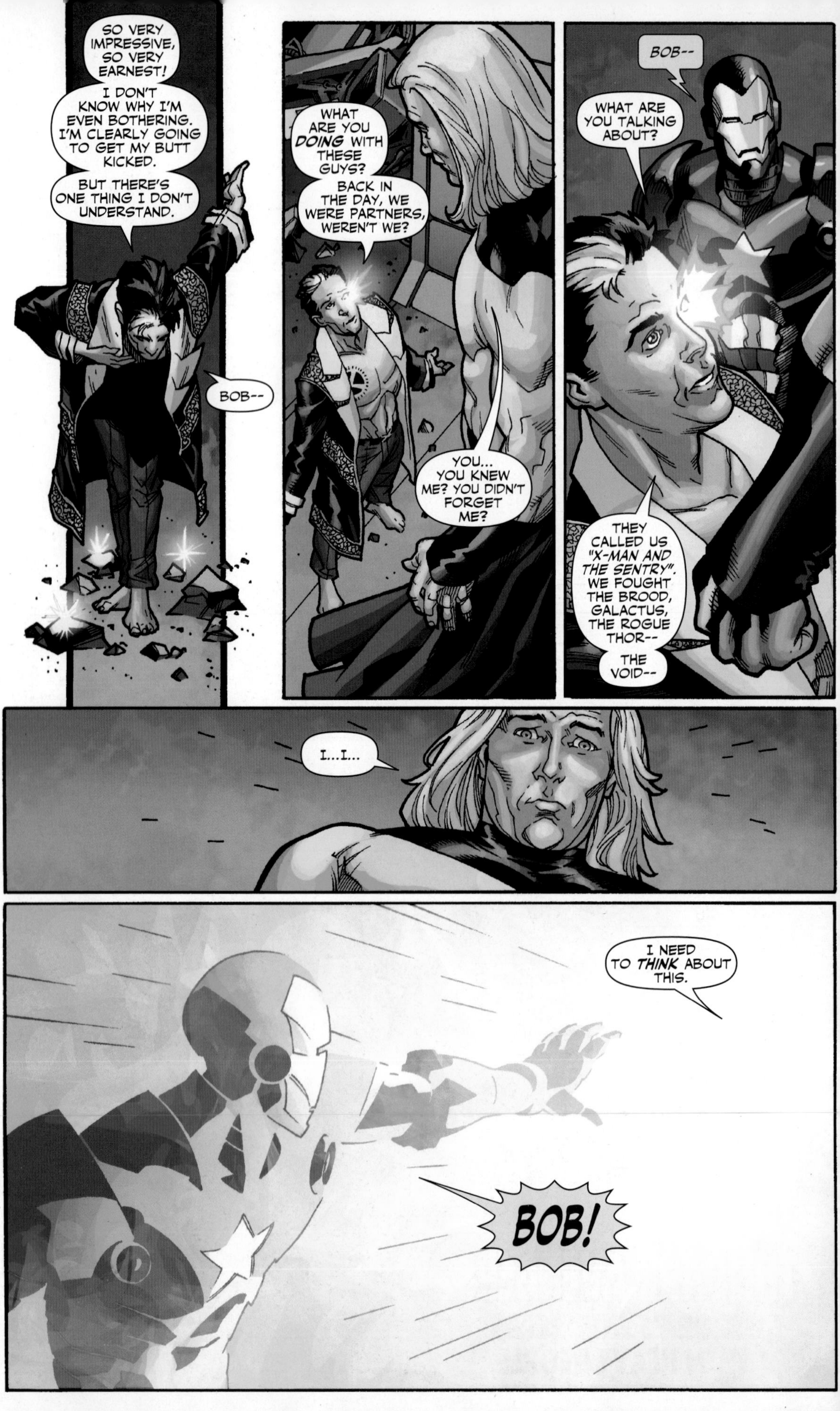

SO VERY IMPRESSIVE, SO VERY EARNEST!
I DON'T KNOW WHY I'M EVEN BOTHERING. I'M CLEARLY GOING TO GET MY BUTT KICKED.
BUT THERE'S ONE THING I DON'T UNDERSTAND.
BOB--
WHAT ARE YOU DOING WITH THESE GUYS?
BACK IN THE DAY, WE WERE PARTNERS, WEREN'T WE?
YOU... YOU KNEW ME? YOU DIDN'T FORGET ME?
BOB--
WHAT ARE YOU TALKING ABOUT?
THEY CALLED US "X-MAN AND THE SENTRY". WE FOUGHT THE BROOD, GALACTUS, THE ROGUE THOR--
THE VOID--
I...I...
I NEED TO THINK ABOUT THIS.
BOB!

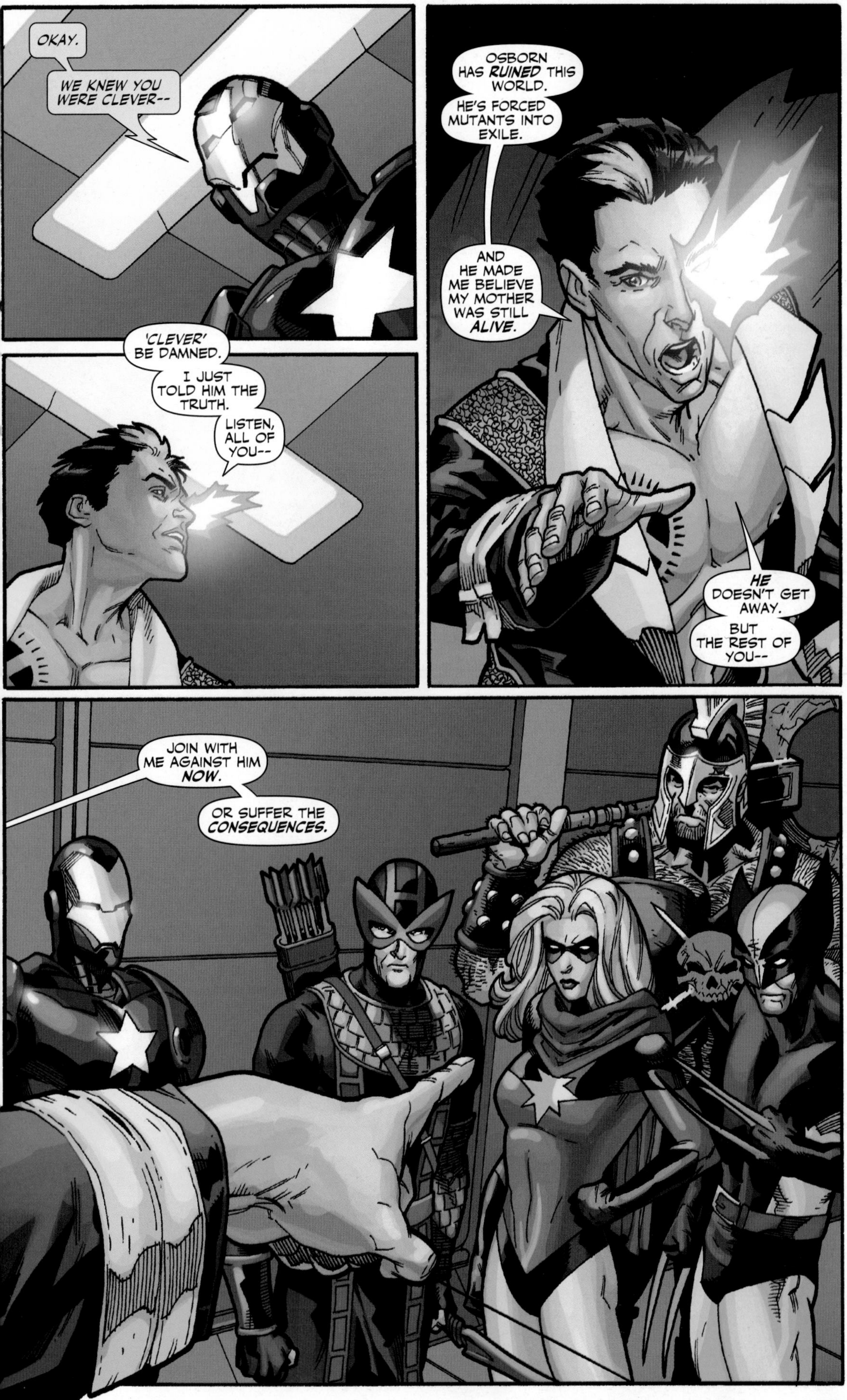
OKAY.
WE KNEW YOU WERE CLEVER--
OSBORN HAS RUINED THIS WORLD.
HE'S FORCED MUTANTS INTO EXILE.
AND HE MADE ME BELIEVE MY MOTHER WAS STILL ALIVE.
'CLEVER' BE DAMNED.
I JUST TOLD HIM THE TRUTH.
LISTEN, ALL OF YOU--
HE DOESN'T GET AWAY.
BUT THE REST OF YOU--
JOIN WITH ME AGAINST HIM NOW.
OR SUFFER THE CONSEQUENCES.

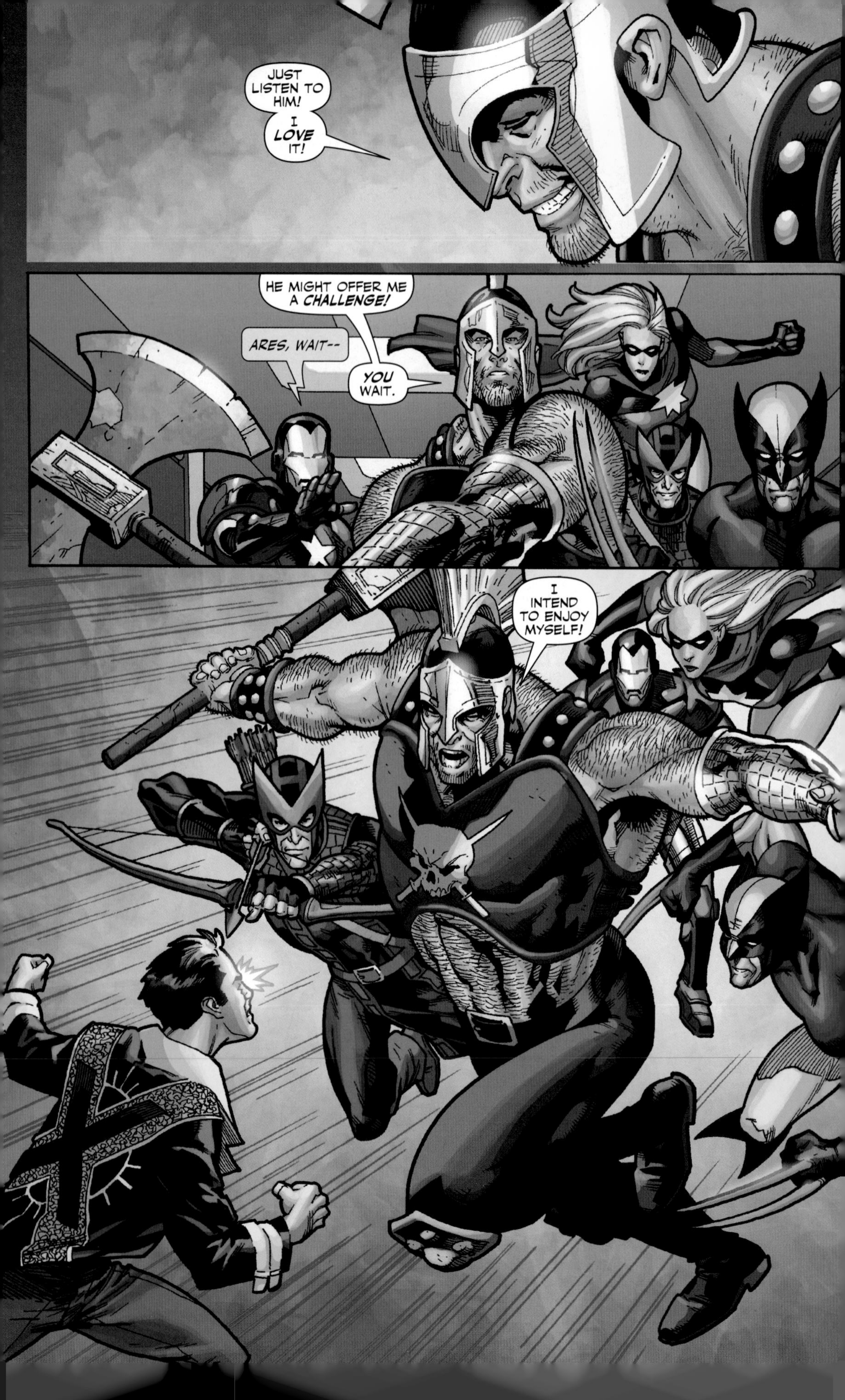
JUST LISTEN TO HIM!
I LOVE IT!
HE MIGHT OFFER ME A CHALLENGE!
ARES, WAIT--
YOU WAIT.
I INTEND TO ENJOY MYSELF!

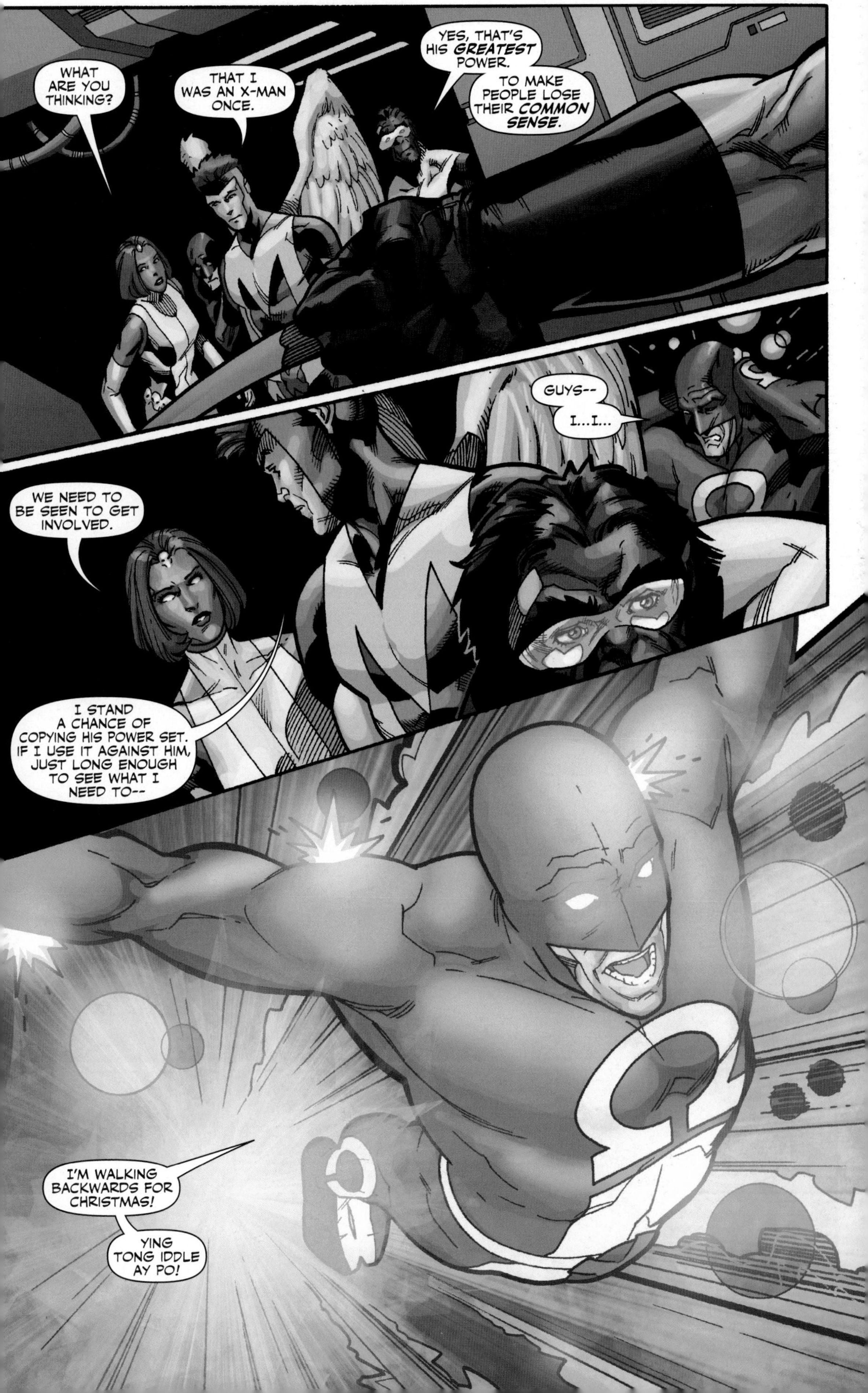
WHAT ARE YOU THINKING?
THAT I WAS AN X-MAN ONCE.
YES, THAT'S HIS *GREATEST* POWER.
TO MAKE PEOPLE LOSE THEIR *COMMON SENSE*.
GUYS--
I...I...
WE NEED TO BE SEEN TO GET INVOLVED.
I STAND A CHANCE OF COPYING HIS POWER SET. IF I USE IT AGAINST HIM, JUST LONG ENOUGH TO SEE WHAT I NEED TO--
I'M WALKING BACKWARDS FOR CHRISTMAS!
YING TONG IDDLE AY PO!

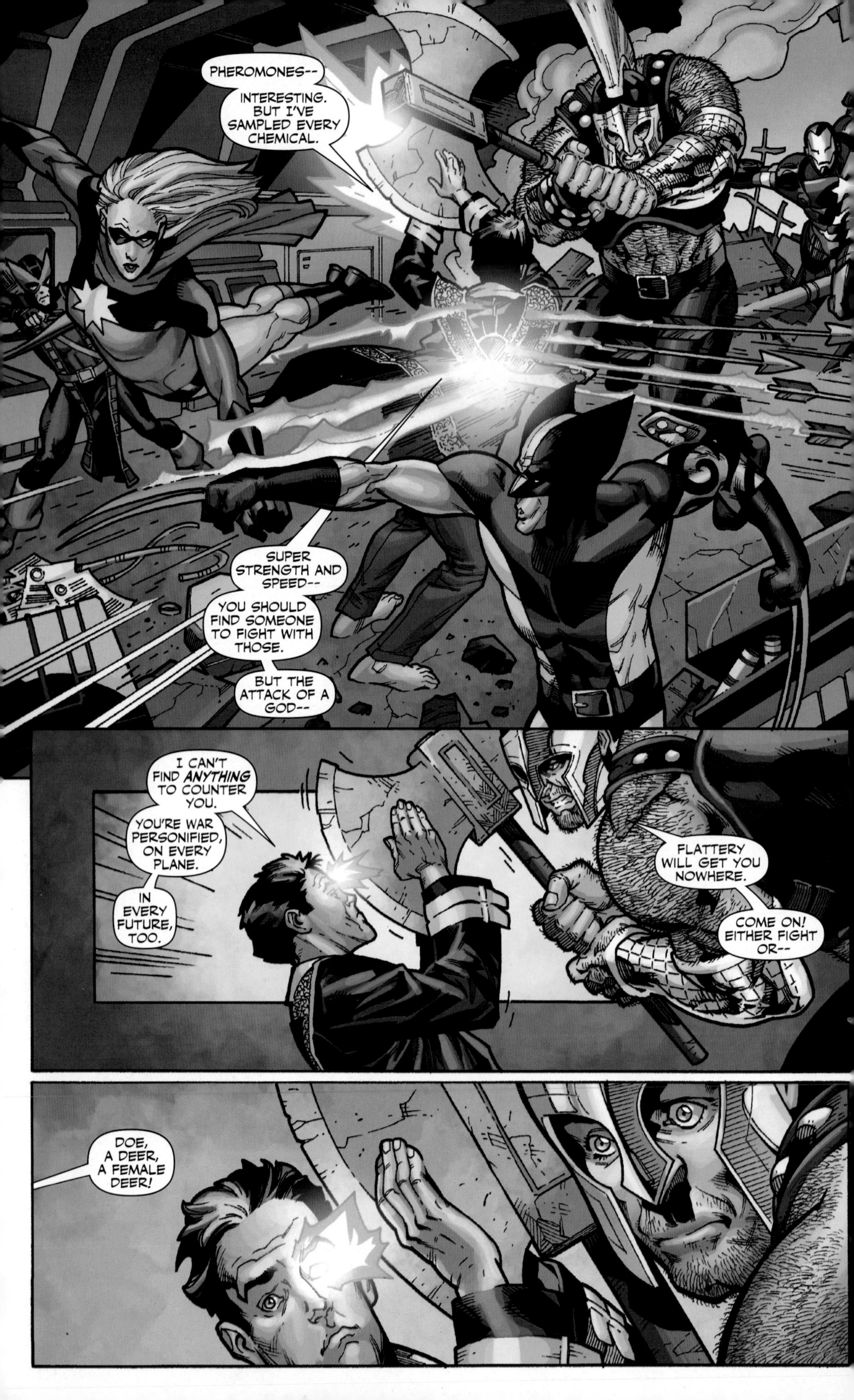
PHEROMONES--
INTERESTING. BUT I'VE SAMPLED EVERY CHEMICAL.
SUPER STRENGTH AND SPEED--
YOU SHOULD FIND SOMEONE TO FIGHT WITH THOSE.
BUT THE ATTACK OF A GOD--
I CAN'T FIND *ANYTHING* TO COUNTER YOU.
YOU'RE WAR PERSONIFIED, ON EVERY PLANE.
IN EVERY FUTURE, TOO.
FLATTERY WILL GET YOU NOWHERE.
COME ON! EITHER FIGHT OR--
DOE, A DEER, A FEMALE DEER!

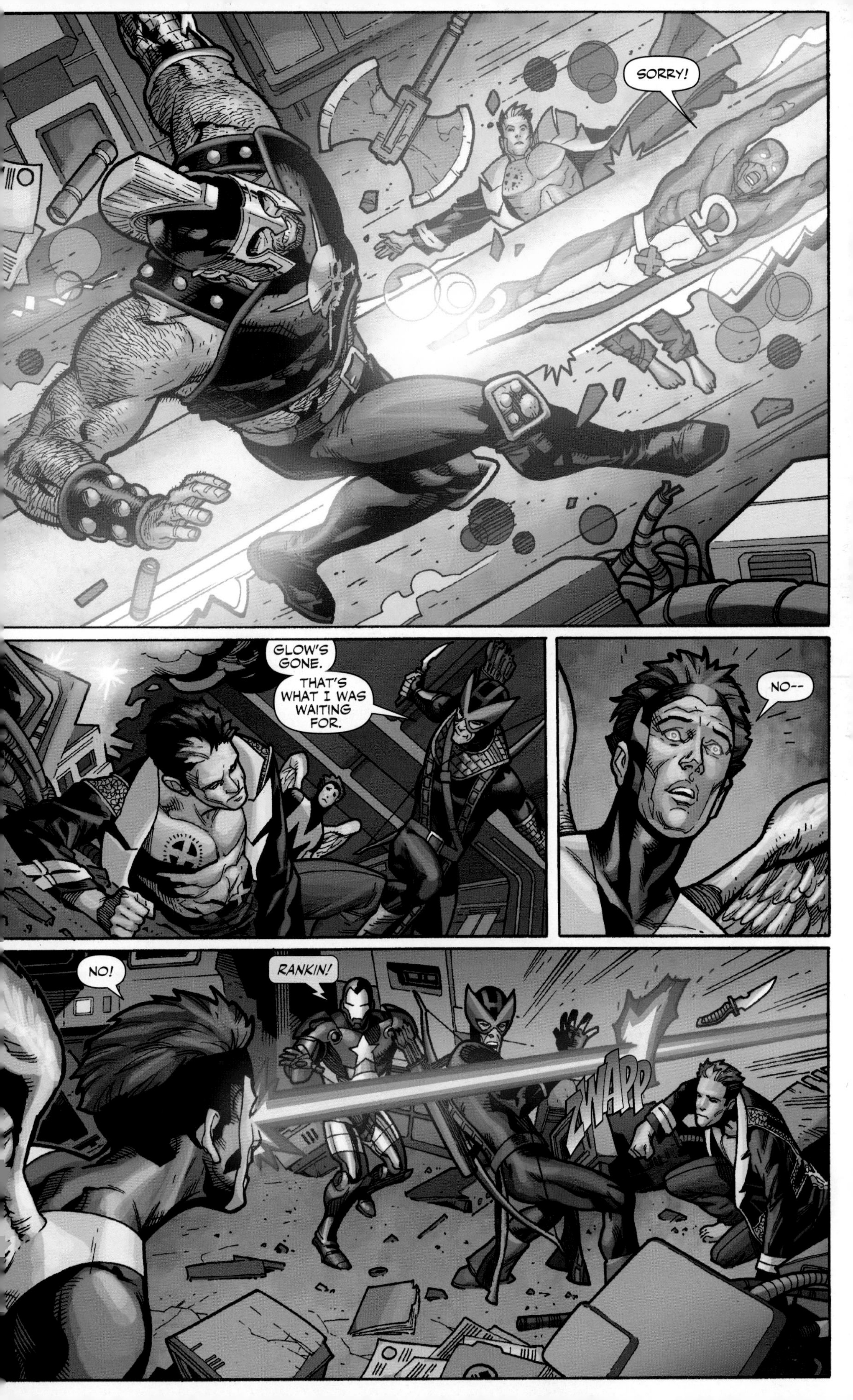
SORRY!
GLOW'S GONE.
THAT'S WHAT I WAS WAITING FOR.
NO--
NO!
RANKIN!
ZWAPP

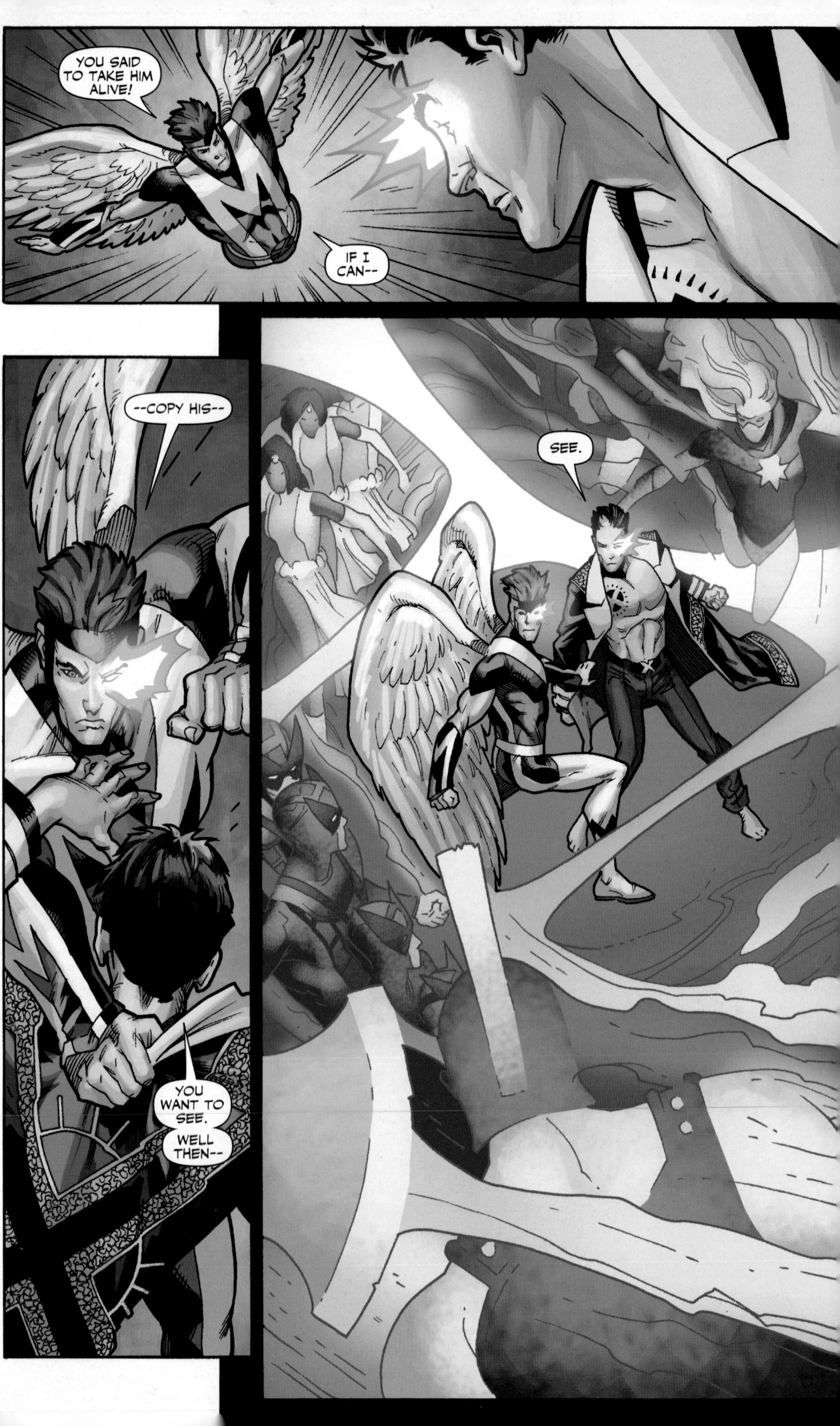
YOU SAID TO TAKE HIM ALIVE!
IF I CAN--
--COPY HIS--
YOU WANT TO SEE. WELL THEN--
SEE.

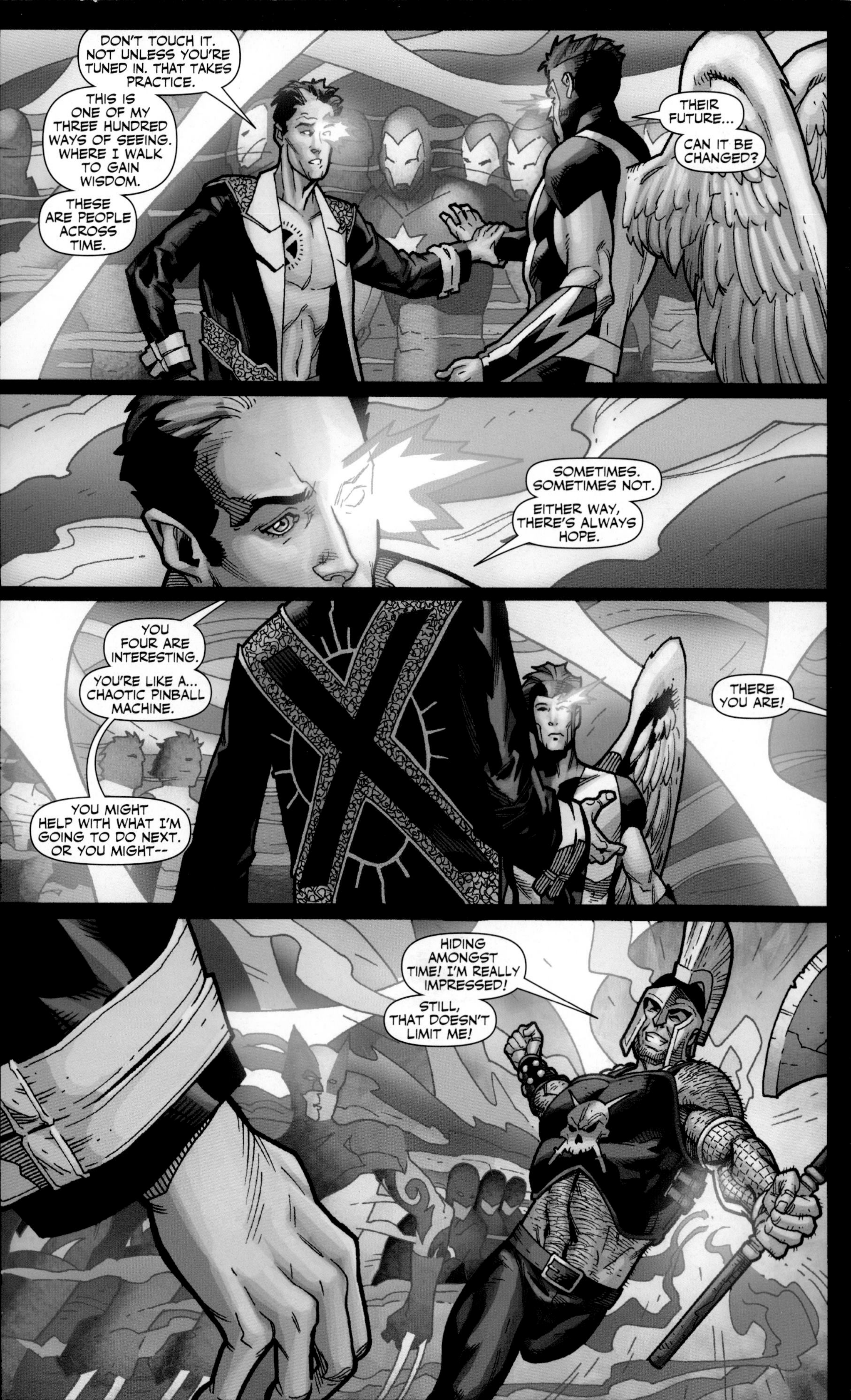
DON'T TOUCH IT. NOT UNLESS YOU'RE TUNED IN. THAT TAKES PRACTICE.
THIS IS ONE OF MY THREE HUNDRED WAYS OF SEEING. WHERE I WALK TO GAIN WISDOM.
THESE ARE PEOPLE ACROSS TIME.
THEIR FUTURE...
CAN IT BE CHANGED?
SOMETIMES. SOMETIMES NOT.
EITHER WAY, THERE'S ALWAYS HOPE.
YOU FOUR ARE INTERESTING.
YOU'RE LIKE A... CHAOTIC PINBALL MACHINE.
YOU MIGHT HELP WITH WHAT I'M GOING TO DO NEXT. OR YOU MIGHT--
THERE YOU ARE!
HIDING AMONGST TIME! I'M REALLY IMPRESSED!
STILL, THAT DOESN'T LIMIT ME!

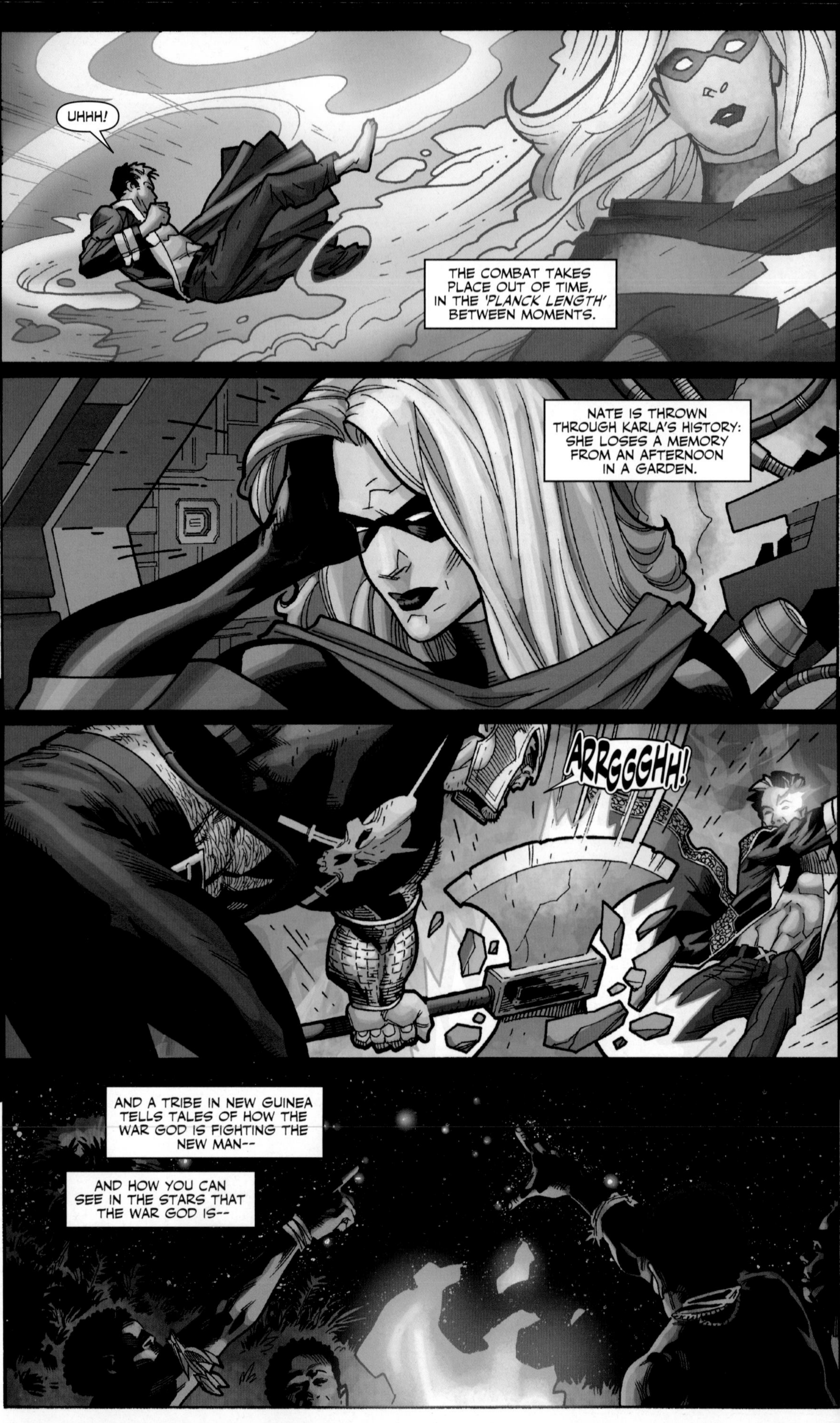
UHHH!
THE COMBAT TAKES PLACE OUT OF TIME, IN THE 'PLANCK LENGTH' BETWEEN MOMENTS.
NATE IS THROWN THROUGH KARLA'S HISTORY: SHE LOSES A MEMORY FROM AN AFTERNOON IN A GARDEN.
ARRGGGHH!
AND A TRIBE IN NEW GUINEA TELLS TALES OF HOW THE WAR GOD IS FIGHTING THE NEW MAN--
AND HOW YOU CAN SEE IN THE STARS THAT THE WAR GOD IS--

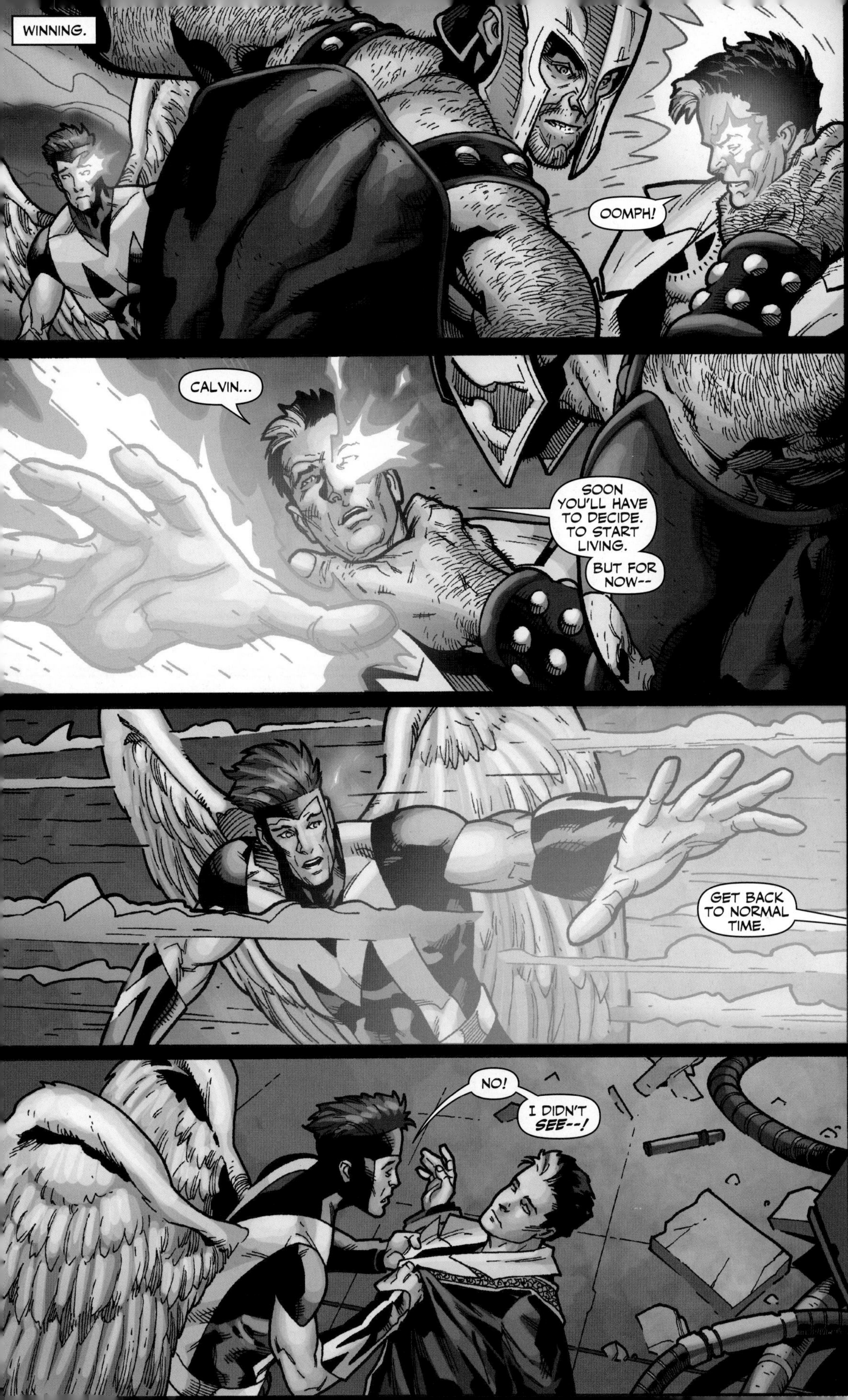
WINNING.
OOMPH!
CALVIN...
SOON YOU'LL HAVE TO DECIDE. TO START LIVING.
BUT FOR NOW--
GET BACK TO NORMAL TIME.
NO!
I DIDN'T SEE--!

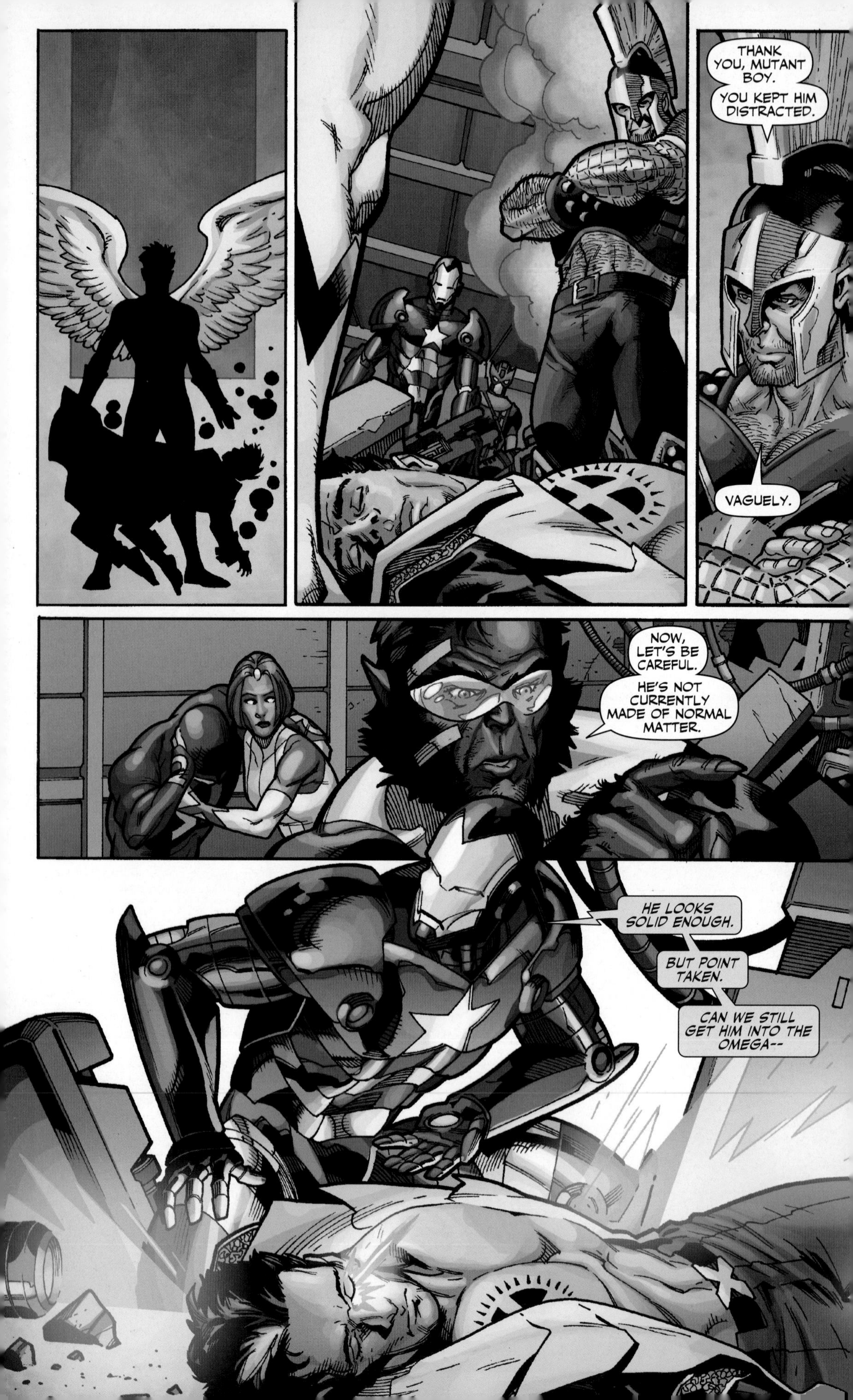
THANK YOU, MUTANT BOY.
YOU KEPT HIM DISTRACTED.
VAGUELY.
NOW, LET'S BE CAREFUL.
HE'S NOT CURRENTLY MADE OF NORMAL MATTER.
HE LOOKS SOLID ENOUGH.
BUT POINT TAKEN.
CAN WE STILL GET HIM INTO THE OMEGA--

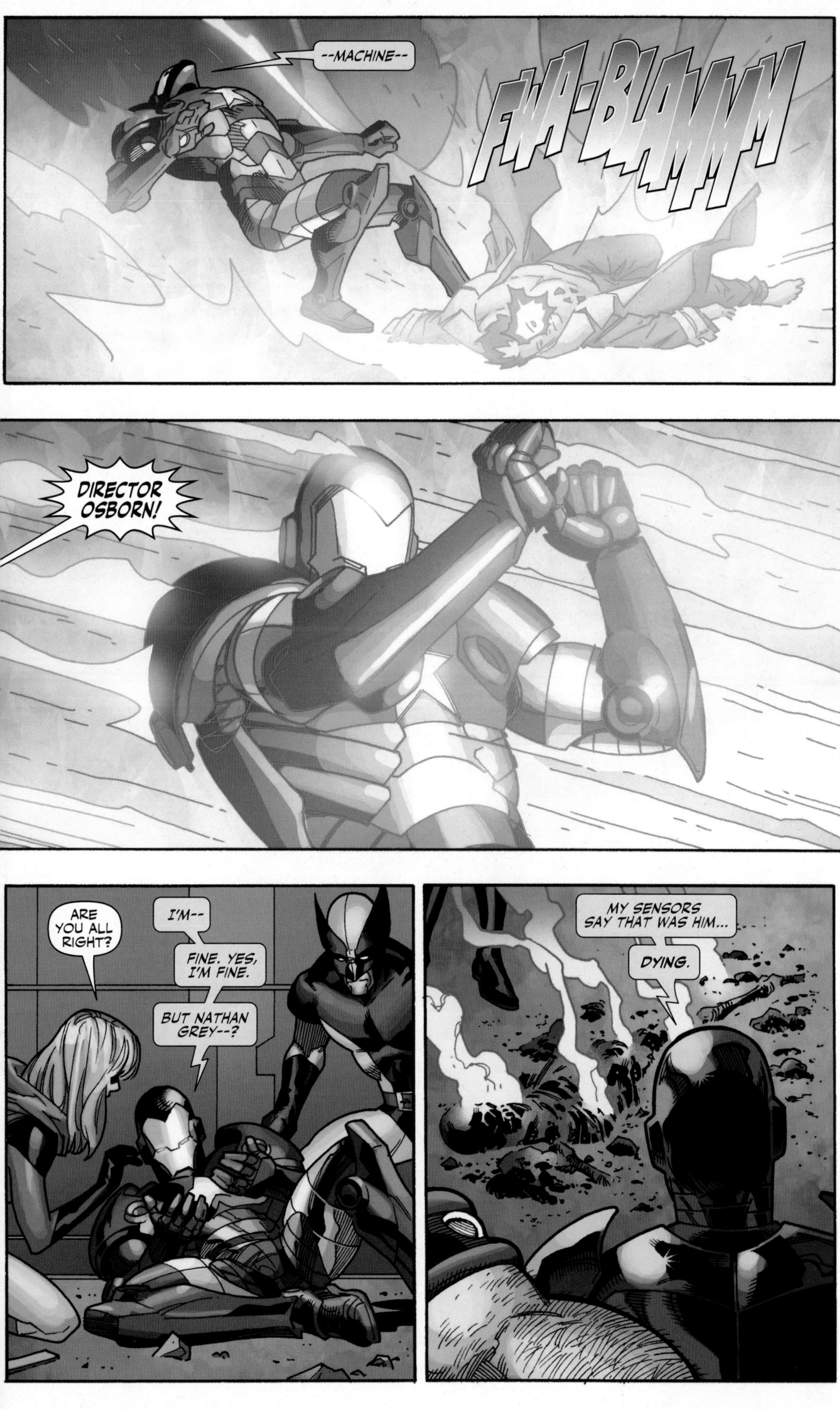
--MACHINE--
FWA-BLAMMM
DIRECTOR OSBORN!
ARE YOU ALL RIGHT?
I'M--
FINE. YES, I'M FINE.
BUT NATHAN GREY--?
MY SENSORS SAY THAT WAS HIM...
DYING.

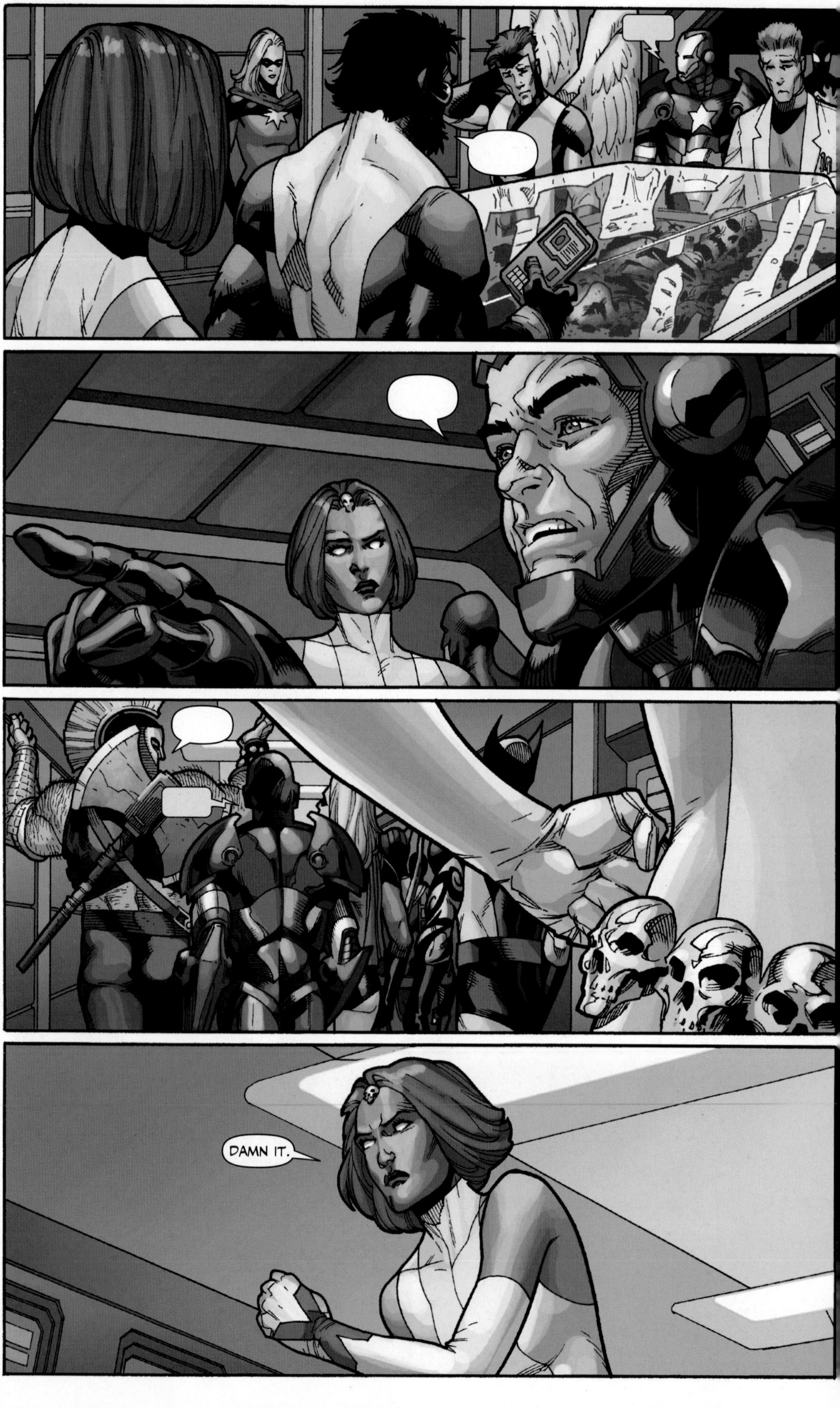
DAMN IT.

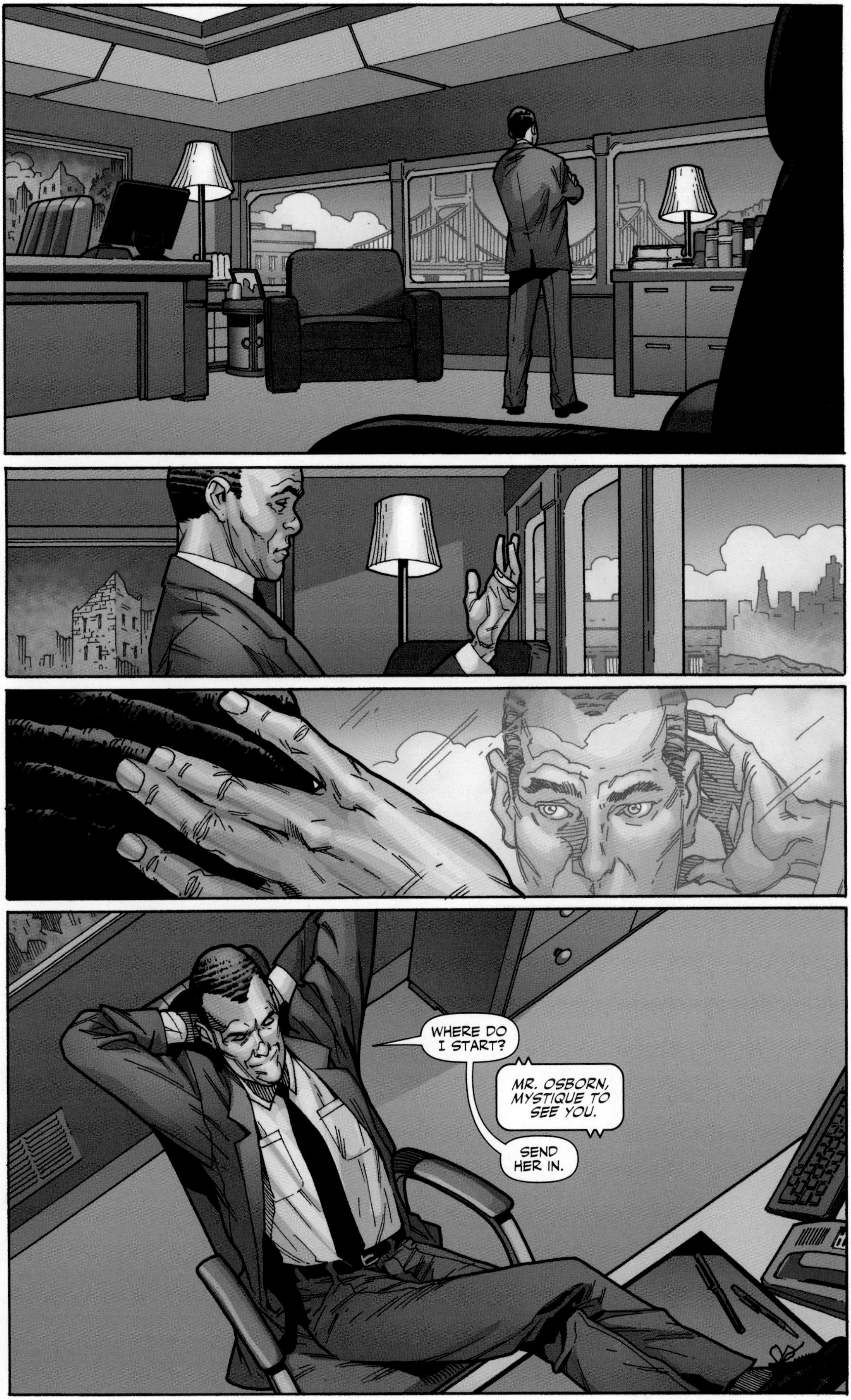
WHERE DO I START?
MR. OSBORN, MYSTIQUE TO SEE YOU.
SEND HER IN.

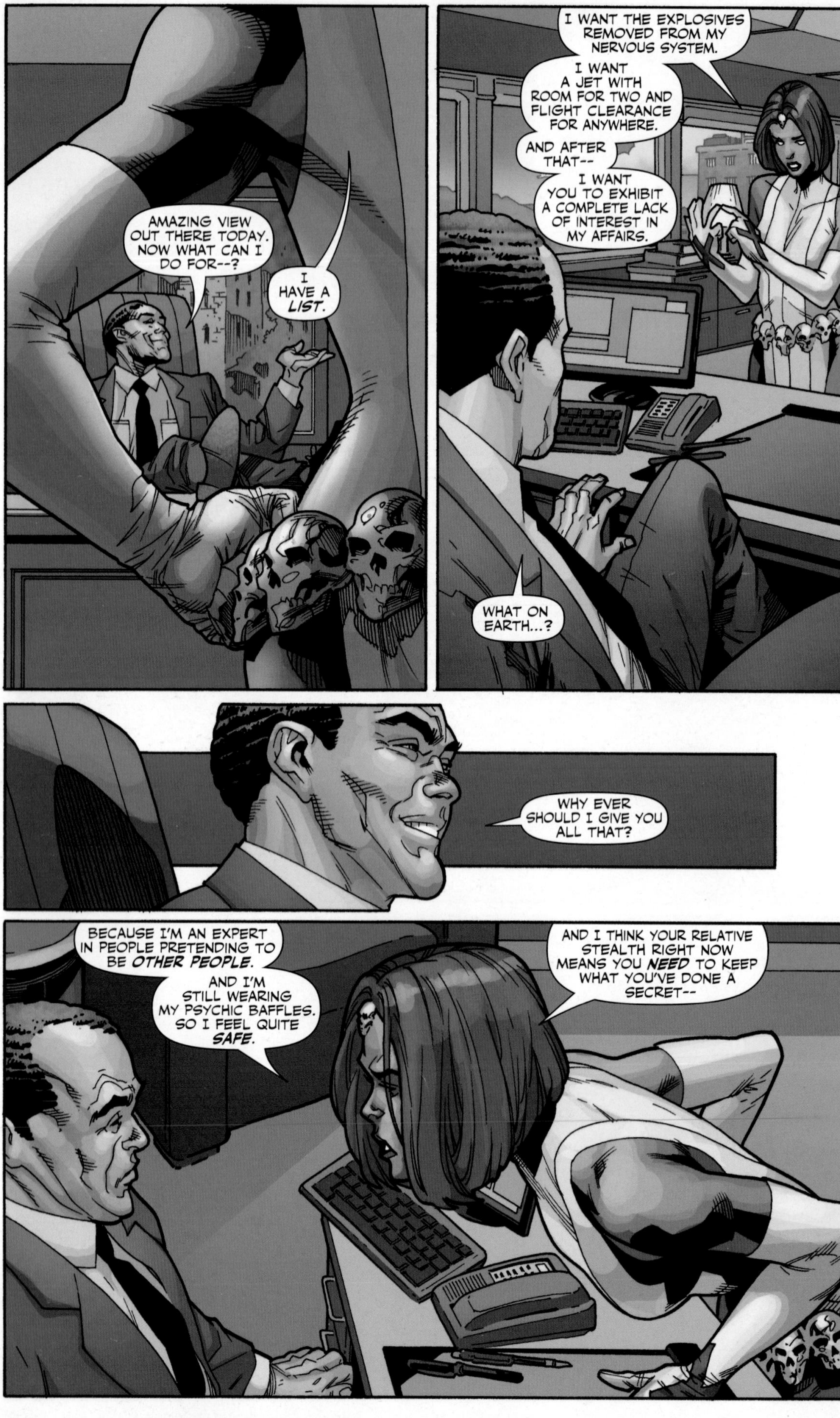
AMAZING VIEW OUT THERE TODAY. NOW WHAT CAN I DO FOR--?
I HAVE A *LIST*.
I WANT THE EXPLOSIVES REMOVED FROM MY NERVOUS SYSTEM.
I WANT A JET WITH ROOM FOR TWO AND FLIGHT CLEARANCE FOR ANYWHERE.
AND AFTER THAT--
I WANT YOU TO EXHIBIT A COMPLETE LACK OF INTEREST IN MY AFFAIRS.
WHAT ON EARTH...?
WHY EVER SHOULD I GIVE YOU ALL THAT?
BECAUSE I'M AN EXPERT IN PEOPLE PRETENDING TO BE *OTHER PEOPLE*.
AND I'M STILL WEARING MY PSYCHIC BAFFLES. SO I FEEL QUITE *SAFE*.
AND I THINK YOUR RELATIVE STEALTH RIGHT NOW MEANS YOU *NEED* TO KEEP WHAT YOU'VE DONE A SECRET--

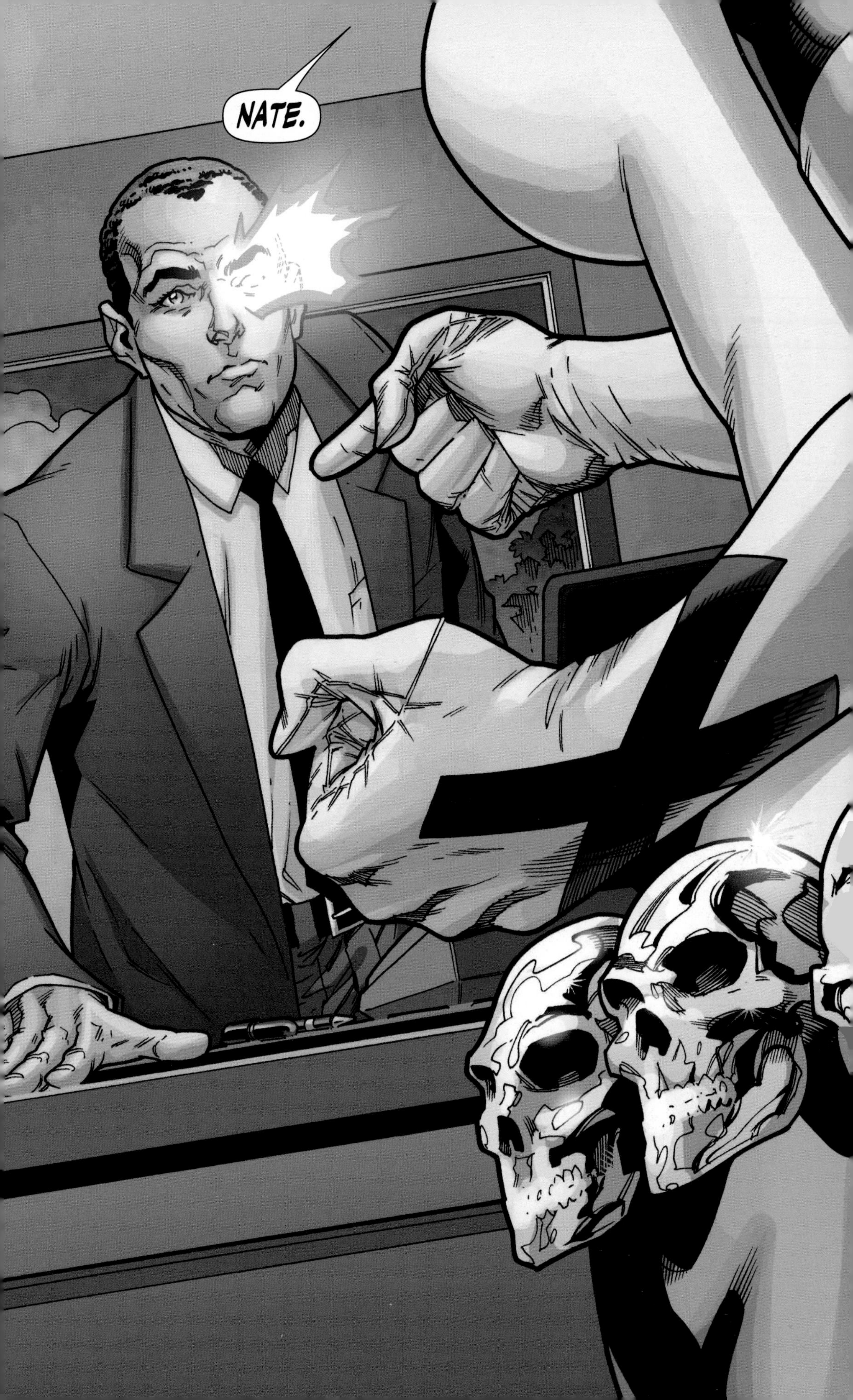
NATE.

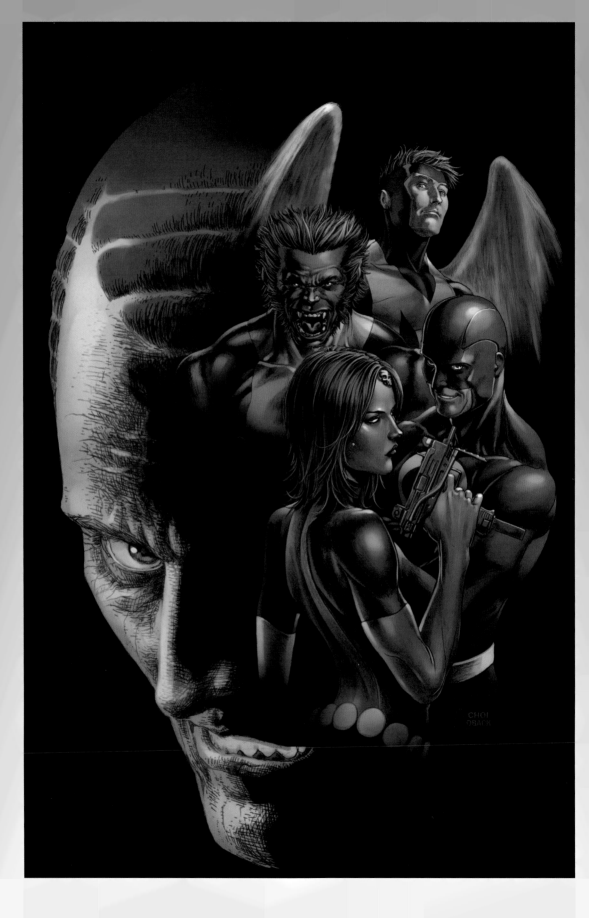
CHOI
OBACK

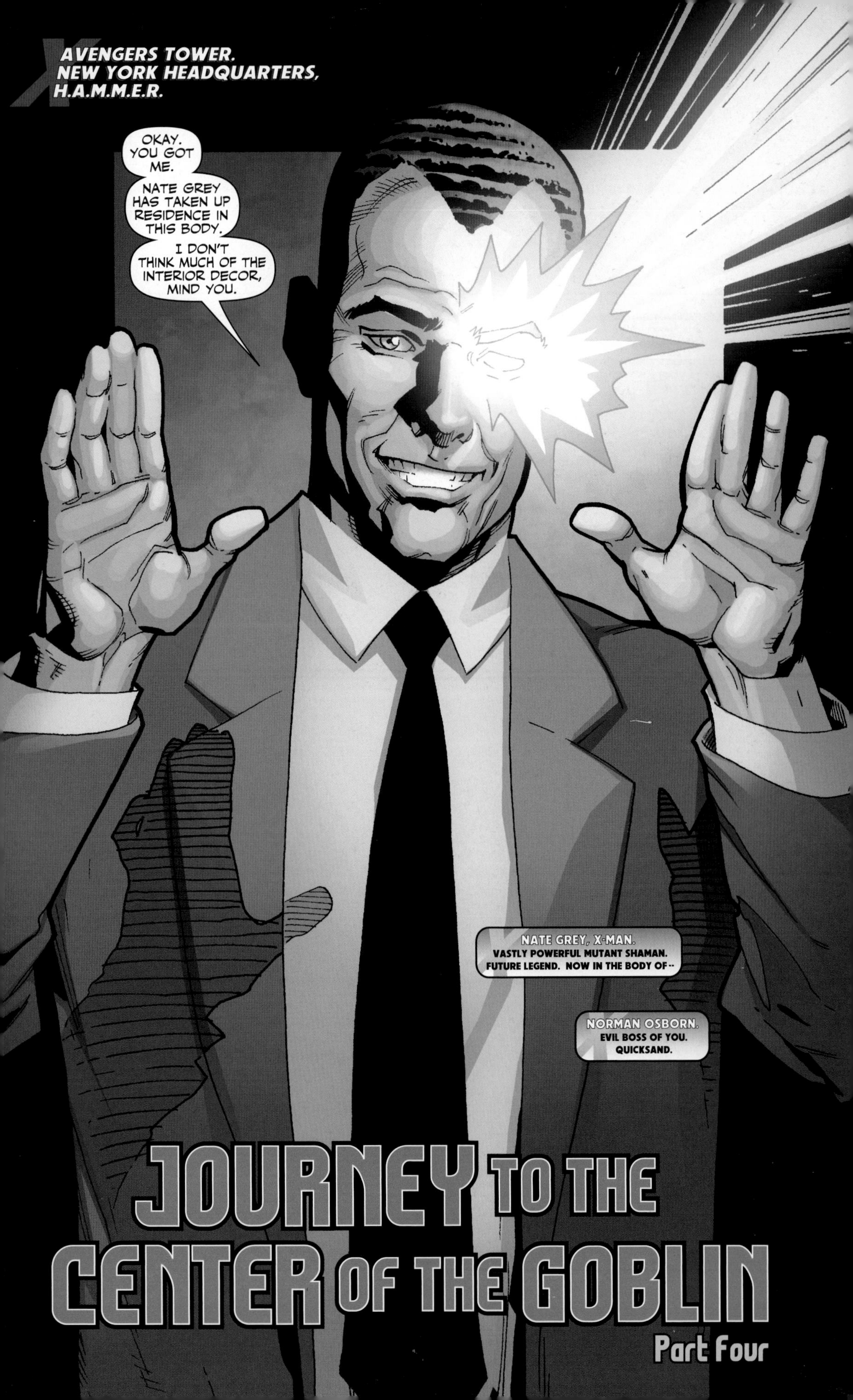
AVENGERS TOWER. NEW YORK HEADQUARTERS, H.A.M.M.E.R.
OKAY. YOU GOT ME.
NATE GREY HAS TAKEN UP RESIDENCE IN THIS BODY.
I DON'T THINK MUCH OF THE INTERIOR DECOR, MIND YOU.
NATE GREY, X-MAN. VASTLY POWERFUL MUTANT SHAMAN. FUTURE LEGEND. NOW IN THE BODY OF--
NORMAN OSBORN. EVIL BOSS OF YOU. QUICKSAND.
JOURNEY TO THE CENTER OF THE GOBLIN
Part Four

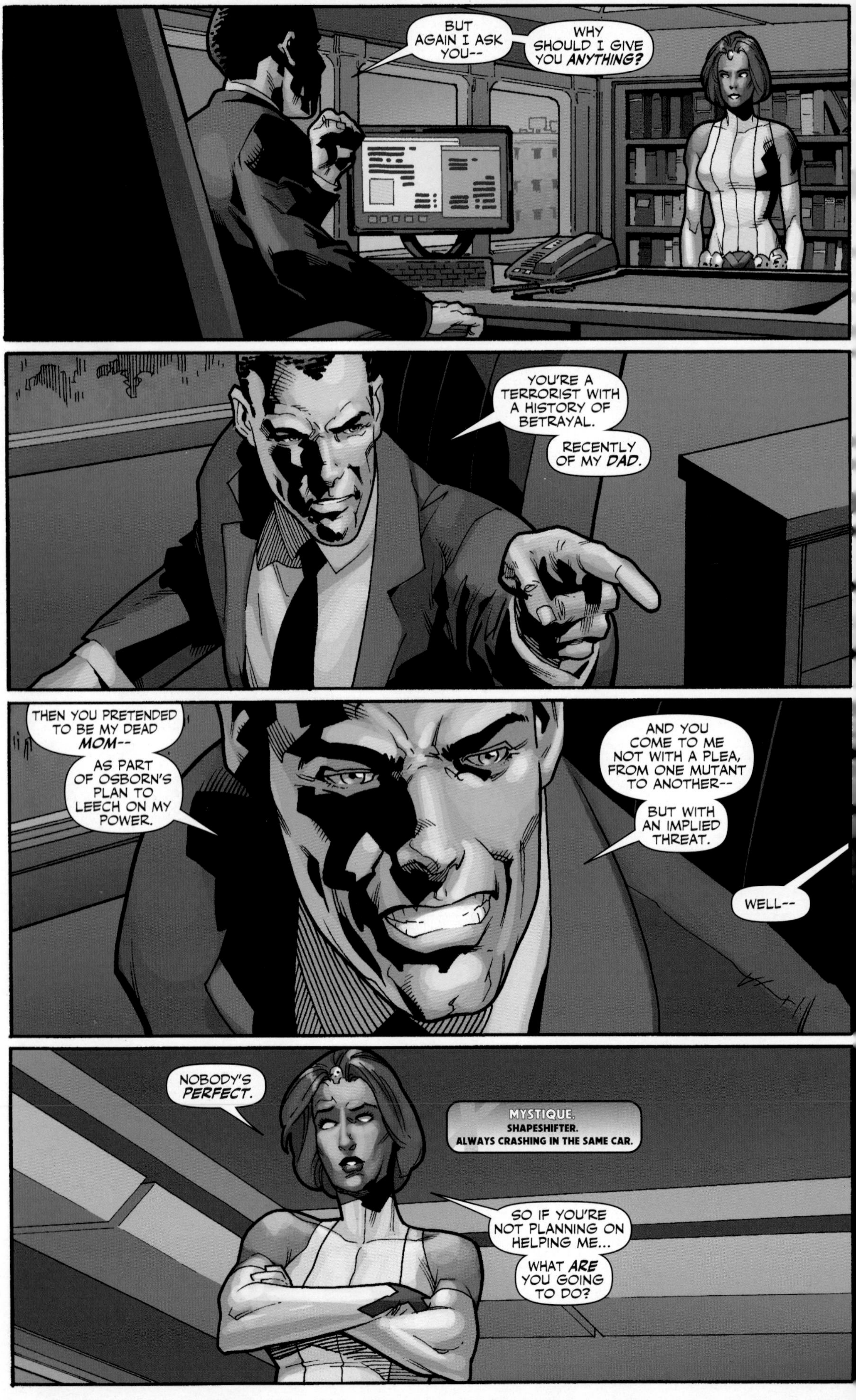
BUT AGAIN I ASK YOU--
WHY SHOULD I GIVE YOU ANYTHING?
YOU'RE A TERRORIST WITH A HISTORY OF BETRAYAL.
RECENTLY OF MY DAD.
THEN YOU PRETENDED TO BE MY DEAD MOM--
AS PART OF OSBORN'S PLAN TO LEECH ON MY POWER.
AND YOU COME TO ME NOT WITH A PLEA, FROM ONE MUTANT TO ANOTHER--
BUT WITH AN IMPLIED THREAT.
WELL--
NOBODY'S PERFECT.
MYSTIQUE.
SHAPESHIFTER.
ALWAYS CRASHING IN THE SAME CAR.
SO IF YOU'RE NOT PLANNING ON HELPING ME...
WHAT ARE YOU GOING TO DO?

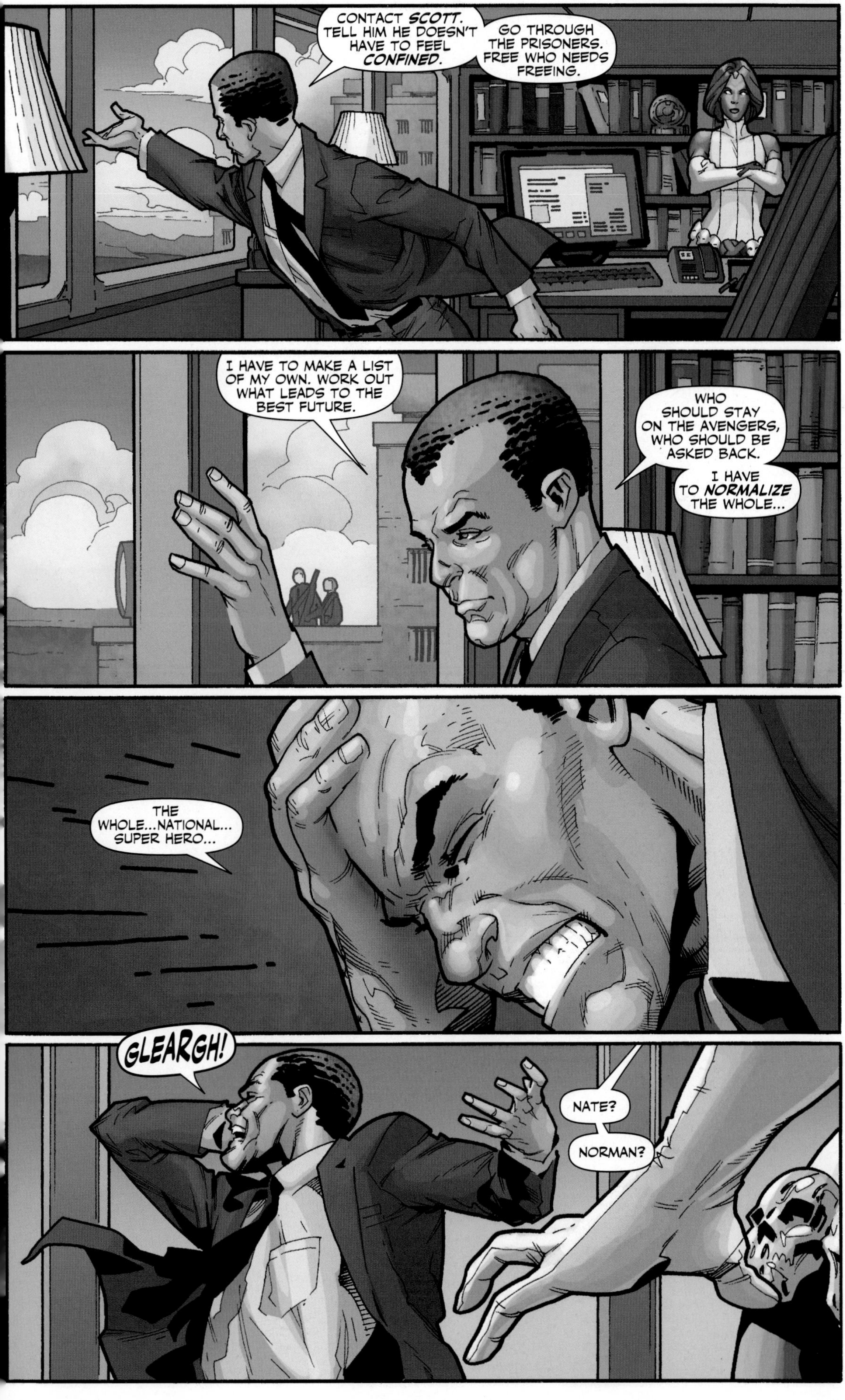
CONTACT SCOTT. TELL HIM HE DOESN'T HAVE TO FEEL CONFINED.
GO THROUGH THE PRISONERS. FREE WHO NEEDS FREEING.
I HAVE TO MAKE A LIST OF MY OWN. WORK OUT WHAT LEADS TO THE BEST FUTURE.
WHO SHOULD STAY ON THE AVENGERS, WHO SHOULD BE ASKED BACK.
I HAVE TO NORMALIZE THE WHOLE...
THE WHOLE...NATIONAL... SUPER HERO...
GLEARGH!
NATE?
NORMAN?

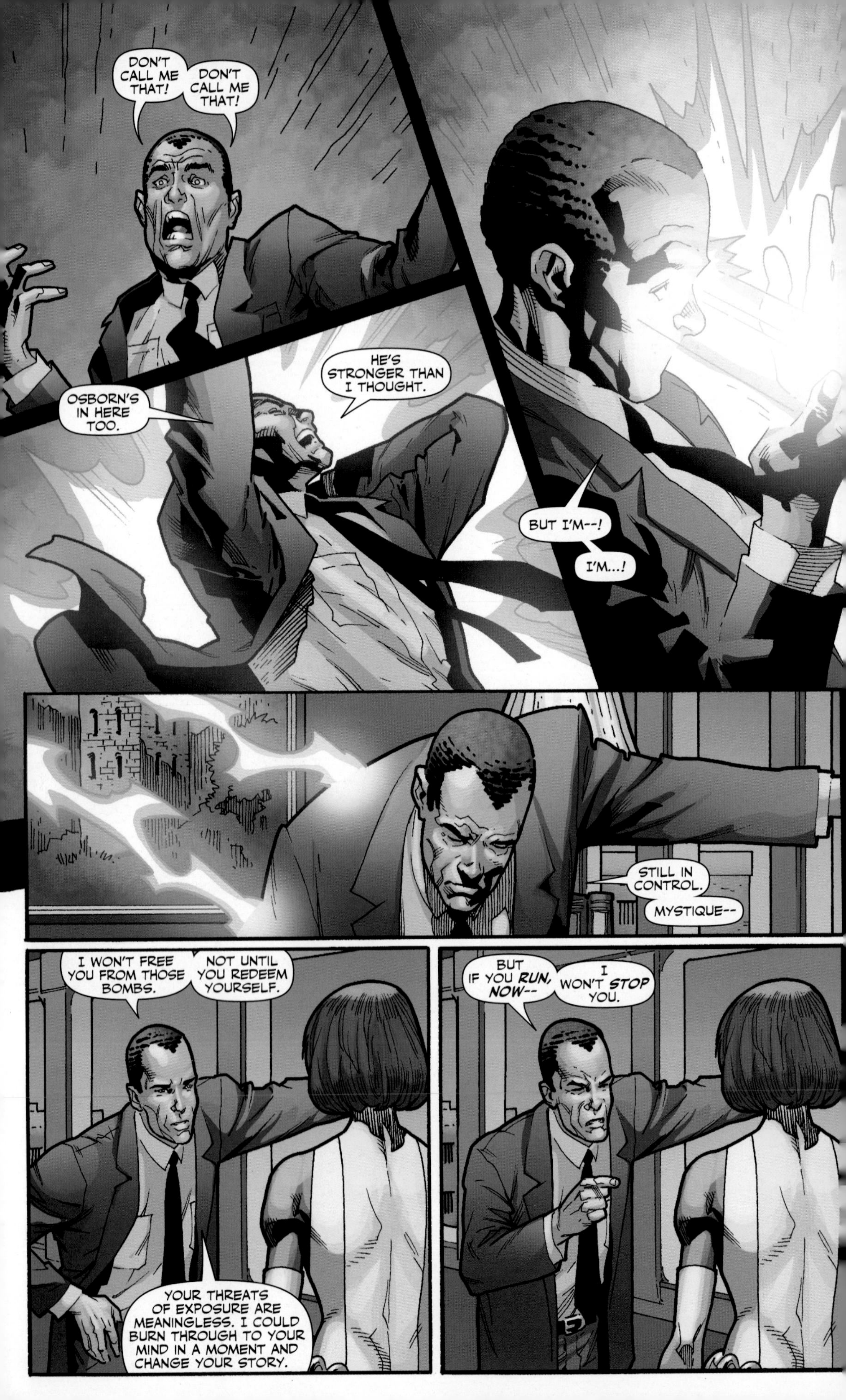
DON'T CALL ME THAT!
DON'T CALL ME THAT!
OSBORN'S IN HERE TOO.
HE'S STRONGER THAN I THOUGHT.
BUT I'M--!
I'M...!
STILL IN CONTROL.
MYSTIQUE--
I WON'T FREE YOU FROM THOSE BOMBS.
NOT UNTIL YOU REDEEM YOURSELF.
YOUR THREATS OF EXPOSURE ARE MEANINGLESS. I COULD BURN THROUGH TO YOUR MIND IN A MOMENT AND CHANGE YOUR STORY.
BUT IF YOU RUN, NOW--
I WON'T STOP YOU.

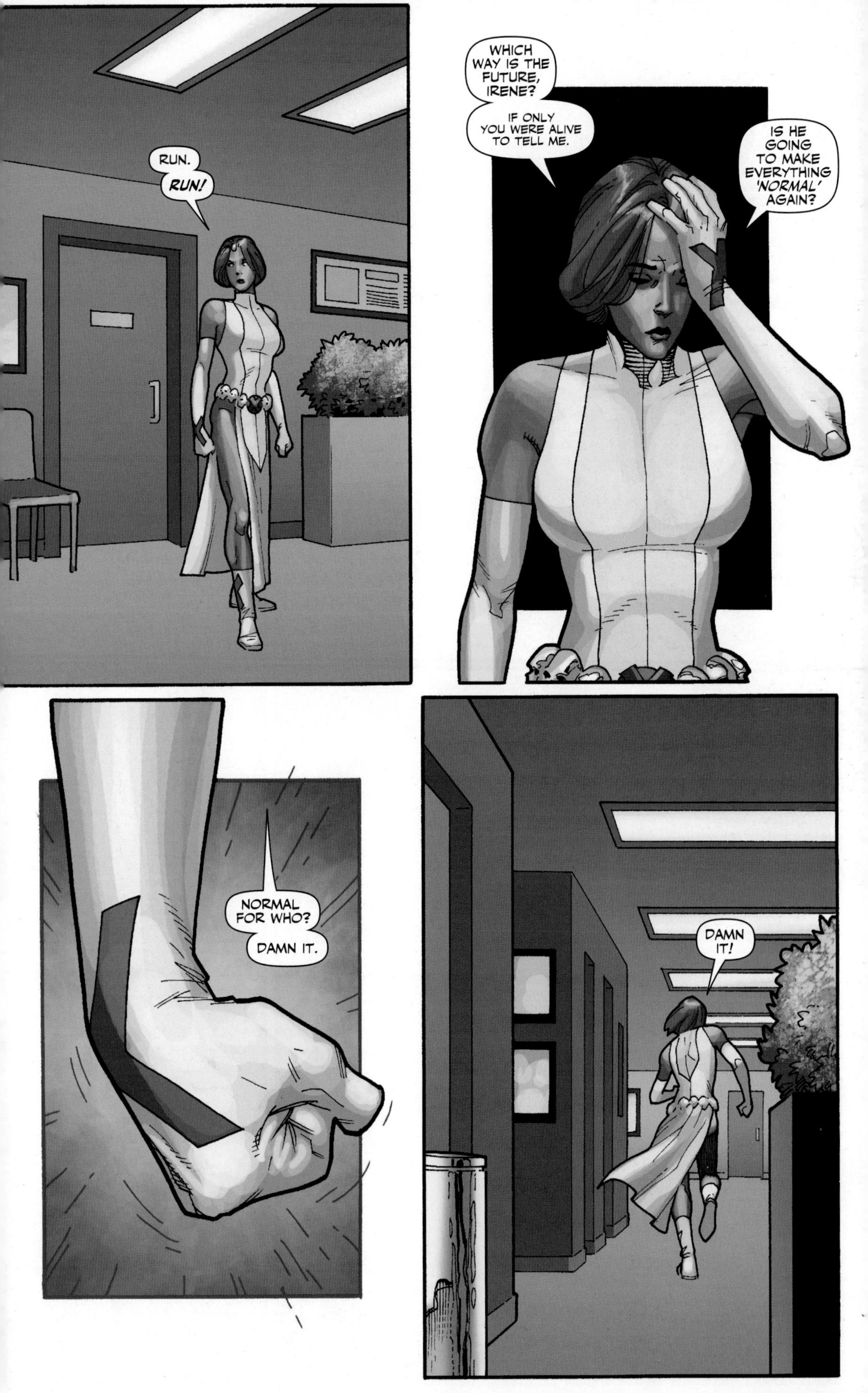
RUN.
RUN!
WHICH WAY IS THE FUTURE, IRENE?
IF ONLY YOU WERE ALIVE TO TELL ME.
IS HE GOING TO MAKE EVERYTHING 'NORMAL' AGAIN?
NORMAL FOR WHO?
DAMN IT.
DAMN IT!

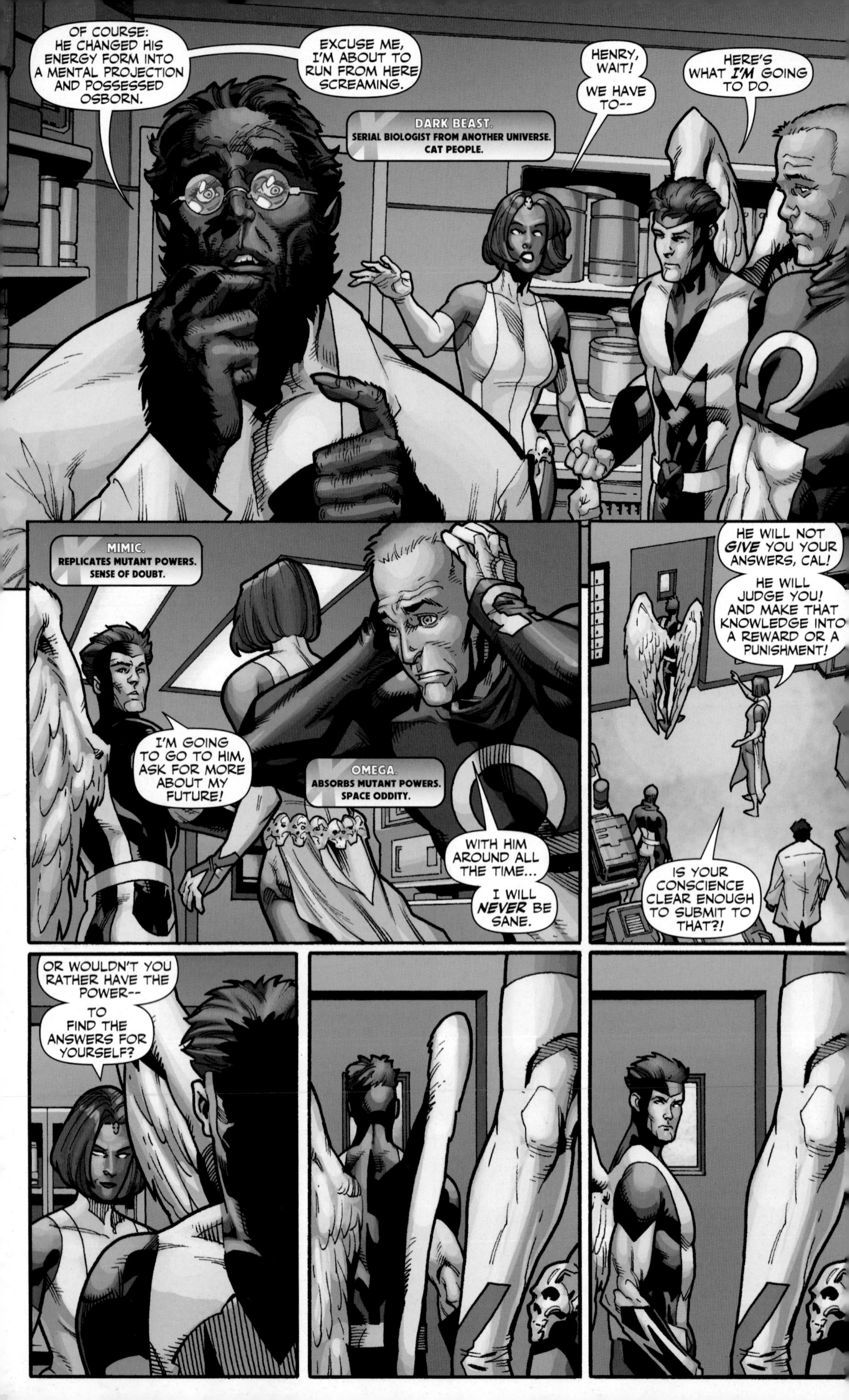

OF COURSE: HE CHANGED HIS ENERGY FORM INTO A MENTAL PROJECTION AND POSSESSED OSBORN.
EXCUSE ME, I'M ABOUT TO RUN FROM HERE SCREAMING.
DARK BEAST. SERIAL BIOLOGIST FROM ANOTHER UNIVERSE. CAT PEOPLE.
HENRY, WAIT!
WE HAVE TO--
HERE'S WHAT *I'M* GOING TO DO.
MIMIC. REPLICATES MUTANT POWERS. SENSE OF DOUBT.
I'M GOING TO GO TO HIM, ASK FOR MORE ABOUT MY FUTURE!
OMEGA. ABSORBS MUTANT POWERS. SPACE ODDITY.
WITH HIM AROUND ALL THE TIME...
I WILL *NEVER* BE SANE.
HE WILL NOT *GIVE* YOU YOUR ANSWERS, CAL!
HE WILL JUDGE YOU! AND MAKE THAT KNOWLEDGE INTO A REWARD OR A PUNISHMENT!
IS YOUR CONSCIENCE CLEAR ENOUGH TO SUBMIT TO THAT?!
OR WOULDN'T YOU RATHER HAVE THE POWER--
TO FIND THE ANSWERS FOR YOURSELF?

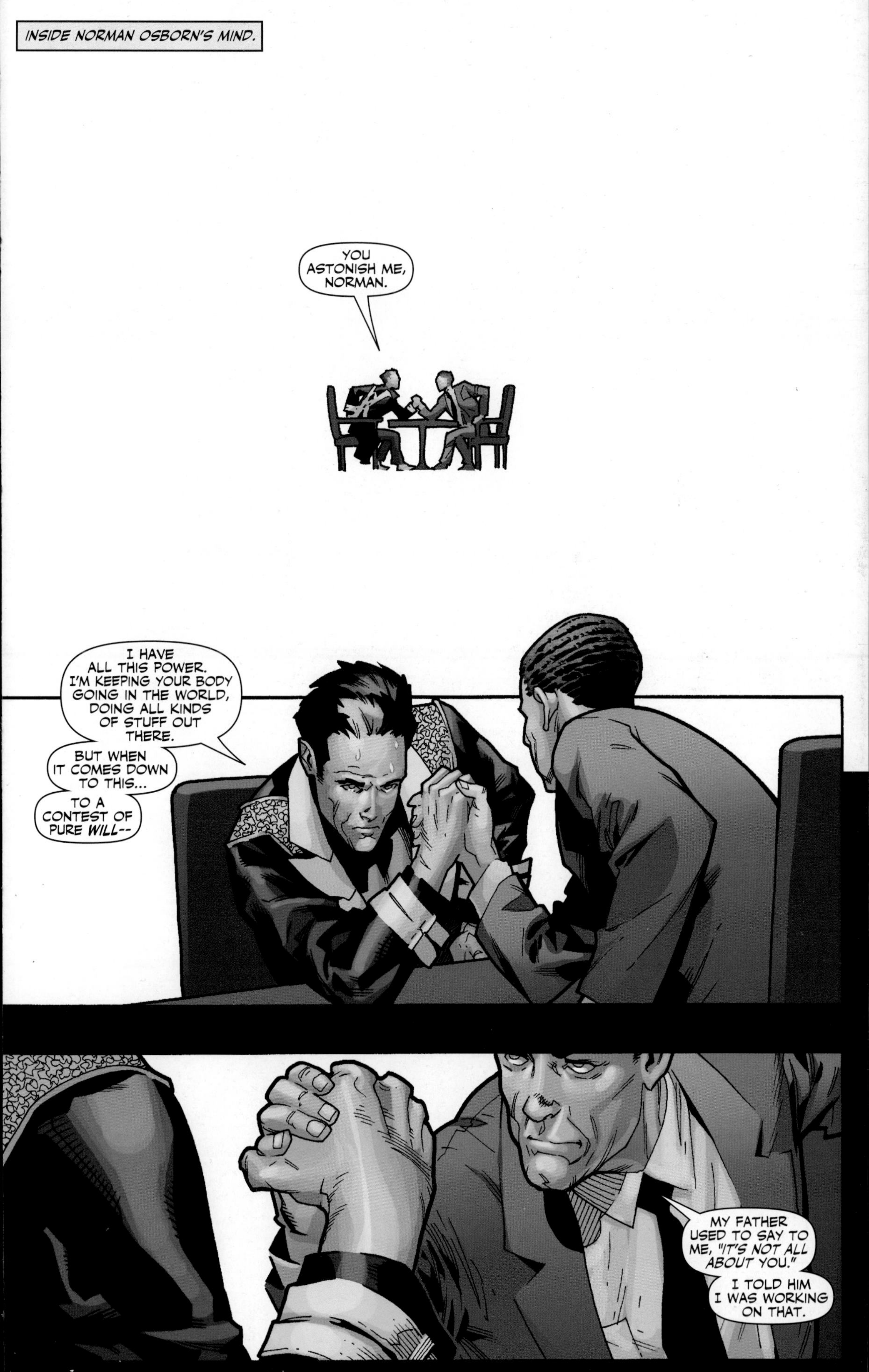
INSIDE NORMAN OSBORN'S MIND.
YOU ASTONISH ME, NORMAN.
I HAVE ALL THIS POWER. I'M KEEPING YOUR BODY GOING IN THE WORLD, DOING ALL KINDS OF STUFF OUT THERE.
BUT WHEN IT COMES DOWN TO THIS...
TO A CONTEST OF PURE WILL--
MY FATHER USED TO SAY TO ME, "IT'S NOT ALL ABOUT YOU."
I TOLD HIM I WAS WORKING ON THAT.

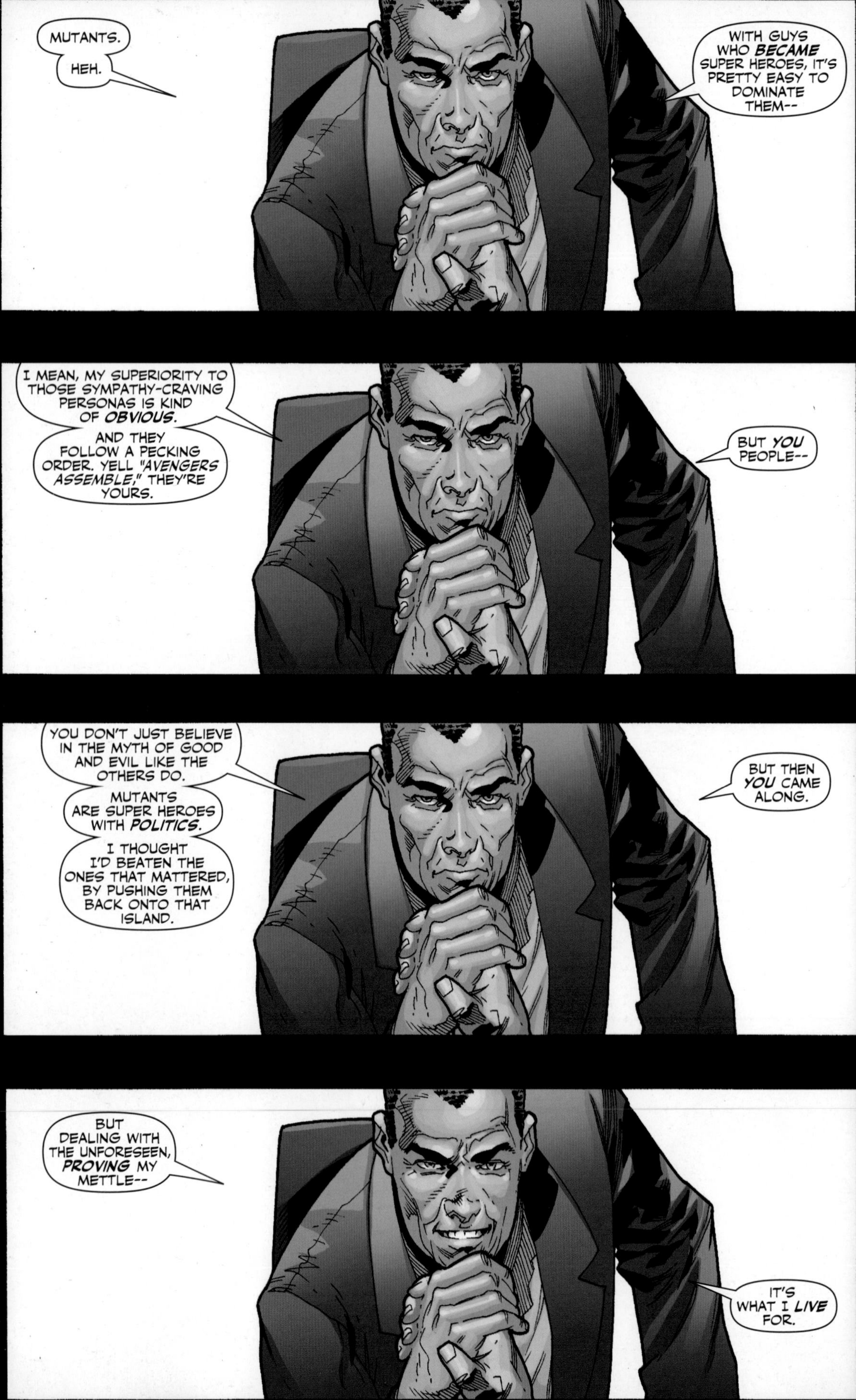

MUTANTS.
HEH.
WITH GUYS WHO BECAME SUPER HEROES, IT'S PRETTY EASY TO DOMINATE THEM--
I MEAN, MY SUPERIORITY TO THOSE SYMPATHY-CRAVING PERSONAS IS KIND OF OBVIOUS.
AND THEY FOLLOW A PECKING ORDER. YELL "AVENGERS ASSEMBLE," THEY'RE YOURS.
BUT YOU PEOPLE--
YOU DON'T JUST BELIEVE IN THE MYTH OF GOOD AND EVIL LIKE THE OTHERS DO.
MUTANTS ARE SUPER HEROES WITH POLITICS.
I THOUGHT I'D BEATEN THE ONES THAT MATTERED, BY PUSHING THEM BACK ONTO THAT ISLAND.
BUT THEN YOU CAME ALONG.
BUT DEALING WITH THE UNFORESEEN, PROVING MY METTLE--
IT'S WHAT I LIVE FOR.

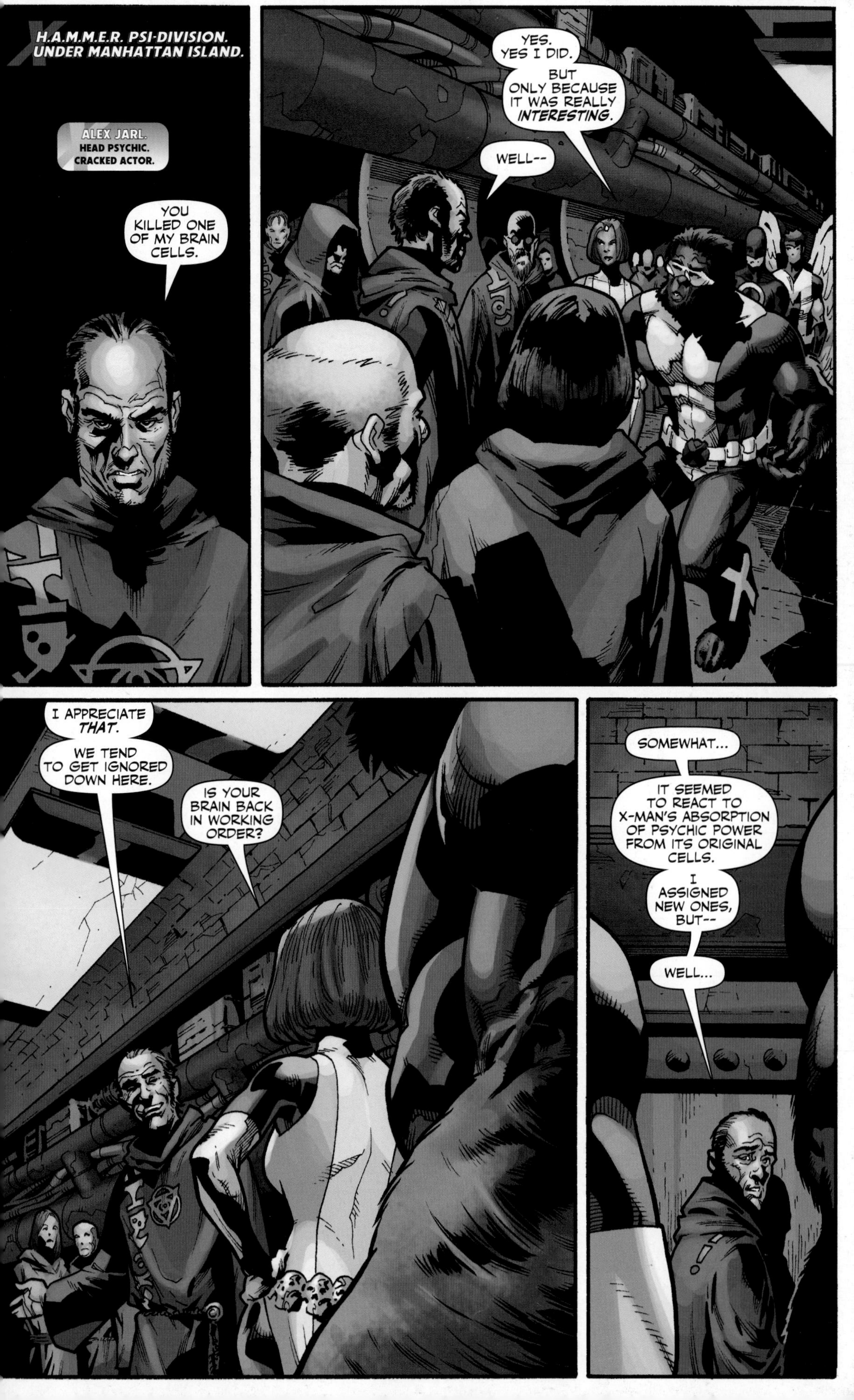
H.A.M.M.E.R. PSI-DIVISION. UNDER MANHATTAN ISLAND.
ALEX JARL. HEAD PSYCHIC. CRACKED ACTOR.
YOU KILLED ONE OF MY BRAIN CELLS.
WELL--
YES. YES I DID.
BUT ONLY BECAUSE IT WAS REALLY INTERESTING.
I APPRECIATE THAT.
WE TEND TO GET IGNORED DOWN HERE.
IS YOUR BRAIN BACK IN WORKING ORDER?
SOMEWHAT...
IT SEEMED TO REACT TO X-MAN'S ABSORPTION OF PSYCHIC POWER FROM ITS ORIGINAL CELLS.
I ASSIGNED NEW ONES, BUT--
WELL...

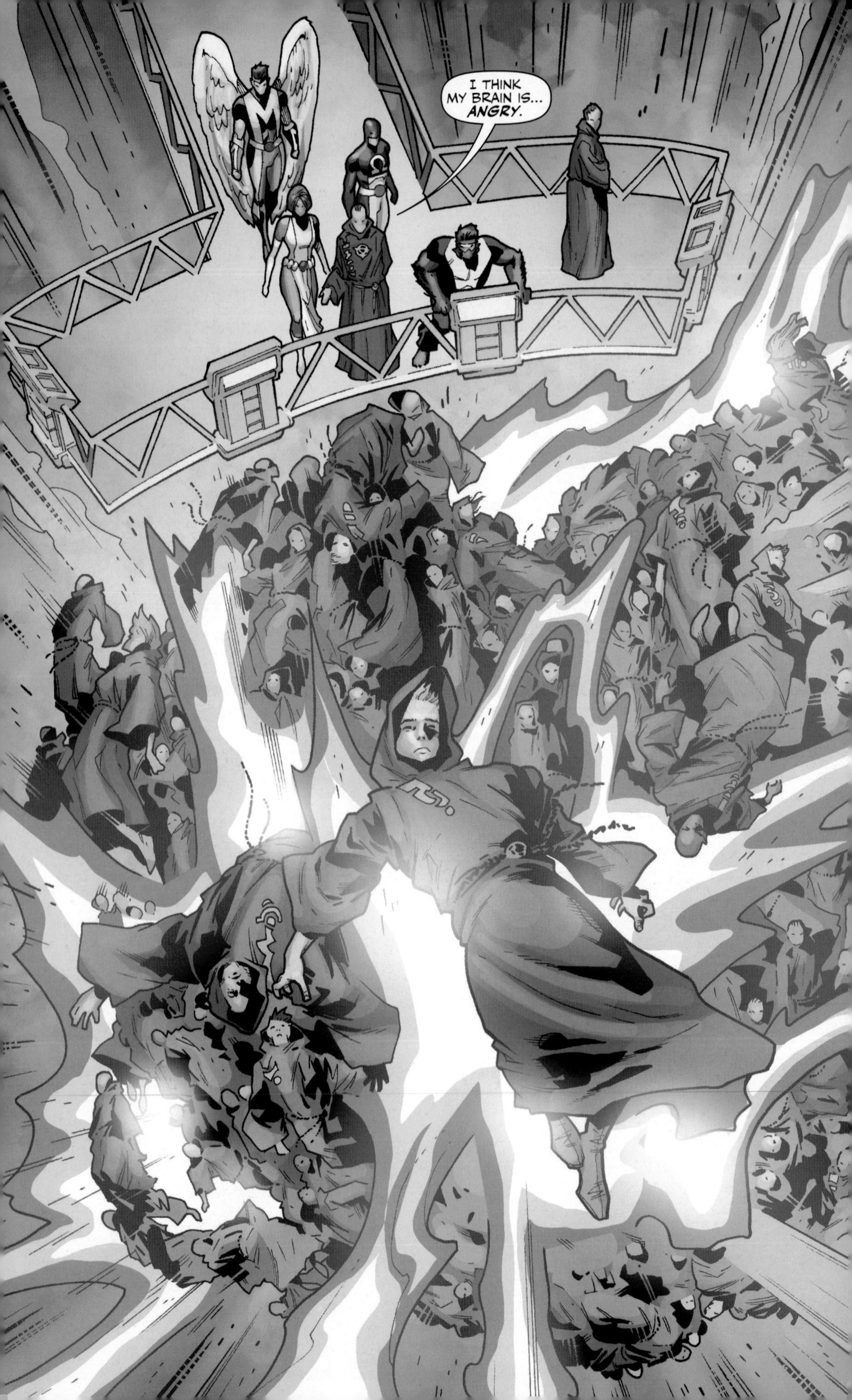
I THINK MY BRAIN IS... ANGRY.

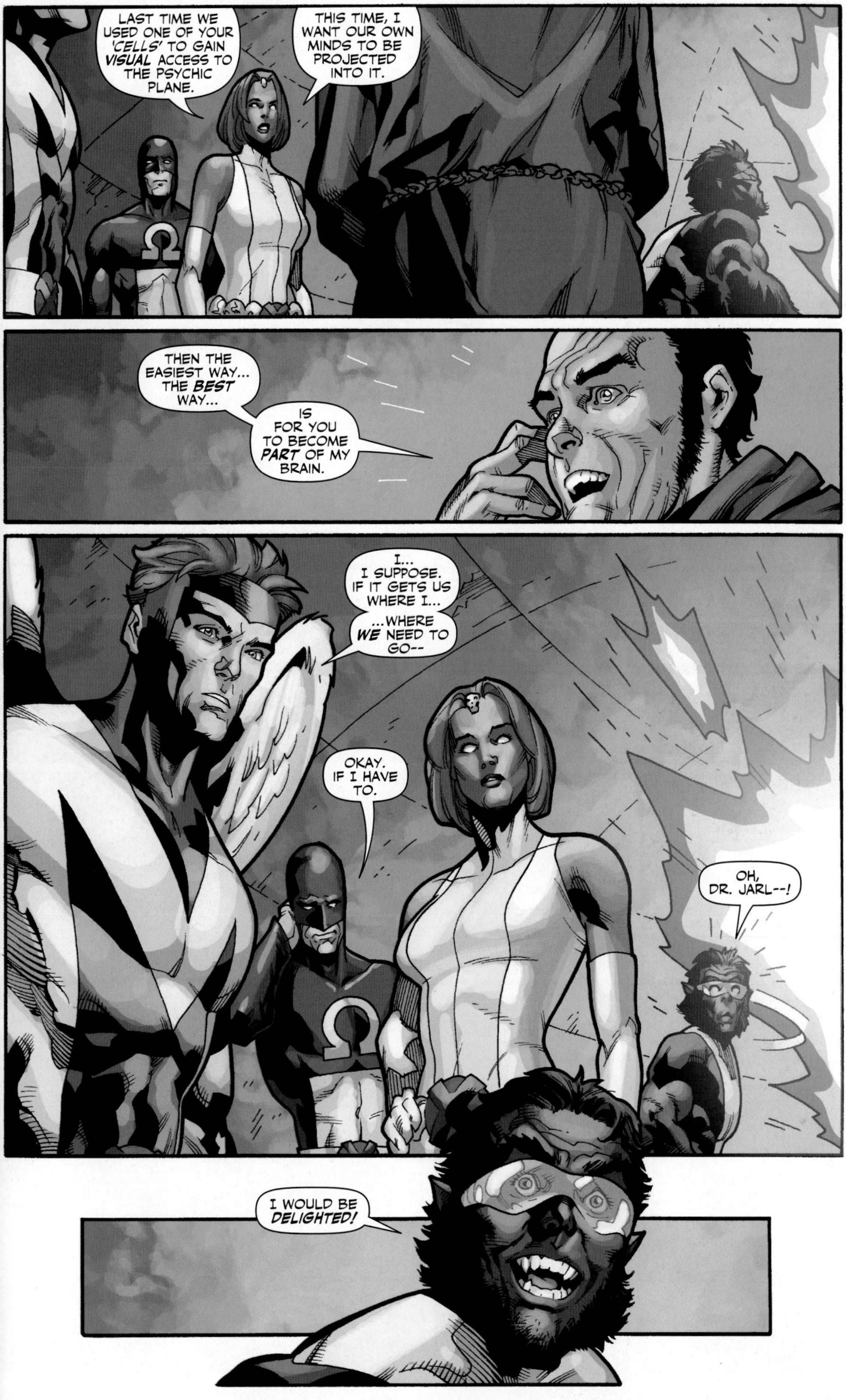
LAST TIME WE USED ONE OF YOUR 'CELLS' TO GAIN VISUAL ACCESS TO THE PSYCHIC PLANE.
THIS TIME, I WANT OUR OWN MINDS TO BE PROJECTED INTO IT.
THEN THE EASIEST WAY... THE BEST WAY...
IS FOR YOU TO BECOME PART OF MY BRAIN.
I... I SUPPOSE. IF IT GETS US WHERE I... ...WHERE WE NEED TO GO--
OKAY. IF I HAVE TO.
OH, DR. JARL--!
I WOULD BE DELIGHTED!

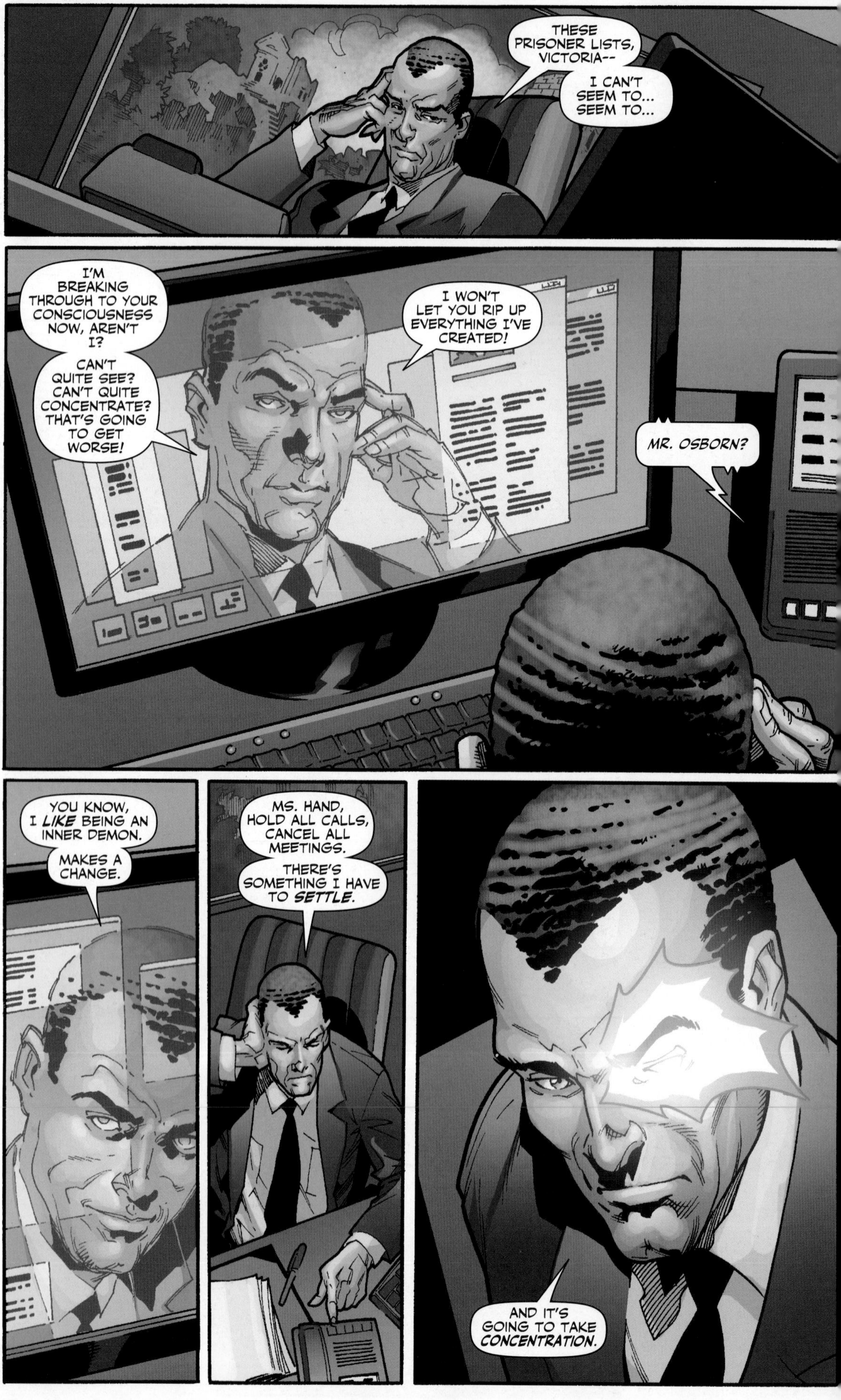
THESE PRISONER LISTS, VICTORIA--
I CAN'T SEEM TO... SEEM TO...
I'M BREAKING THROUGH TO YOUR CONSCIOUSNESS NOW, AREN'T I?
CAN'T QUITE SEE? CAN'T QUITE CONCENTRATE? THAT'S GOING TO GET WORSE!
I WON'T LET YOU RIP UP EVERYTHING I'VE CREATED!
MR. OSBORN?
YOU KNOW, I LIKE BEING AN INNER DEMON.
MAKES A CHANGE.
MS. HAND, HOLD ALL CALLS, CANCEL ALL MEETINGS.
THERE'S SOMETHING I HAVE TO SETTLE.
AND IT'S GOING TO TAKE CONCENTRATION.

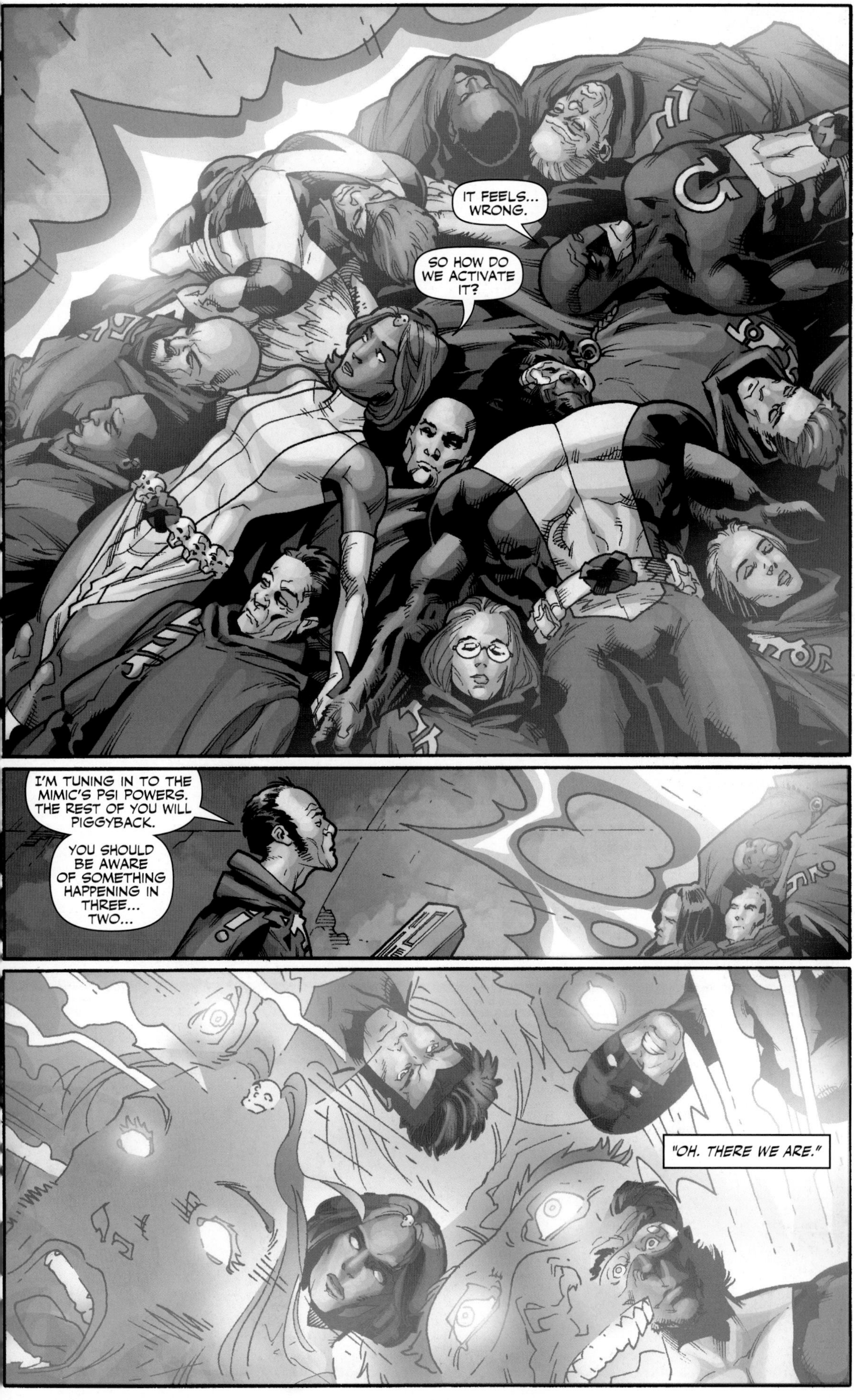
IT FEELS... WRONG.
SO HOW DO WE ACTIVATE IT?
I'M TUNING IN TO THE MIMIC'S PSI POWERS. THE REST OF YOU WILL PIGGYBACK.
YOU SHOULD BE AWARE OF SOMETHING HAPPENING IN THREE... TWO...
"OH. THERE WE ARE."

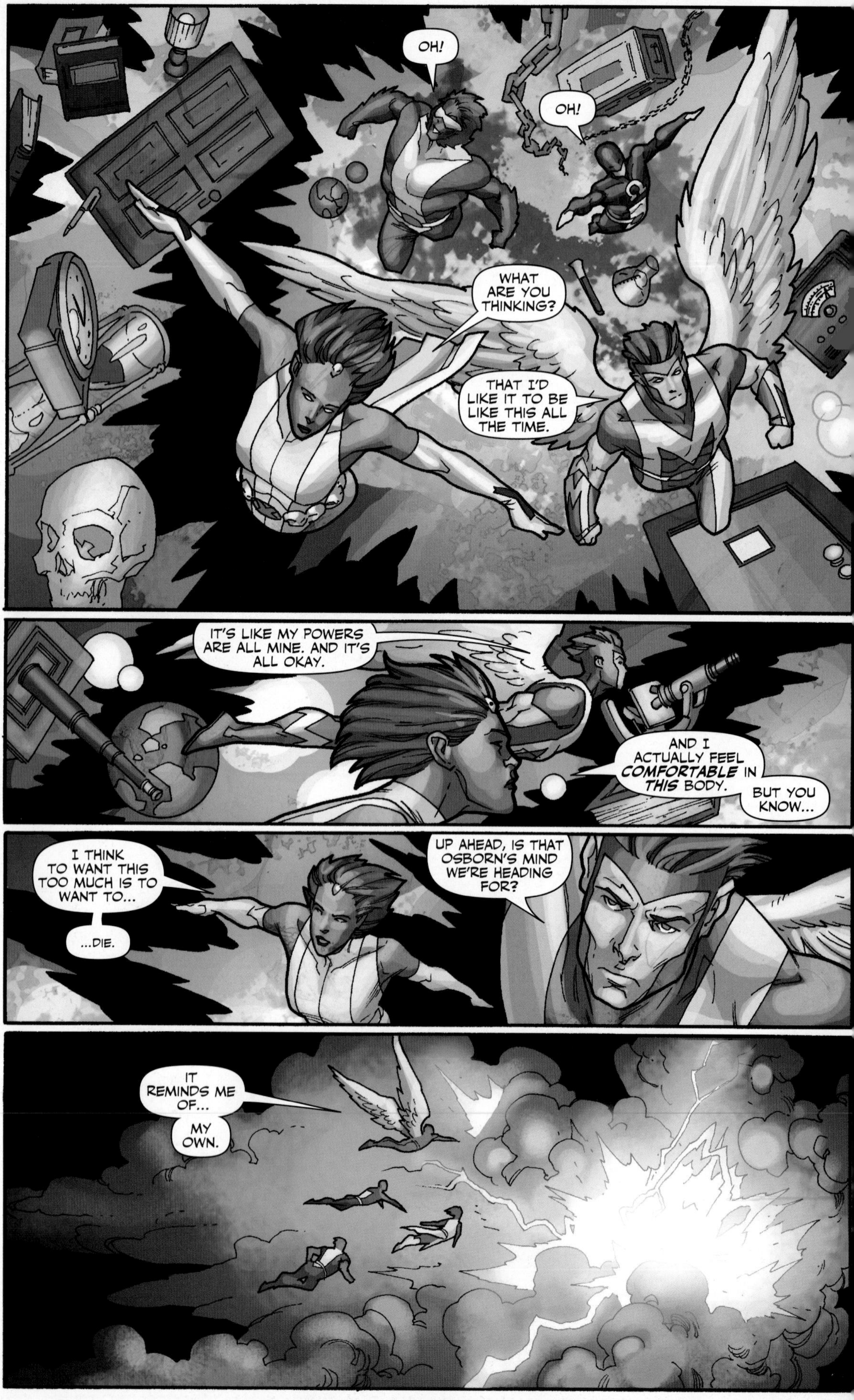
OH!
OH!
WHAT ARE YOU THINKING?
THAT I'D LIKE IT TO BE LIKE THIS ALL THE TIME.
IT'S LIKE MY POWERS ARE ALL MINE. AND IT'S ALL OKAY.
AND I ACTUALLY FEEL COMFORTABLE IN THIS BODY.
BUT YOU KNOW...
I THINK TO WANT THIS TOO MUCH IS TO WANT TO...
...DIE.
UP AHEAD, IS THAT OSBORN'S MIND WE'RE HEADING FOR?
IT REMINDS ME OF...
MY OWN.

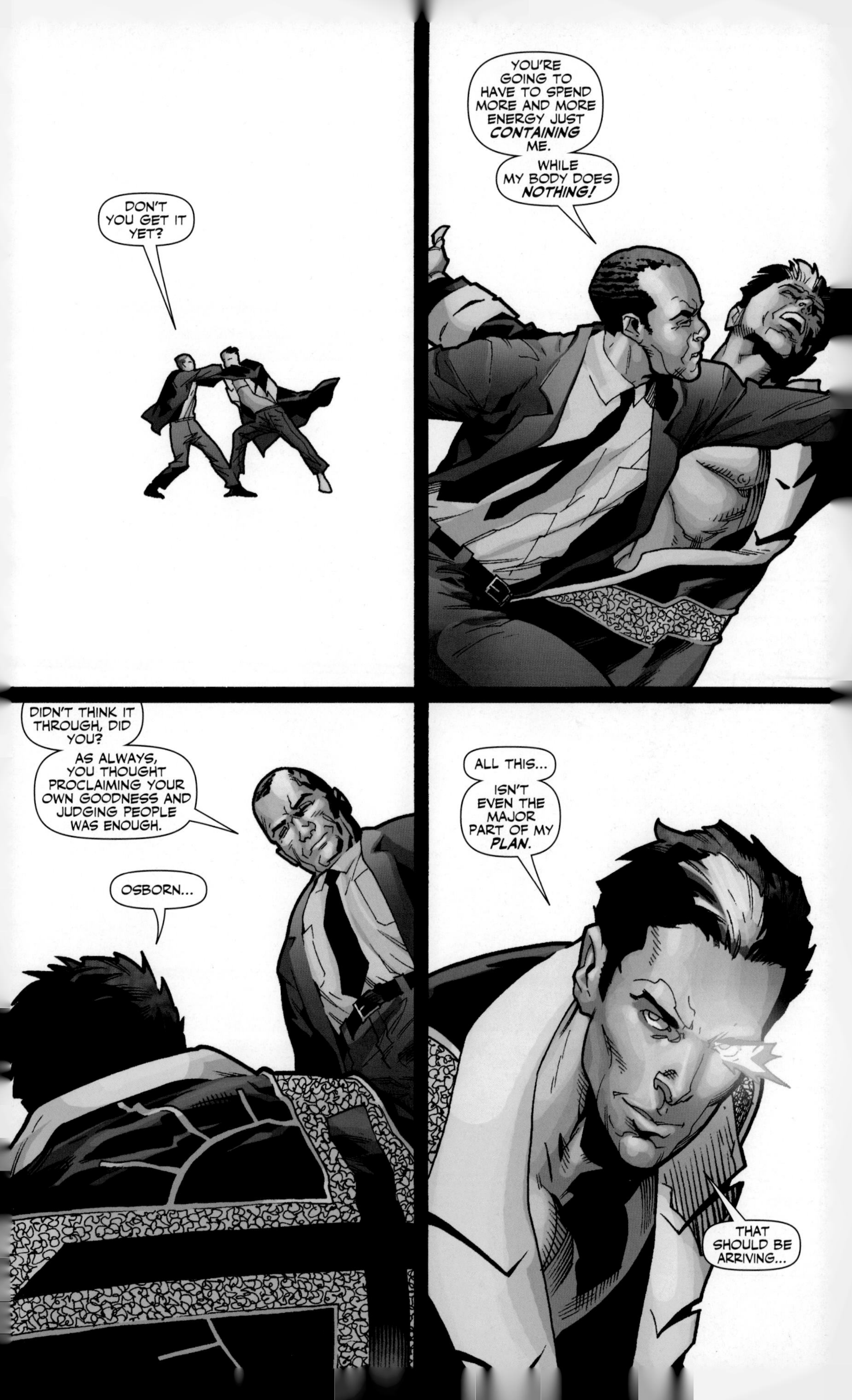
DON'T YOU GET IT YET?
YOU'RE GOING TO HAVE TO SPEND MORE AND MORE ENERGY JUST CONTAINING ME.
WHILE MY BODY DOES NOTHING!
DIDN'T THINK IT THROUGH, DID YOU?
AS ALWAYS, YOU THOUGHT PROCLAIMING YOUR OWN GOODNESS AND JUDGING PEOPLE WAS ENOUGH.
OSBORN...
ALL THIS...
ISN'T EVEN THE MAJOR PART OF MY PLAN.
THAT SHOULD BE ARRIVING...

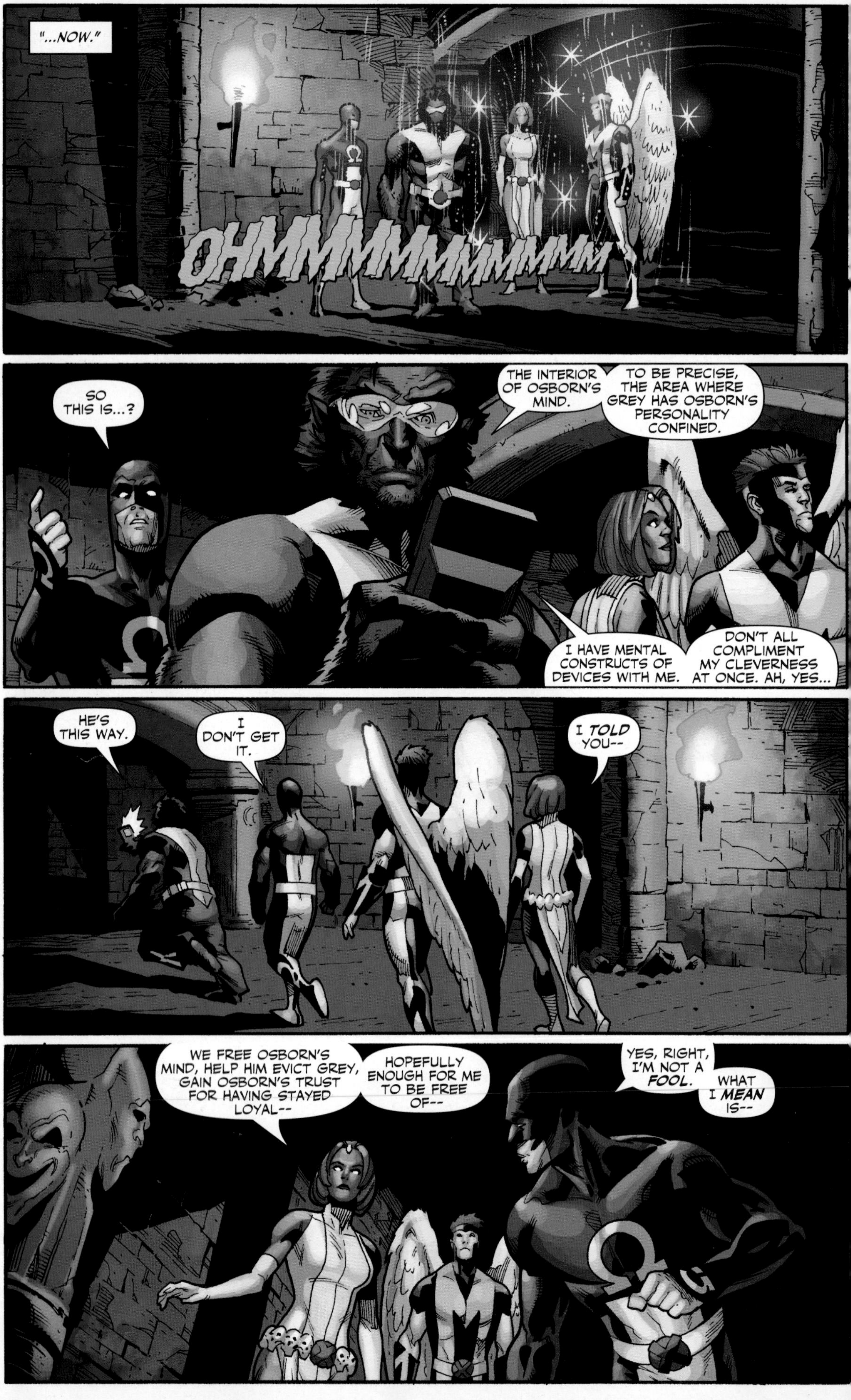
"...NOW."
OHMMMMMMMMMMM
SO THIS IS...?
THE INTERIOR OF OSBORN'S MIND.
TO BE PRECISE, THE AREA WHERE GREY HAS OSBORN'S PERSONALITY CONFINED.
I HAVE MENTAL CONSTRUCTS OF DEVICES WITH ME.
DON'T ALL COMPLIMENT MY CLEVERNESS AT ONCE. AH, YES...
HE'S THIS WAY.
I DON'T GET IT.
I TOLD YOU--
WE FREE OSBORN'S MIND, HELP HIM EVICT GREY, GAIN OSBORN'S TRUST FOR HAVING STAYED LOYAL--
HOPEFULLY ENOUGH FOR ME TO BE FREE OF--
YES, RIGHT, I'M NOT A FOOL.
WHAT I MEAN IS--

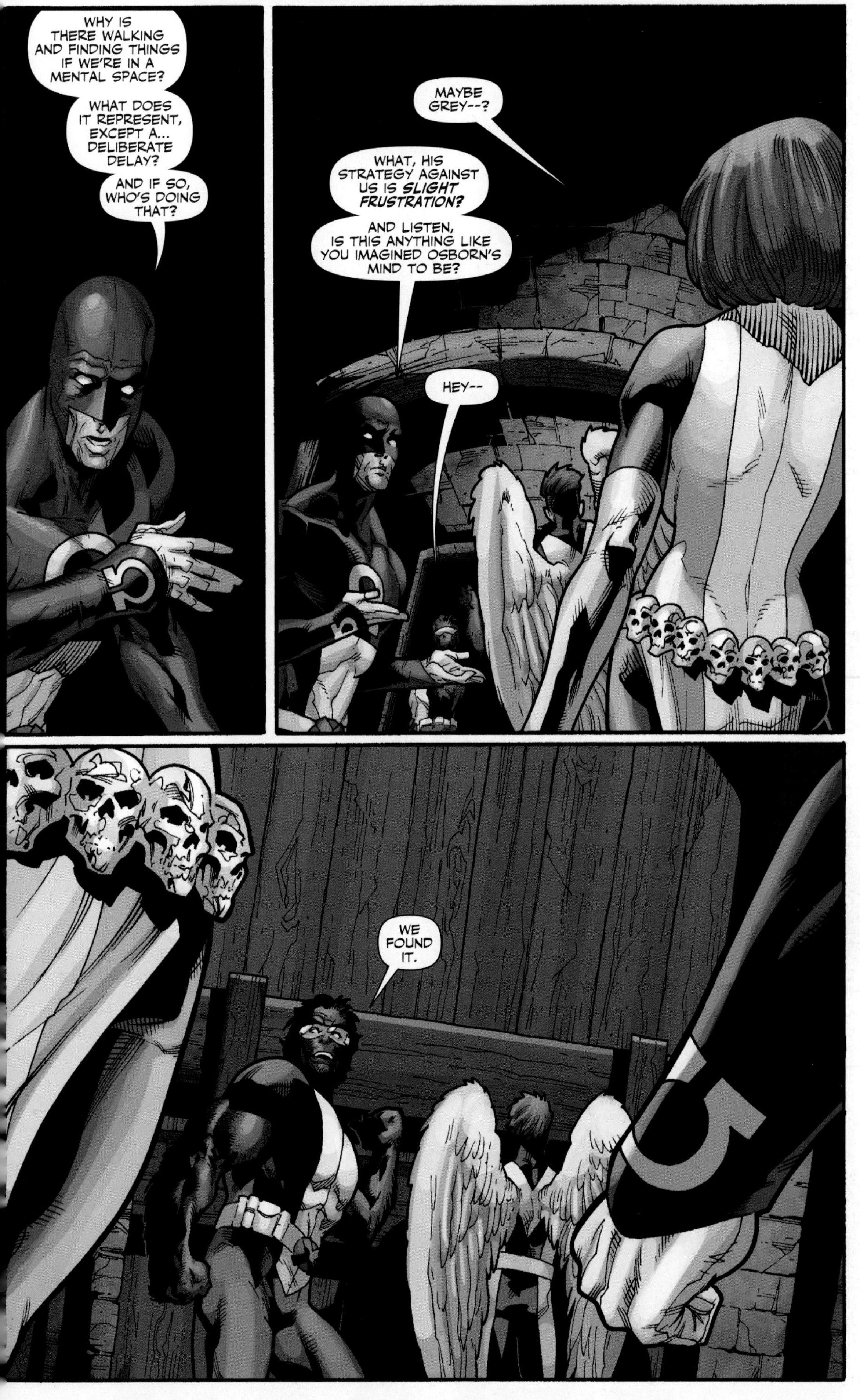
WHY IS THERE WALKING AND FINDING THINGS IF WE'RE IN A MENTAL SPACE?
WHAT DOES IT REPRESENT, EXCEPT A... DELIBERATE DELAY?
AND IF SO, WHO'S DOING THAT?
MAYBE GREY--?
WHAT, HIS STRATEGY AGAINST US IS *SLIGHT FRUSTRATION?*
AND LISTEN, IS THIS ANYTHING LIKE YOU IMAGINED OSBORN'S MIND TO BE?
HEY--
WE FOUND IT.

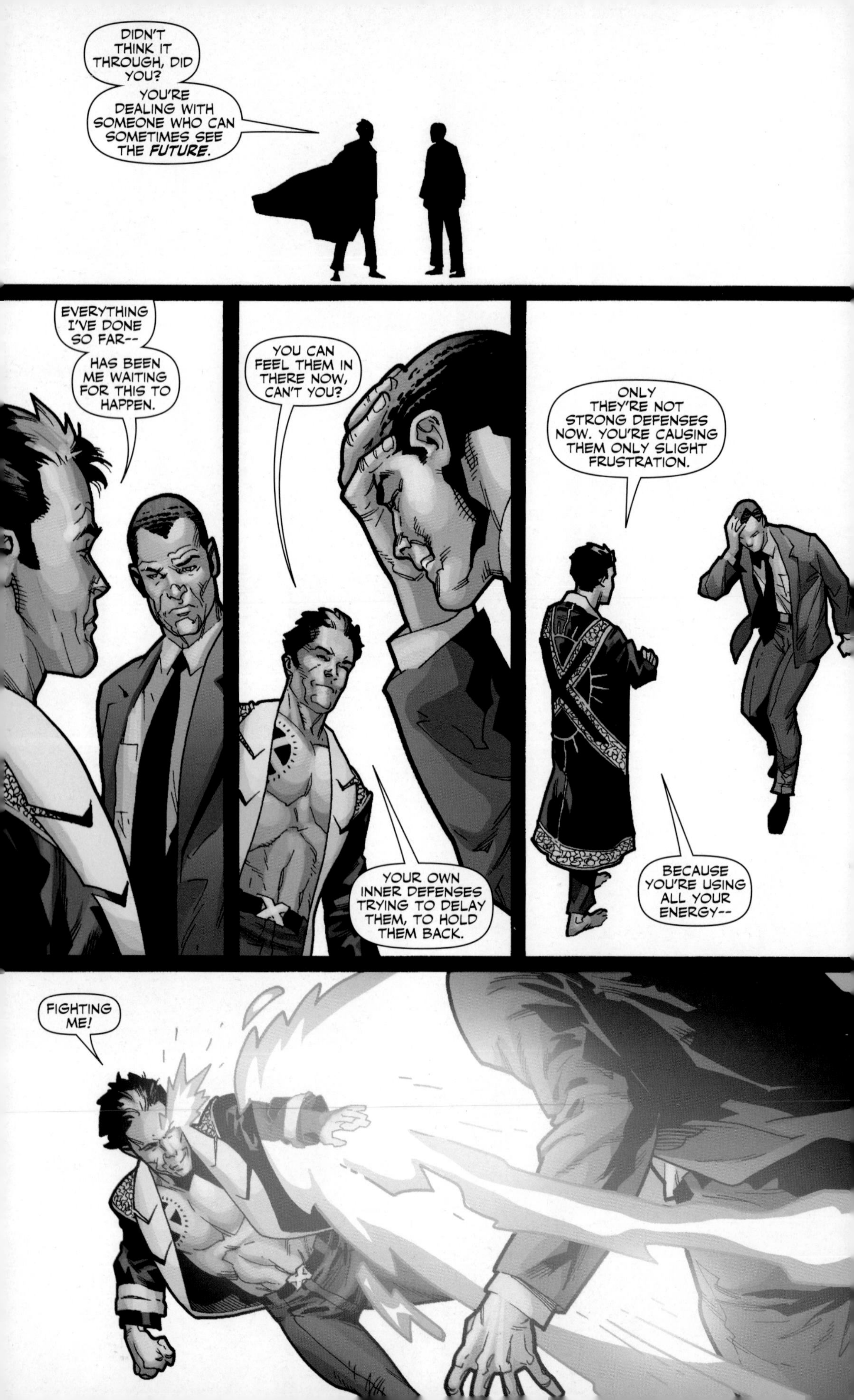
DIDN'T THINK IT THROUGH, DID YOU?
YOU'RE DEALING WITH SOMEONE WHO CAN SOMETIMES SEE THE *FUTURE*.
EVERYTHING I'VE DONE SO FAR--
HAS BEEN ME WAITING FOR THIS TO HAPPEN.
YOU CAN FEEL THEM IN THERE NOW, CAN'T YOU?
YOUR OWN INNER DEFENSES TRYING TO DELAY THEM, TO HOLD THEM BACK.
ONLY THEY'RE NOT STRONG DEFENSES NOW. YOU'RE CAUSING THEM ONLY SLIGHT FRUSTRATION.
BECAUSE YOU'RE USING ALL YOUR ENERGY--
FIGHTING ME!

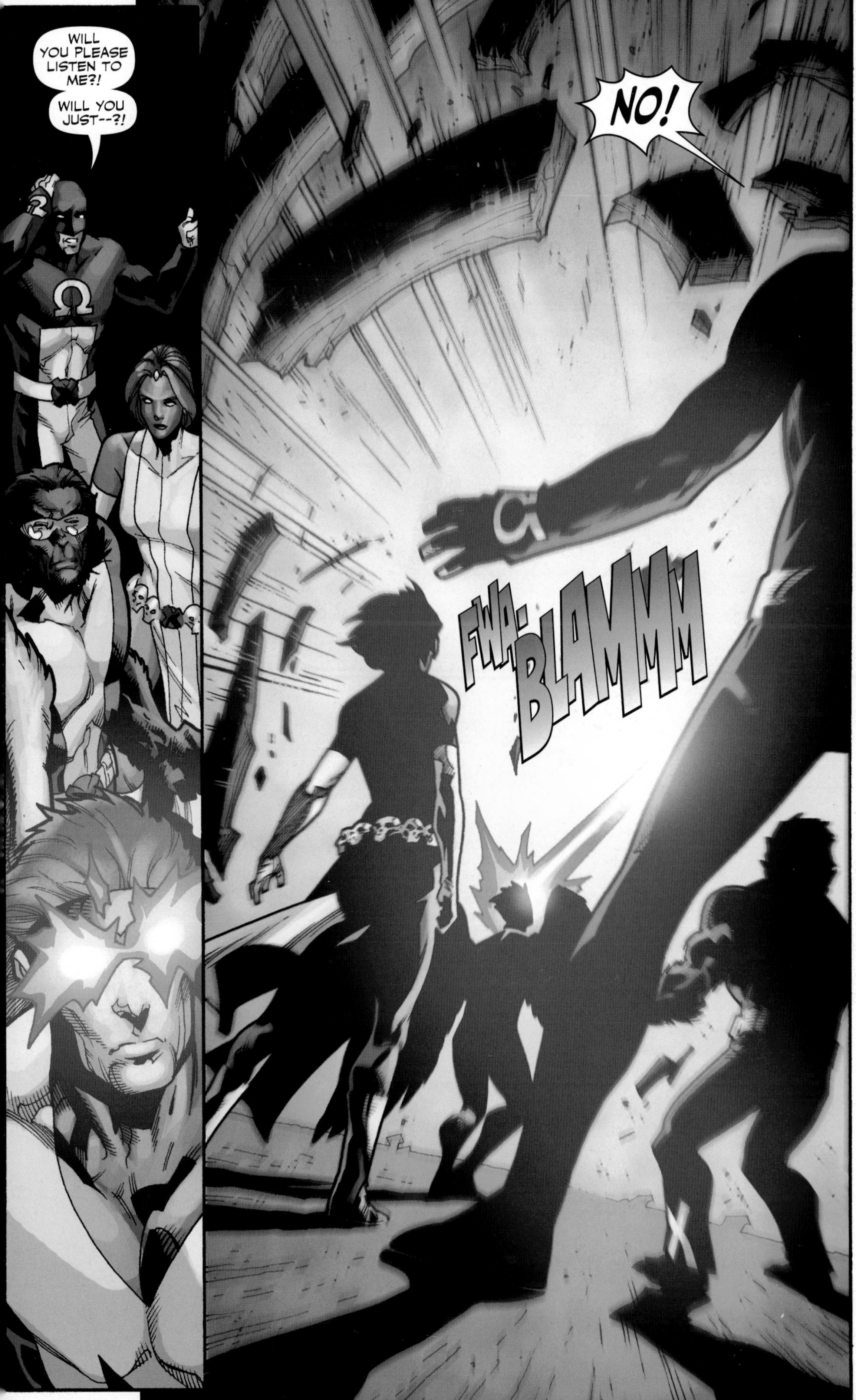

WILL YOU PLEASE LISTEN TO ME?!
WILL YOU JUST--?!
NO!
FWA-BLAMMM

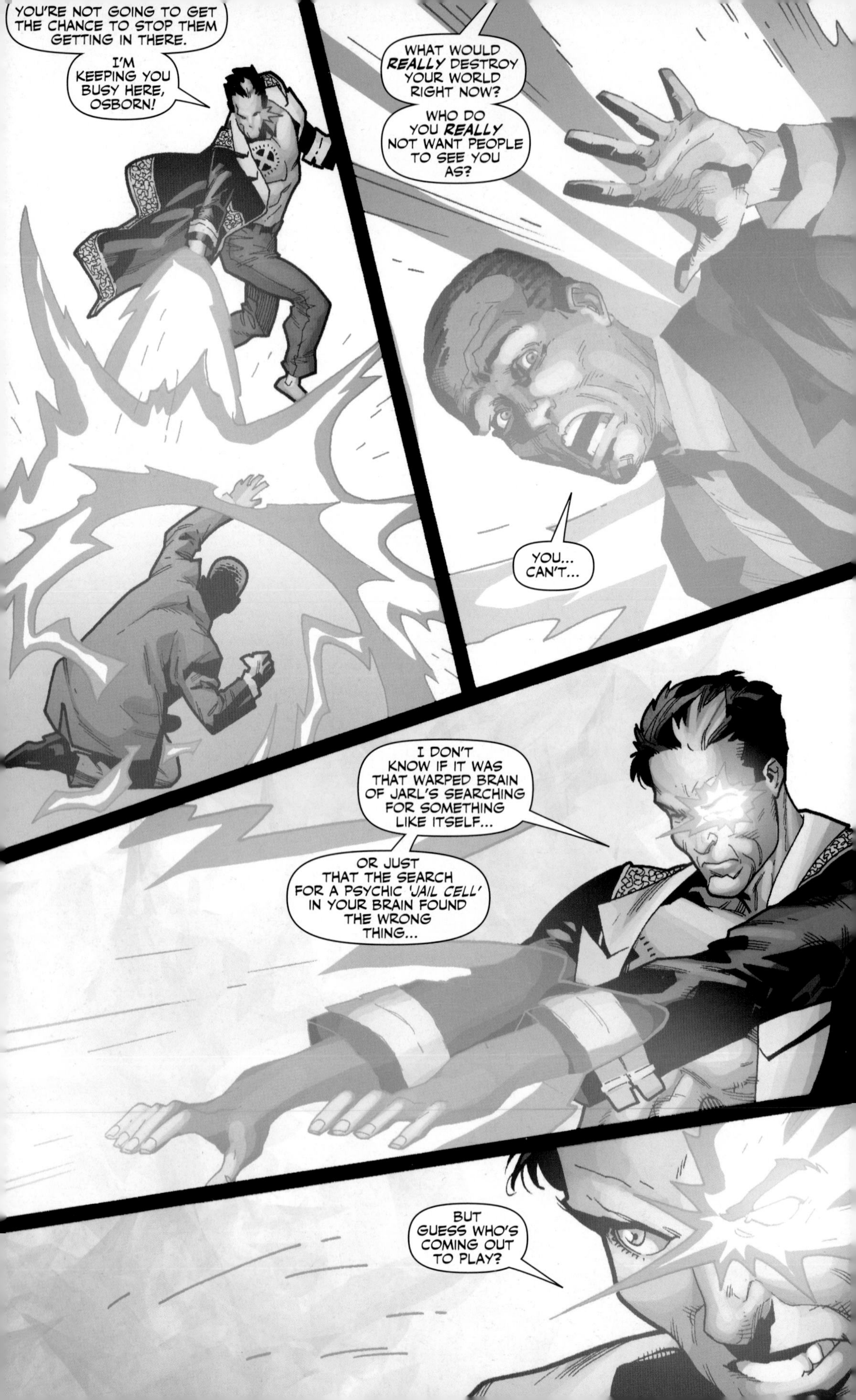
YOU'RE NOT GOING TO GET THE CHANCE TO STOP THEM GETTING IN THERE.
I'M KEEPING YOU BUSY HERE, OSBORN!
WHAT WOULD REALLY DESTROY YOUR WORLD RIGHT NOW?
WHO DO YOU REALLY NOT WANT PEOPLE TO SEE YOU AS?
YOU... CAN'T...
I DON'T KNOW IF IT WAS THAT WARPED BRAIN OF JARL'S SEARCHING FOR SOMETHING LIKE ITSELF...
OR JUST THAT THE SEARCH FOR A PSYCHIC 'JAIL CELL' IN YOUR BRAIN FOUND THE WRONG THING...
BUT GUESS WHO'S COMING OUT TO PLAY?

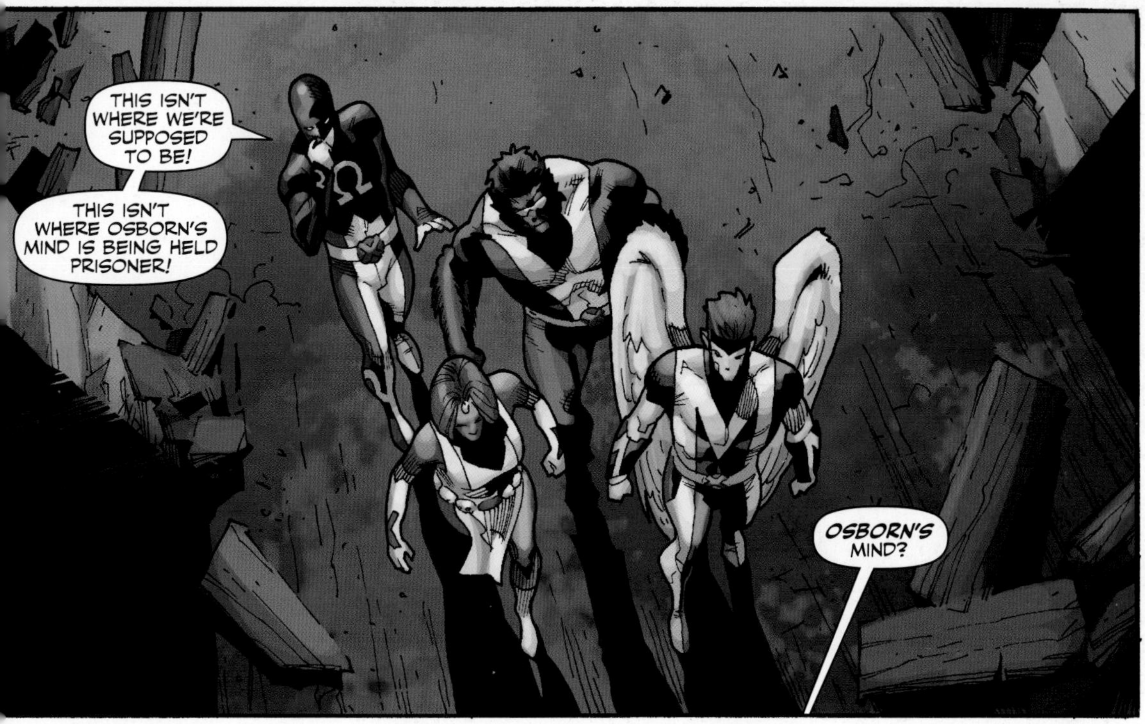
THIS ISN'T WHERE WE'RE SUPPOSED TO BE!
THIS ISN'T WHERE OSBORN'S MIND IS BEING HELD PRISONER!
OSBORN'S MIND?

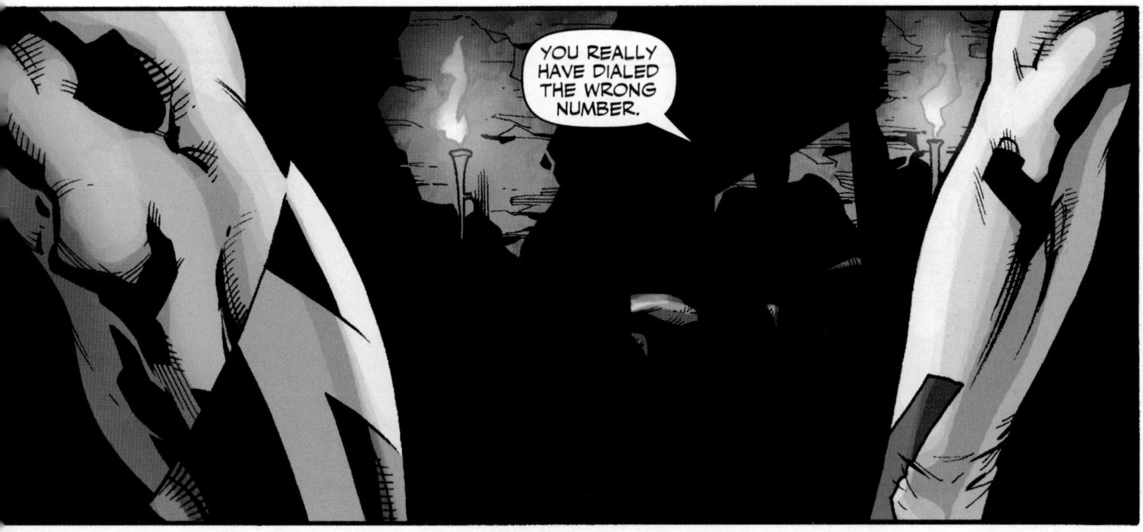
YOU REALLY HAVE DIALED THE WRONG NUMBER.

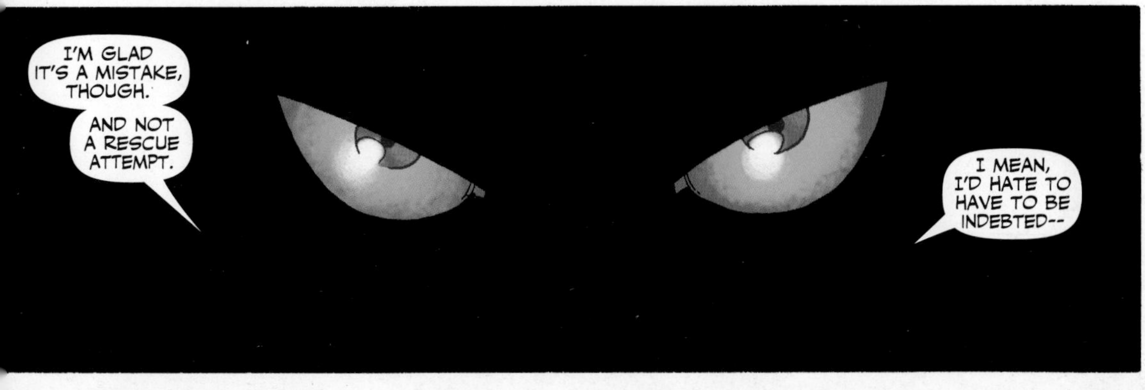
I'M GLAD IT'S A MISTAKE, THOUGH.
AND NOT A RESCUE ATTEMPT.
I MEAN, I'D HATE TO HAVE TO BE INDEBTED--

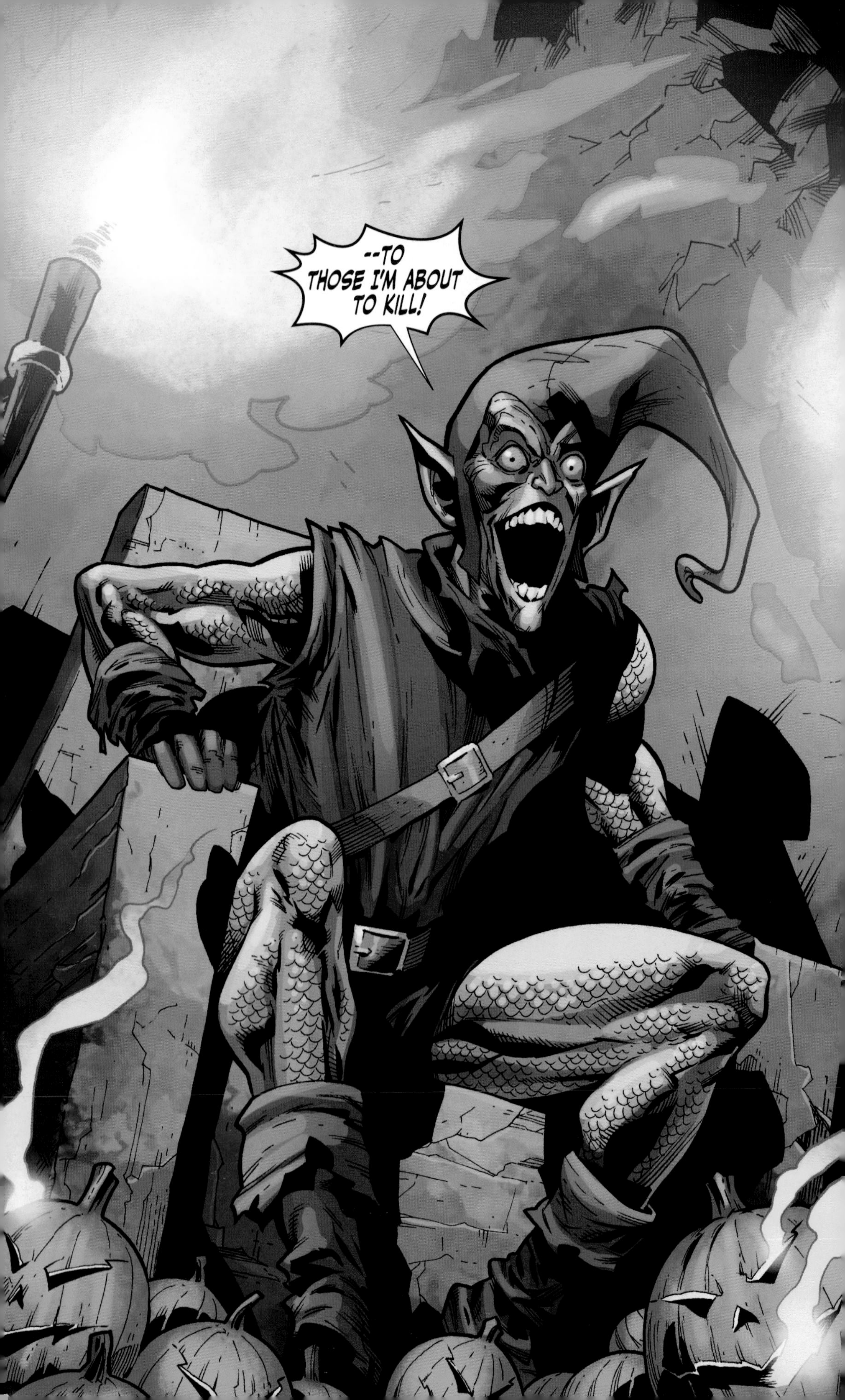
--TO THOSE I'M ABOUT TO KILL!

MYSTIQUE DESIGNS BY LEONARD KIRK

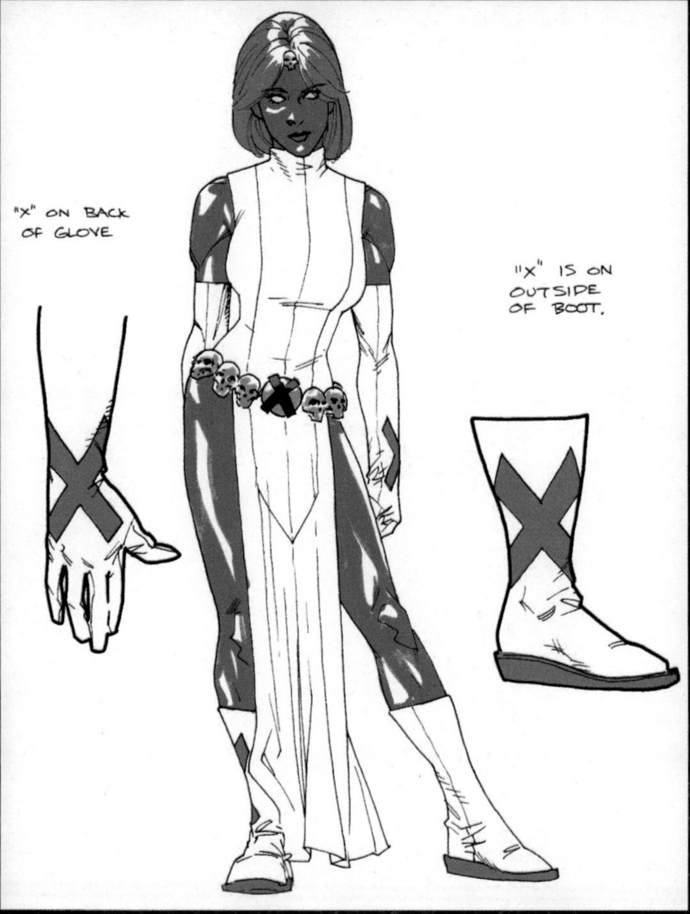
"X" ON BACK OF GLOVE
"X" IS ON OUTSIDE OF BOOT.

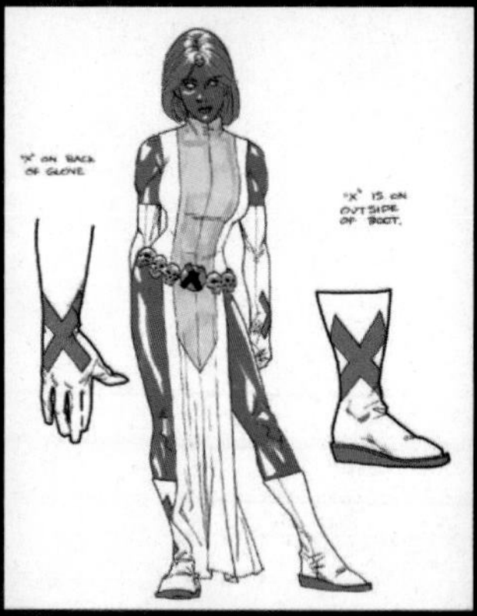

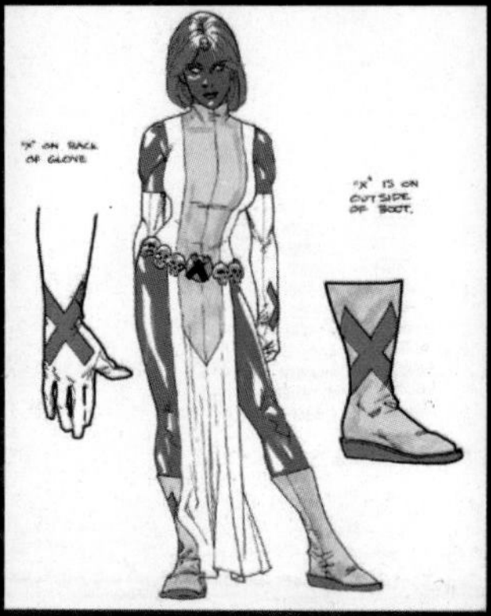

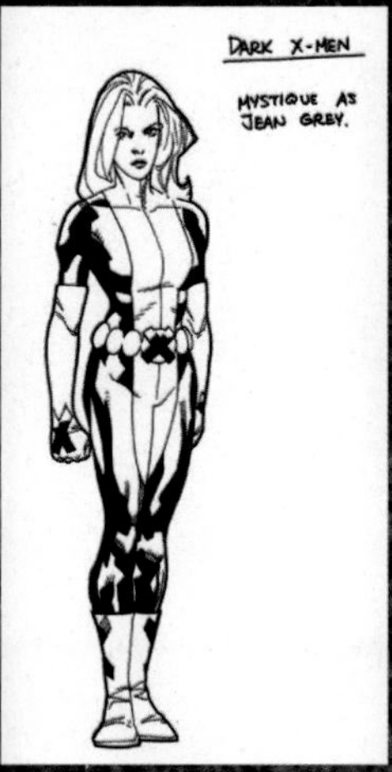
DARK X-MEN
MYSTIQUE AS JEAN GREY.

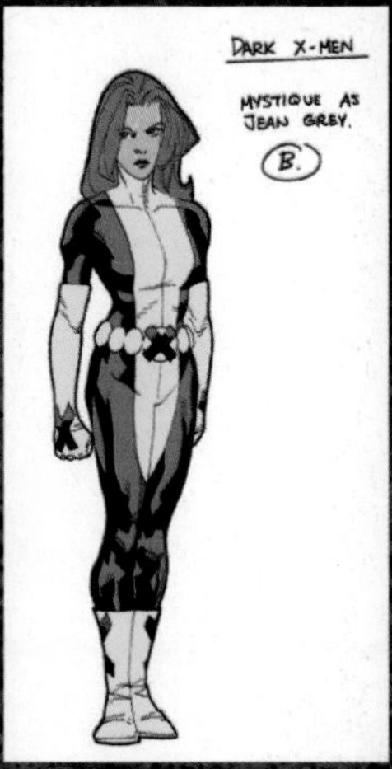
DARK X-MEN
MYSTIQUE AS JEAN GREY.
B.

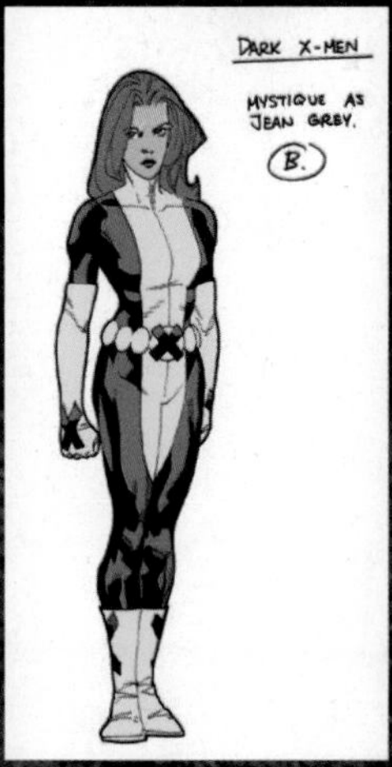
DARK X-MEN
MYSTIQUE AS JEAN GREY.
B.

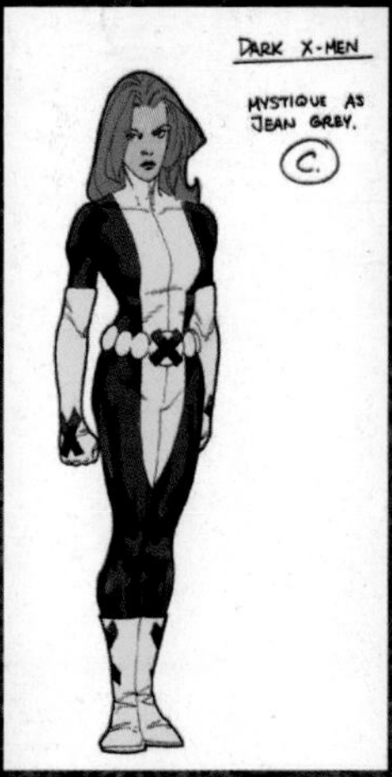
DARK X-MEN
MYSTIQUE AS JEAN GREY.
C.

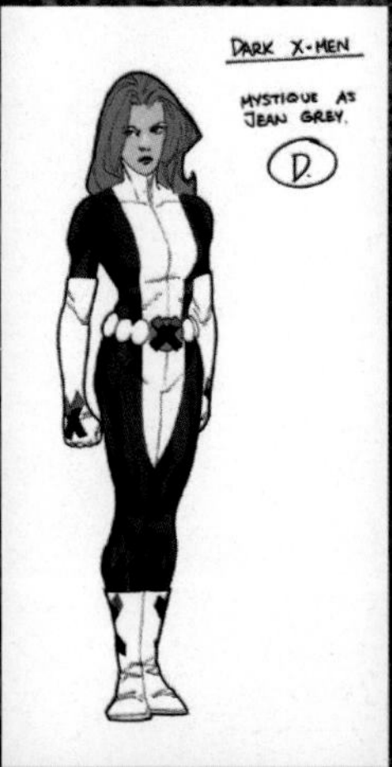
DARK X-MEN
MYSTIQUE AS JEAN GREY.
D.

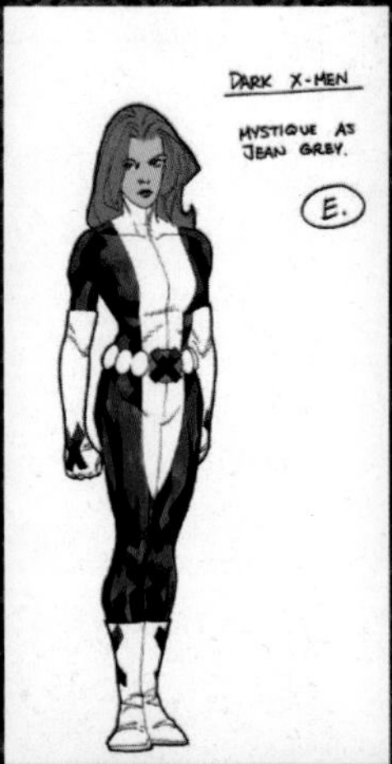
DARK X-MEN
MYSTIQUE AS JEAN GREY.
E.

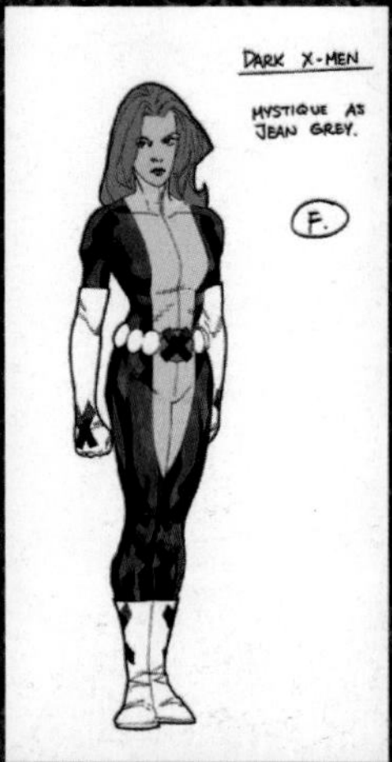
DARK X-MEN
MYSTIQUE AS JEAN GREY.
F.

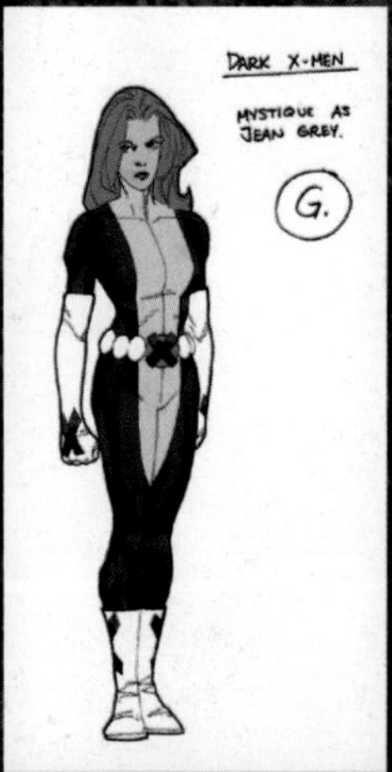
DARK X-MEN
MYSTIQUE AS JEAN GREY.
G.

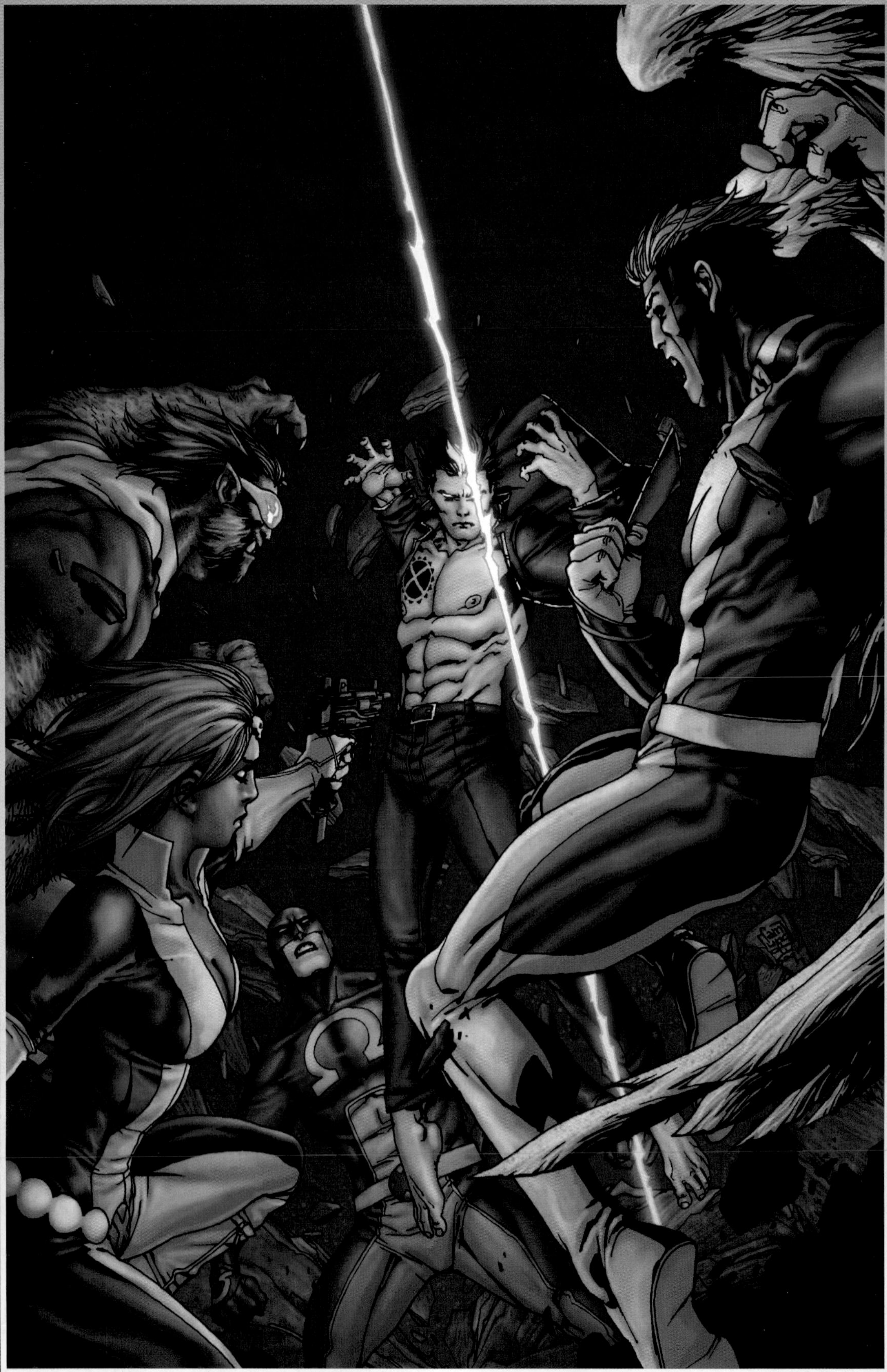

5

INSIDE NORMAN OSBORN'S MIND.

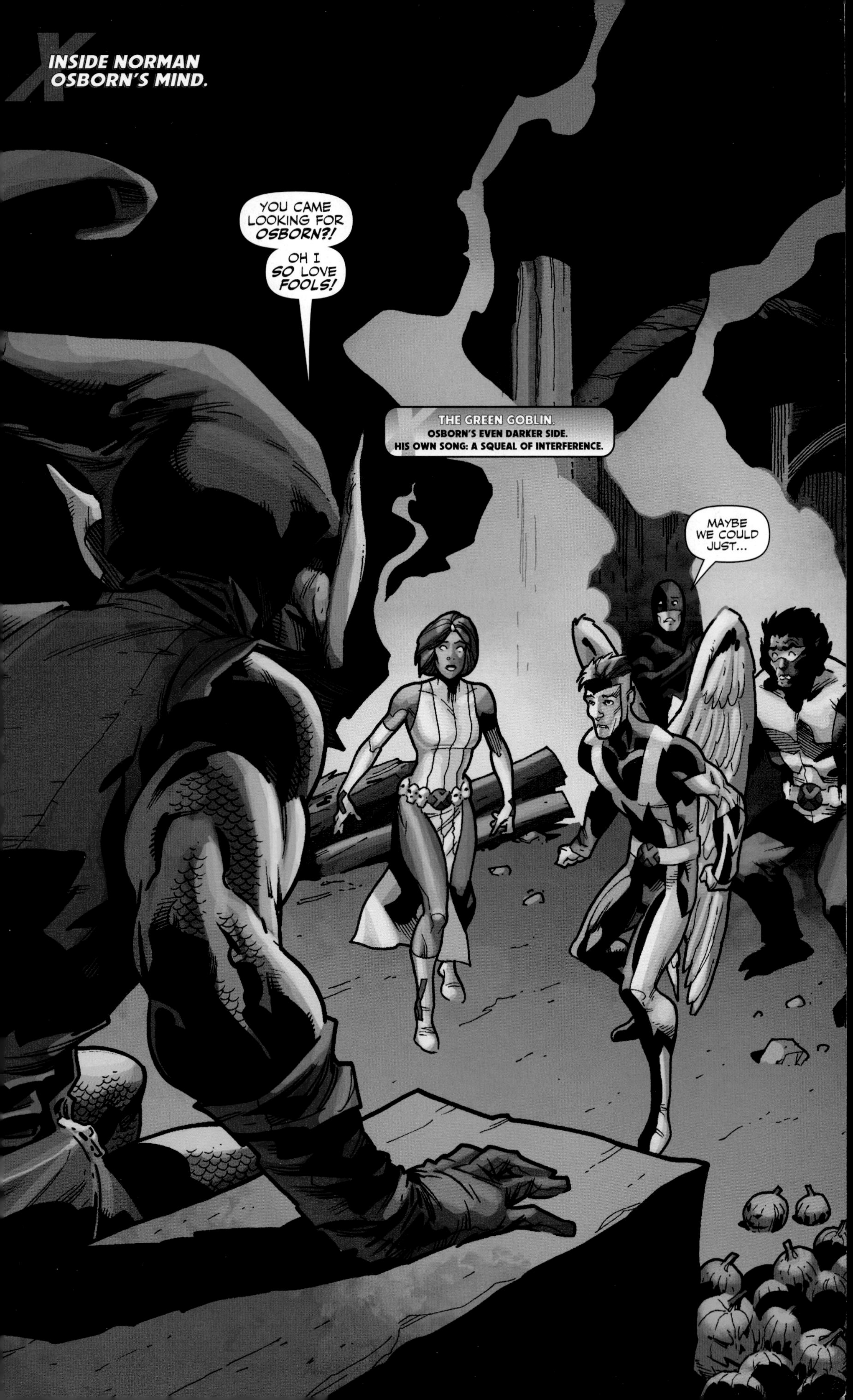
YOU CAME LOOKING FOR OSBORN?!
OH I SO LOVE FOOLS!
THE GREEN GOBLIN.
OSBORN'S EVEN DARKER SIDE.
HIS OWN SONG: A SQUEAL OF INTERFERENCE.
MAYBE WE COULD JUST...

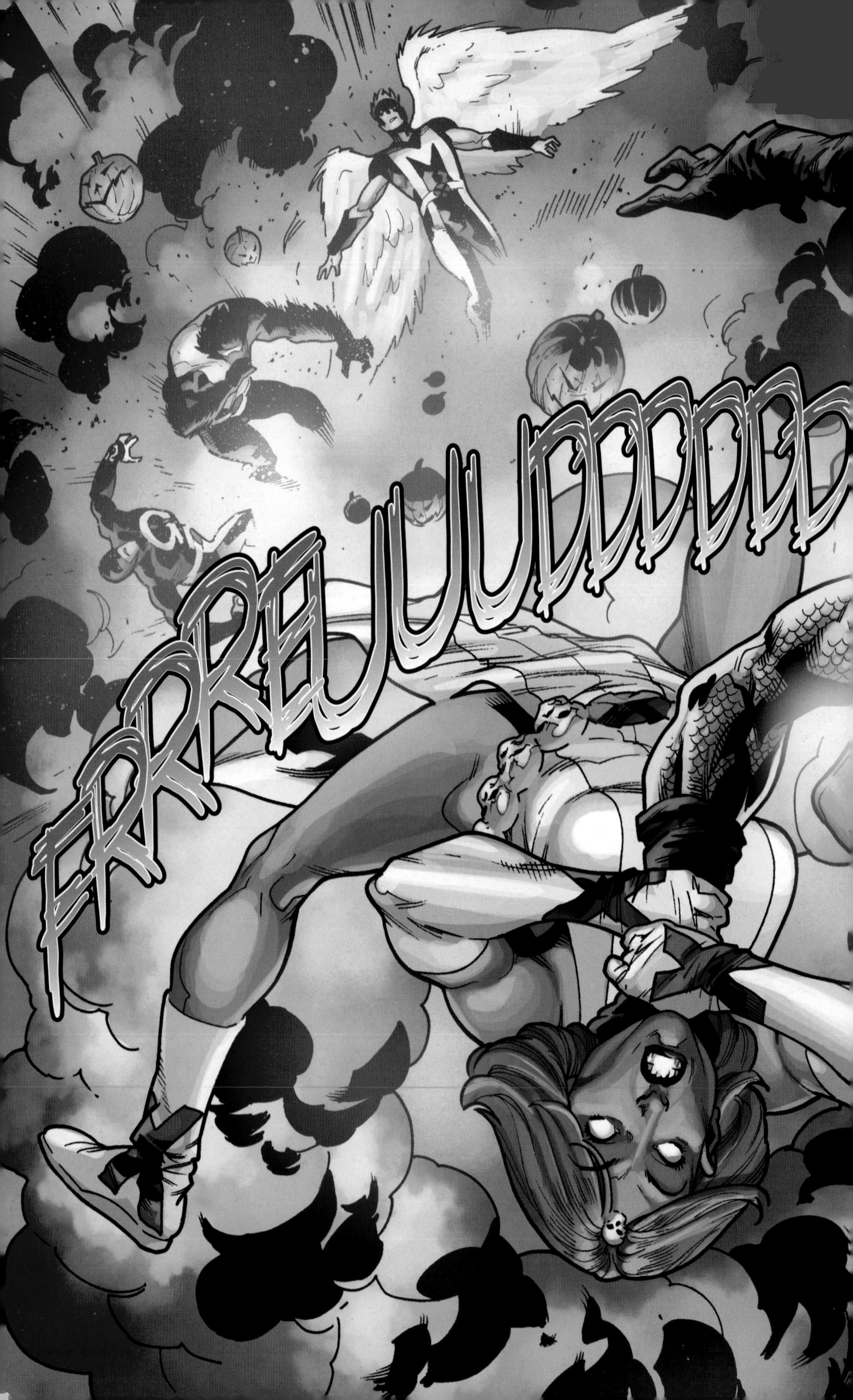
ERRREUUUDDDDDD

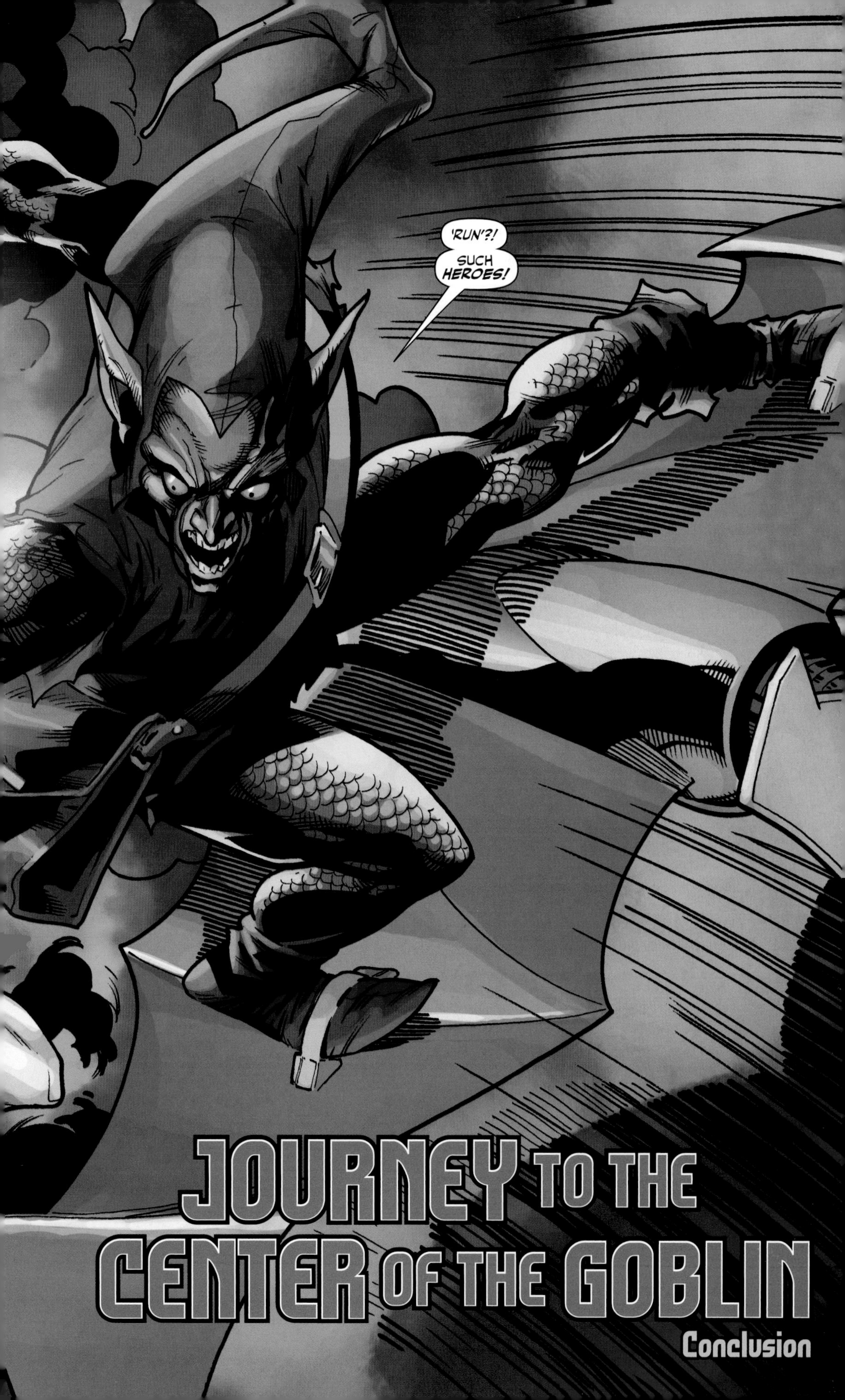
'RUN'?!
SUCH HEROES!
JOURNEY TO THE CENTER OF THE GOBLIN
Conclusion

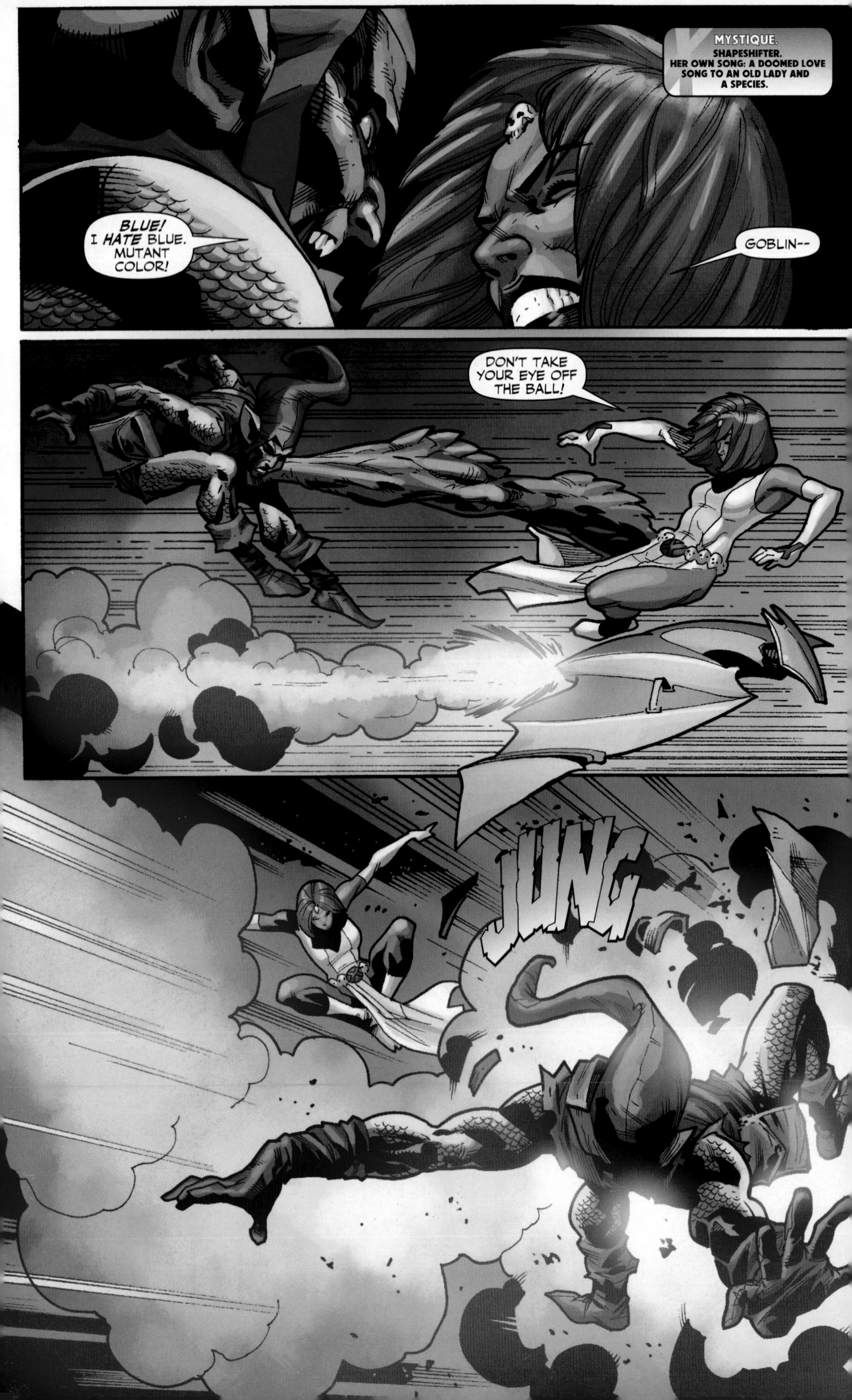
MYSTIQUE.
SHAPESHIFTER.
HER OWN SONG: A DOOMED LOVE SONG TO AN OLD LADY AND A SPECIES.
BLUE! I HATE BLUE. MUTANT COLOR!
GOBLIN--
DON'T TAKE YOUR EYE OFF THE BALL!
JUNG

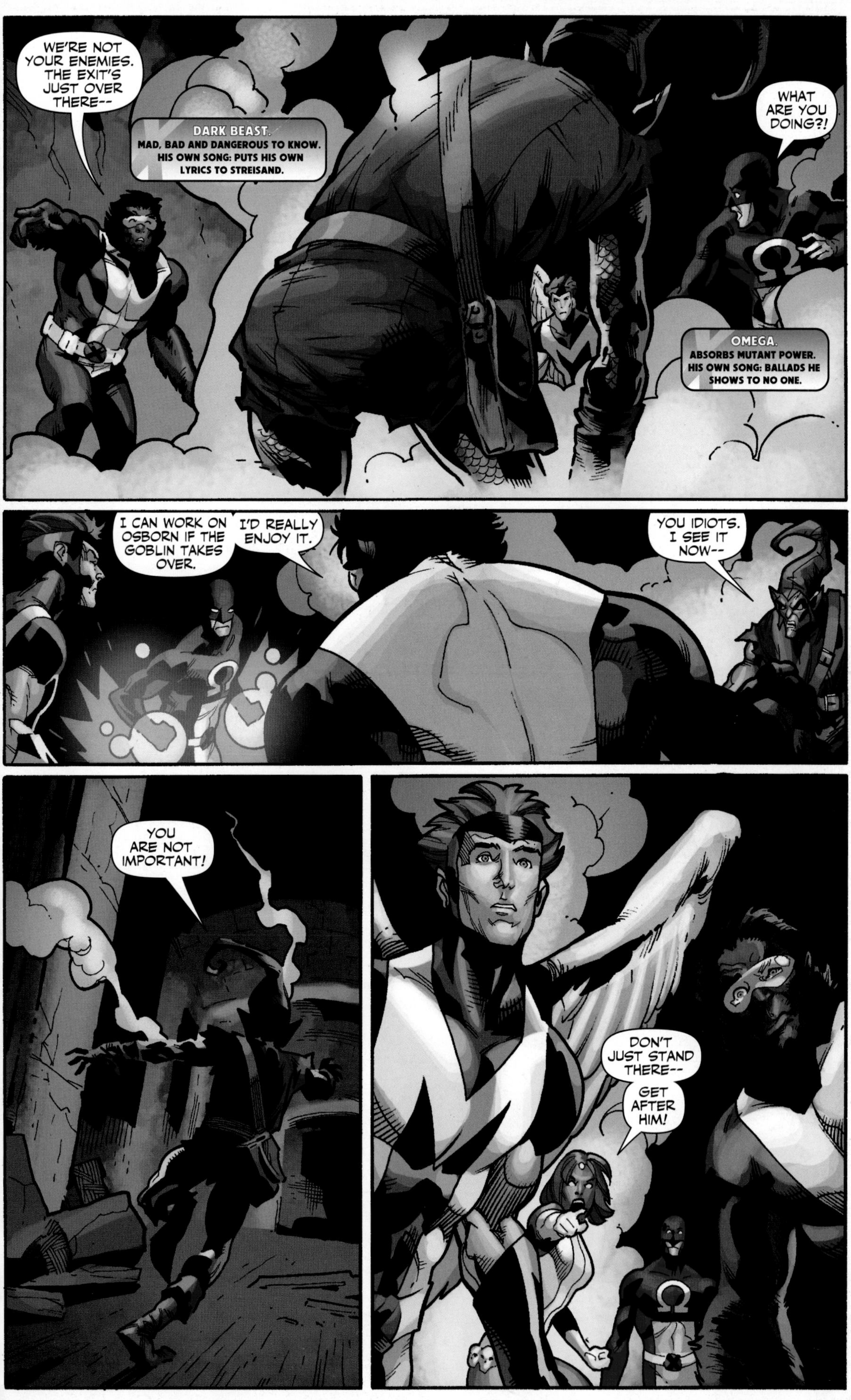
WE'RE NOT YOUR ENEMIES. THE EXIT'S JUST OVER THERE--
DARK BEAST. MAD, BAD AND DANGEROUS TO KNOW. HIS OWN SONG: PUTS HIS OWN LYRICS TO STREISAND.
WHAT ARE YOU DOING?!
OMEGA. ABSORBS MUTANT POWER. HIS OWN SONG: BALLADS HE SHOWS TO NO ONE.
I CAN WORK ON OSBORN IF THE GOBLIN TAKES OVER.
I'D REALLY ENJOY IT.
YOU IDIOTS. I SEE IT NOW--
YOU ARE NOT IMPORTANT!
DON'T JUST STAND THERE--
GET AFTER HIM!

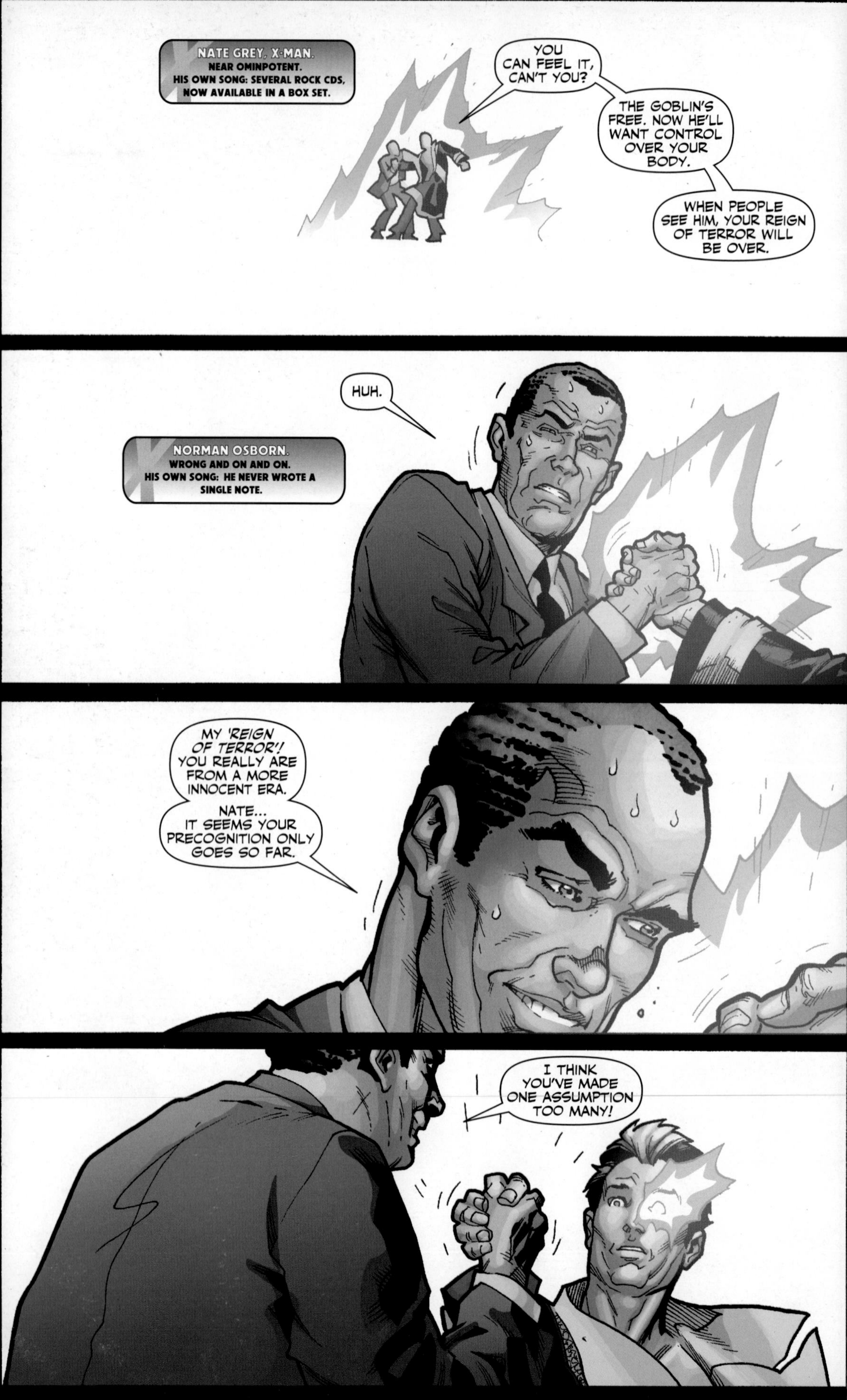
NATE GREY, X-MAN.
NEAR OMINPOTENT.
HIS OWN SONG: SEVERAL ROCK CDS, NOW AVAILABLE IN A BOX SET.
YOU CAN FEEL IT, CAN'T YOU?
THE GOBLIN'S FREE. NOW HE'LL WANT CONTROL OVER YOUR BODY.
WHEN PEOPLE SEE HIM, YOUR REIGN OF TERROR WILL BE OVER.
HUH.
NORMAN OSBORN.
WRONG AND ON AND ON.
HIS OWN SONG: HE NEVER WROTE A SINGLE NOTE.
MY 'REIGN OF TERROR'! YOU REALLY ARE FROM A MORE INNOCENT ERA.
NATE... IT SEEMS YOUR PRECOGNITION ONLY GOES SO FAR.
I THINK YOU'VE MADE ONE ASSUMPTION TOO MANY!

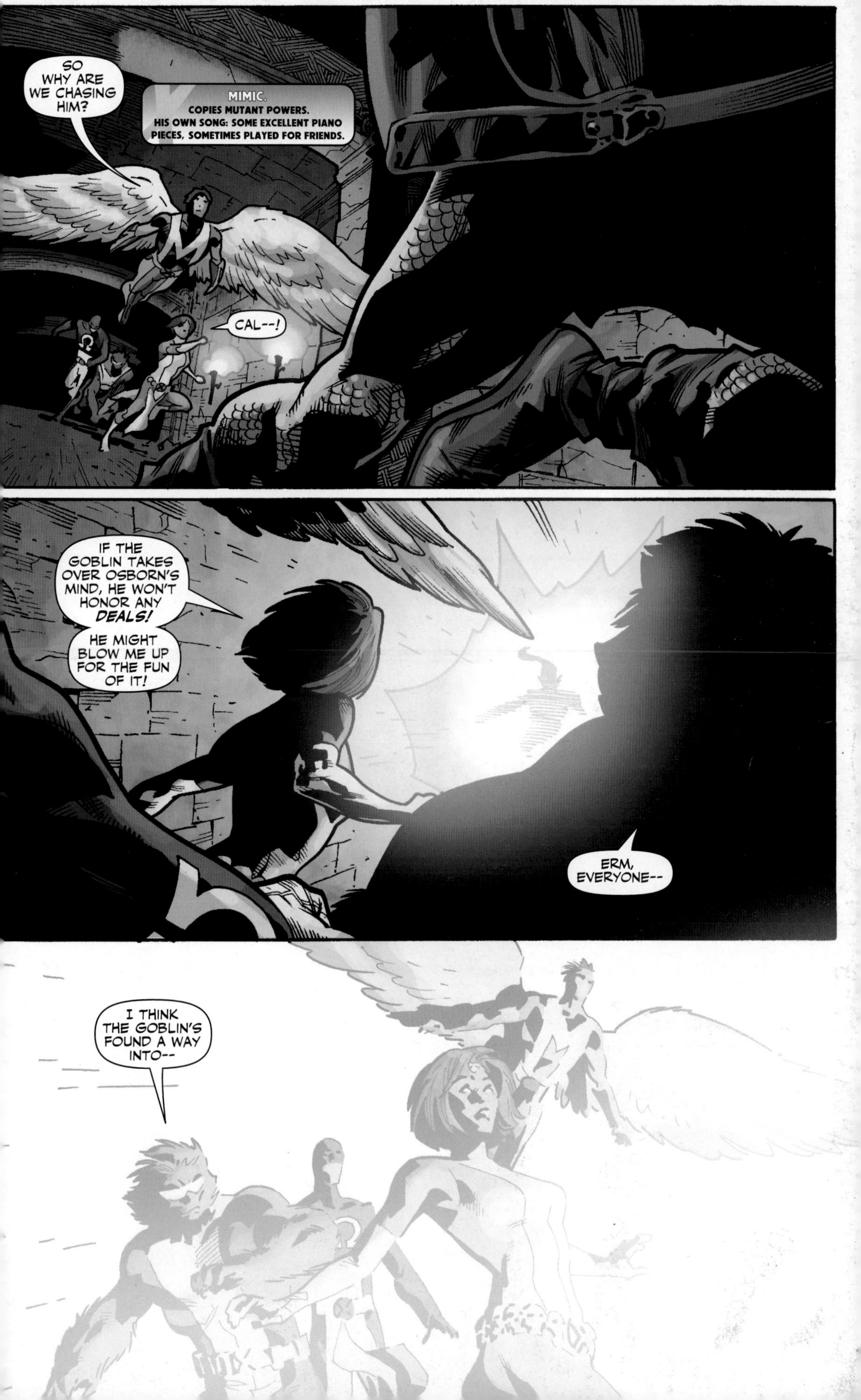
SO WHY ARE WE CHASING HIM?
MIMIC.
COPIES MUTANT POWERS.
HIS OWN SONG: SOME EXCELLENT PIANO PIECES, SOMETIMES PLAYED FOR FRIENDS.
CAL--!
IF THE GOBLIN TAKES OVER OSBORN'S MIND, HE WON'T HONOR ANY *DEALS!*
HE MIGHT BLOW ME UP FOR THE FUN OF IT!
ERM, EVERYONE--
I THINK THE GOBLIN'S FOUND A WAY INTO--

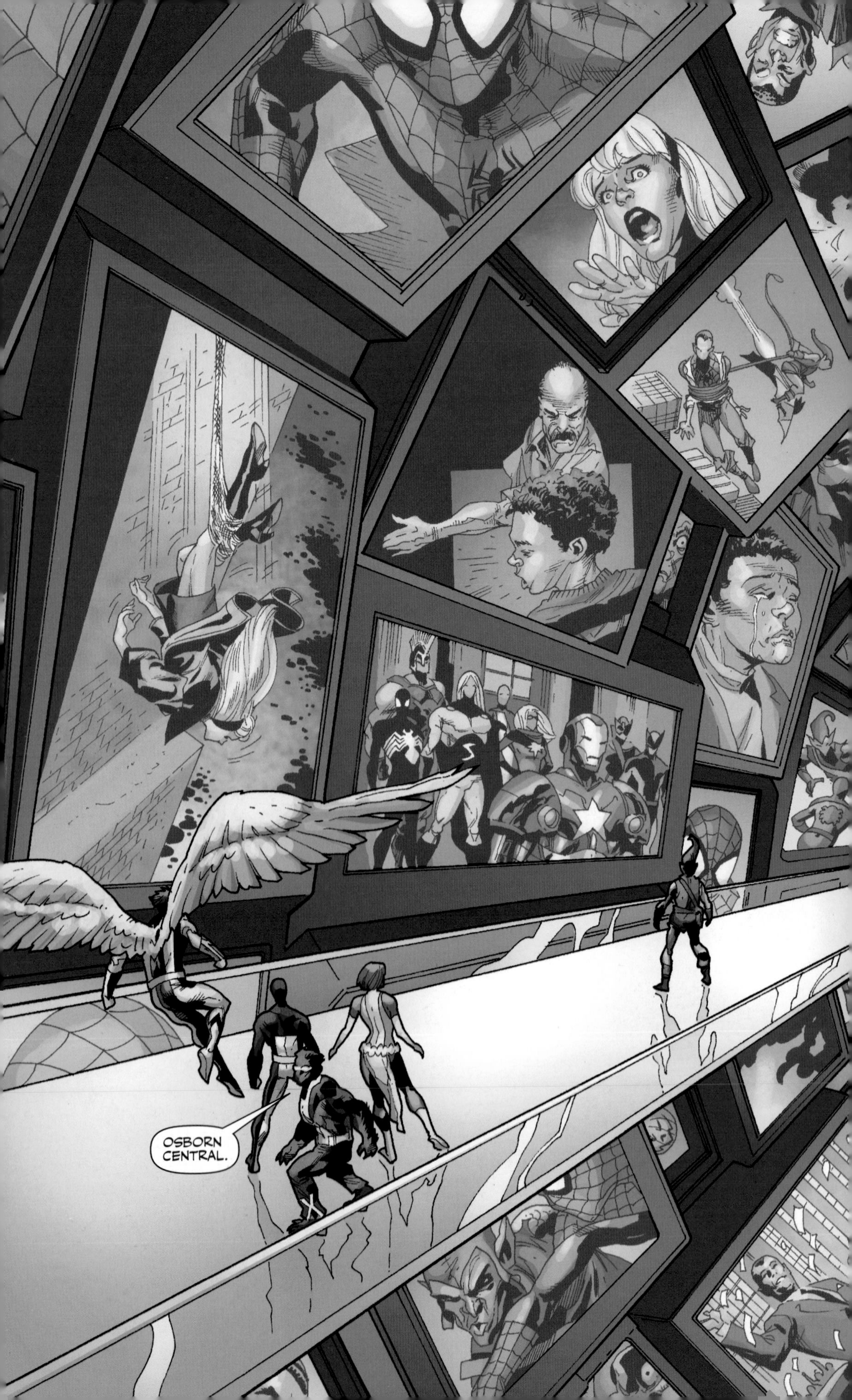
OSBORN CENTRAL.

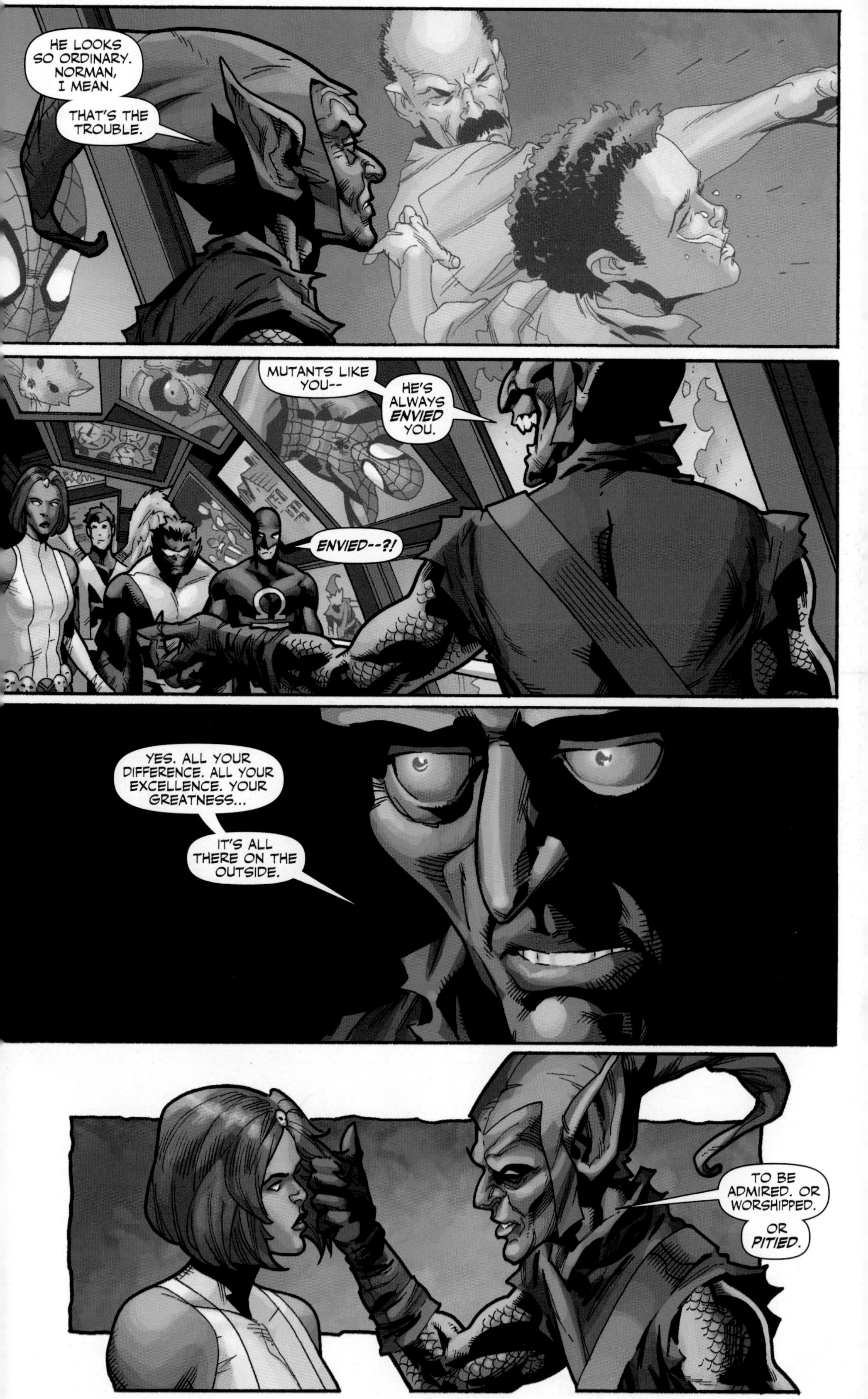
HE LOOKS SO ORDINARY. NORMAN, I MEAN.
THAT'S THE TROUBLE.
MUTANTS LIKE YOU--
HE'S ALWAYS ENVIED YOU.
ENVIED--?!
YES. ALL YOUR DIFFERENCE. ALL YOUR EXCELLENCE. YOUR GREATNESS...
IT'S ALL THERE ON THE OUTSIDE.
TO BE ADMIRED. OR WORSHIPPED.
OR PITIED.

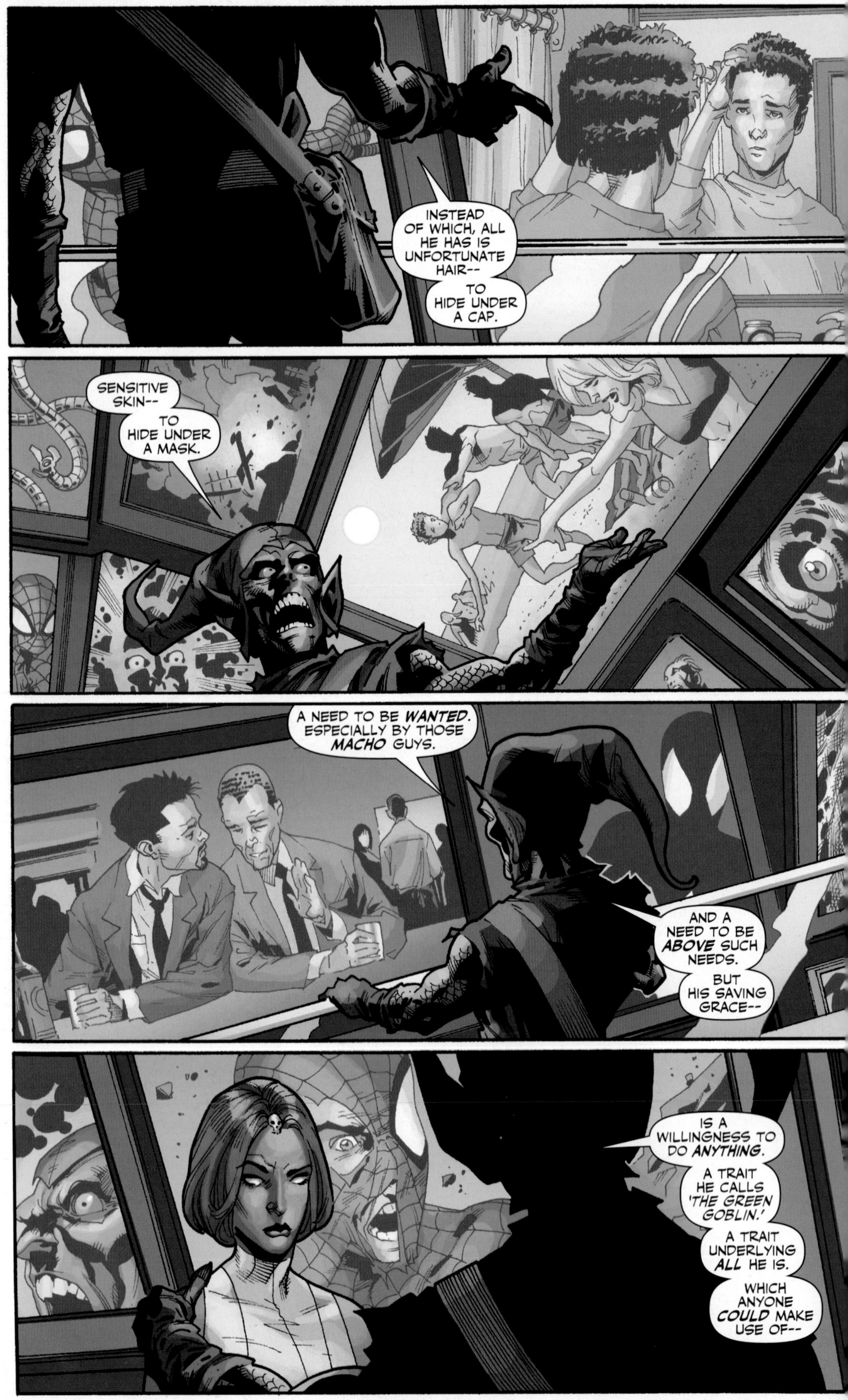
INSTEAD OF WHICH, ALL HE HAS IS UNFORTUNATE HAIR--
TO HIDE UNDER A CAP.
SENSITIVE SKIN--
TO HIDE UNDER A MASK.
A NEED TO BE *WANTED*. ESPECIALLY BY THOSE *MACHO* GUYS.
AND A NEED TO BE *ABOVE* SUCH NEEDS.
BUT HIS SAVING GRACE--
IS A WILLINGNESS TO DO *ANYTHING*.
A TRAIT HE CALLS *'THE GREEN GOBLIN.'*
A TRAIT UNDERLYING *ALL* HE IS.
WHICH ANYONE *COULD* MAKE USE OF--

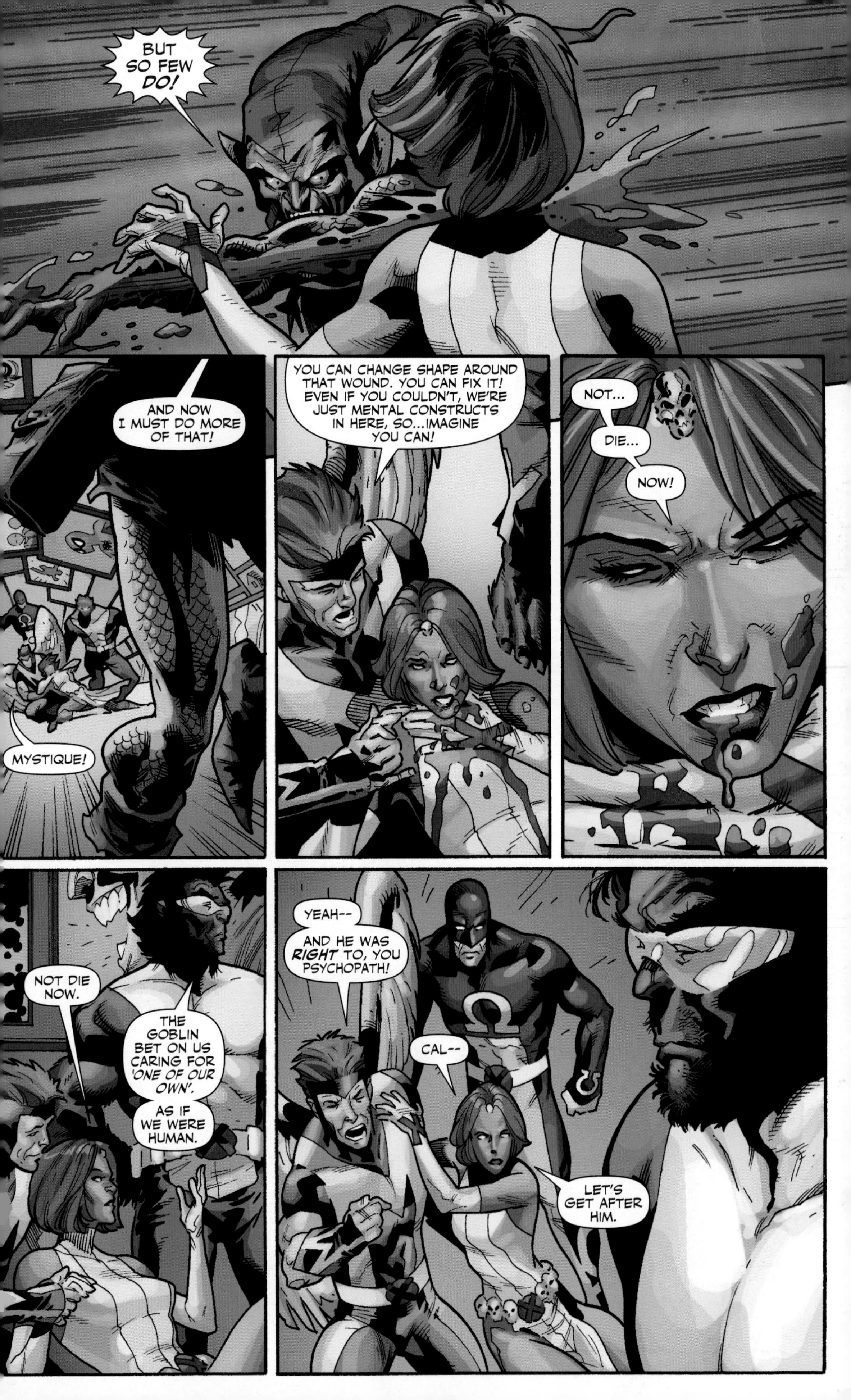
BUT SO FEW *DO!*
AND NOW I MUST DO MORE OF THAT!
MYSTIQUE!
YOU CAN CHANGE SHAPE AROUND THAT WOUND. YOU CAN FIX IT! EVEN IF YOU COULDN'T, WE'RE JUST MENTAL CONSTRUCTS IN HERE, SO...IMAGINE YOU CAN!
NOT...
DIE...
NOW!
NOT DIE NOW.
THE GOBLIN BET ON US CARING FOR *'ONE OF OUR OWN'.*
AS IF WE WERE HUMAN.
YEAH--
AND HE WAS *RIGHT* TO, YOU PSYCHOPATH!
CAL--
LET'S GET AFTER HIM.

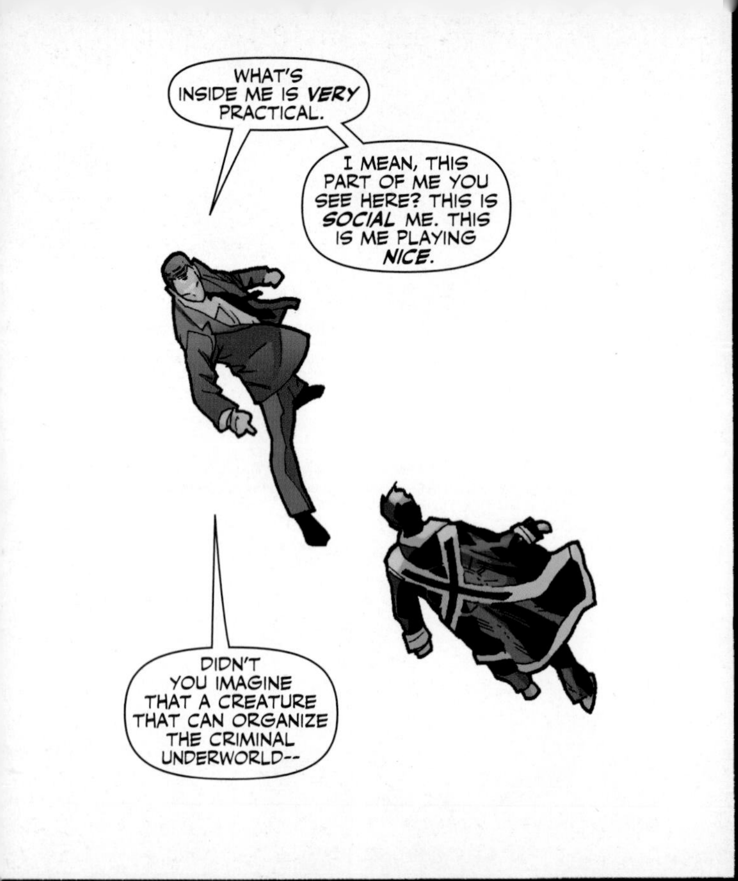
WHAT'S INSIDE ME IS VERY PRACTICAL.
I MEAN, THIS PART OF ME YOU SEE HERE? THIS IS SOCIAL ME. THIS IS ME PLAYING NICE.
DIDN'T YOU IMAGINE THAT A CREATURE THAT CAN ORGANIZE THE CRIMINAL UNDERWORLD--

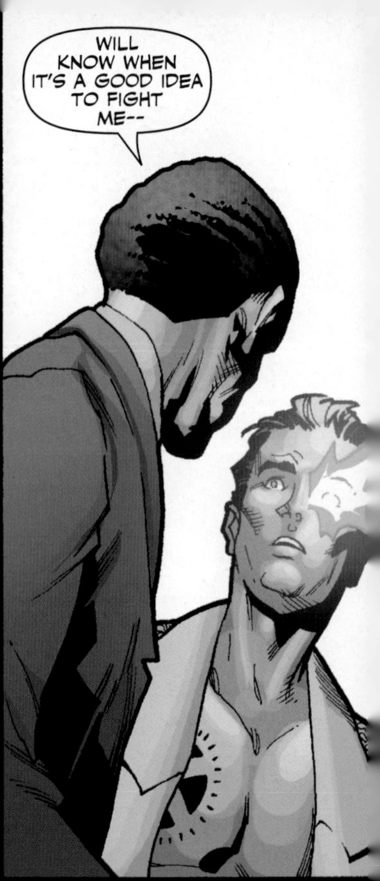
WILL KNOW WHEN IT'S A GOOD IDEA TO FIGHT ME--

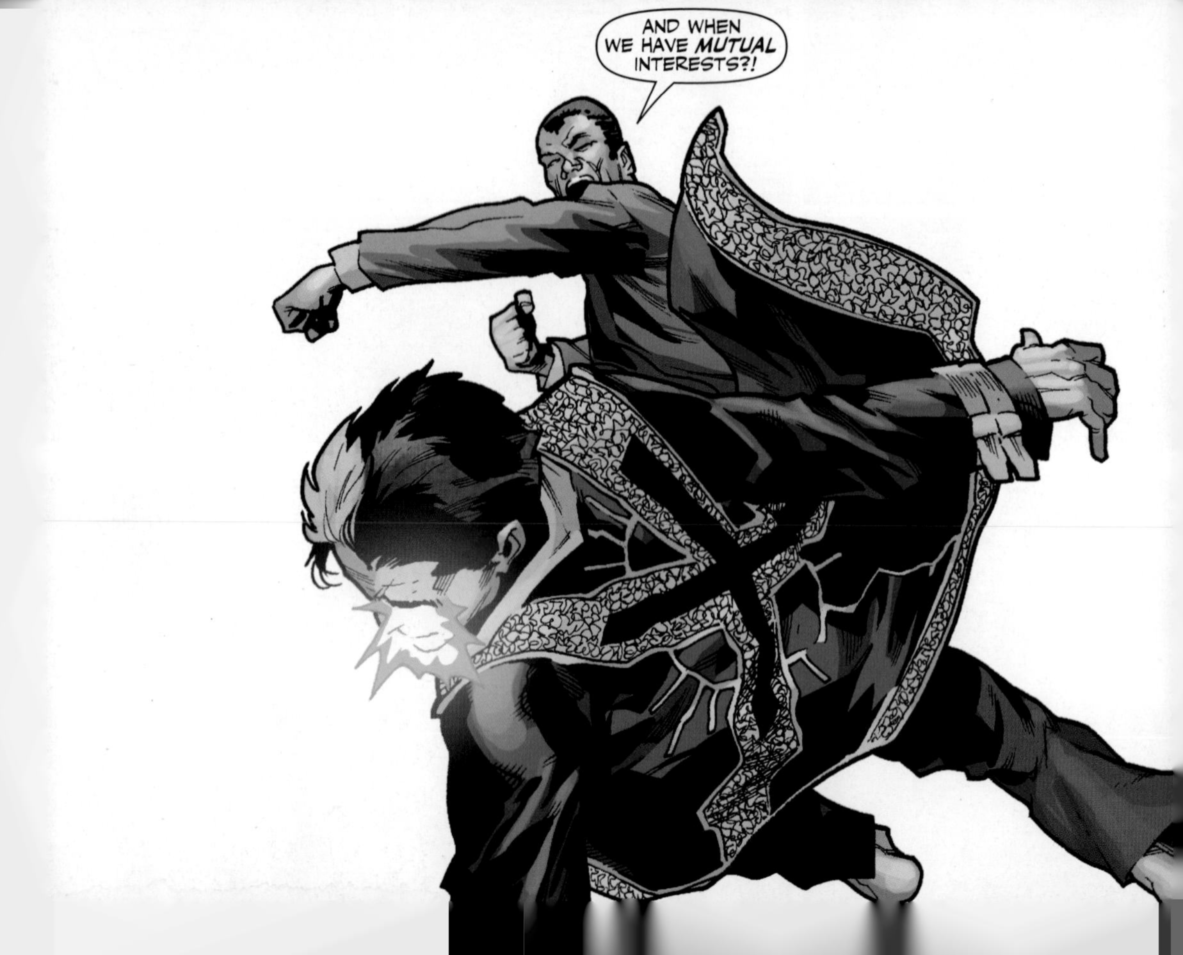
AND WHEN WE HAVE MUTUAL INTERESTS?!

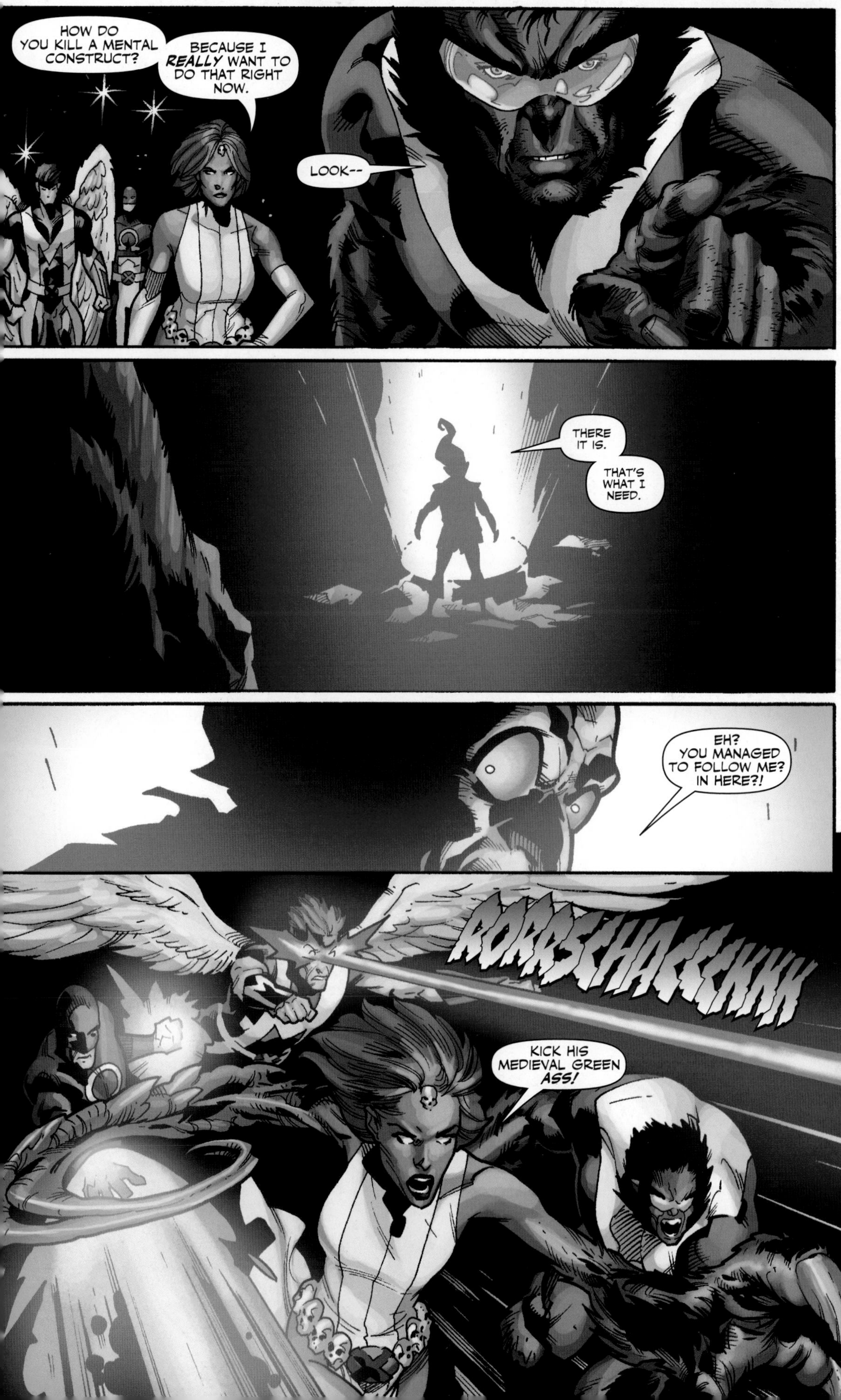
HOW DO YOU KILL A MENTAL CONSTRUCT?
BECAUSE I *REALLY* WANT TO DO THAT RIGHT NOW.
LOOK--
THERE IT IS.
THAT'S WHAT I NEED.
EH? YOU MANAGED TO FOLLOW ME? IN HERE?!
RORRSCHACCCKKK
KICK HIS MEDIEVAL GREEN *ASS!*

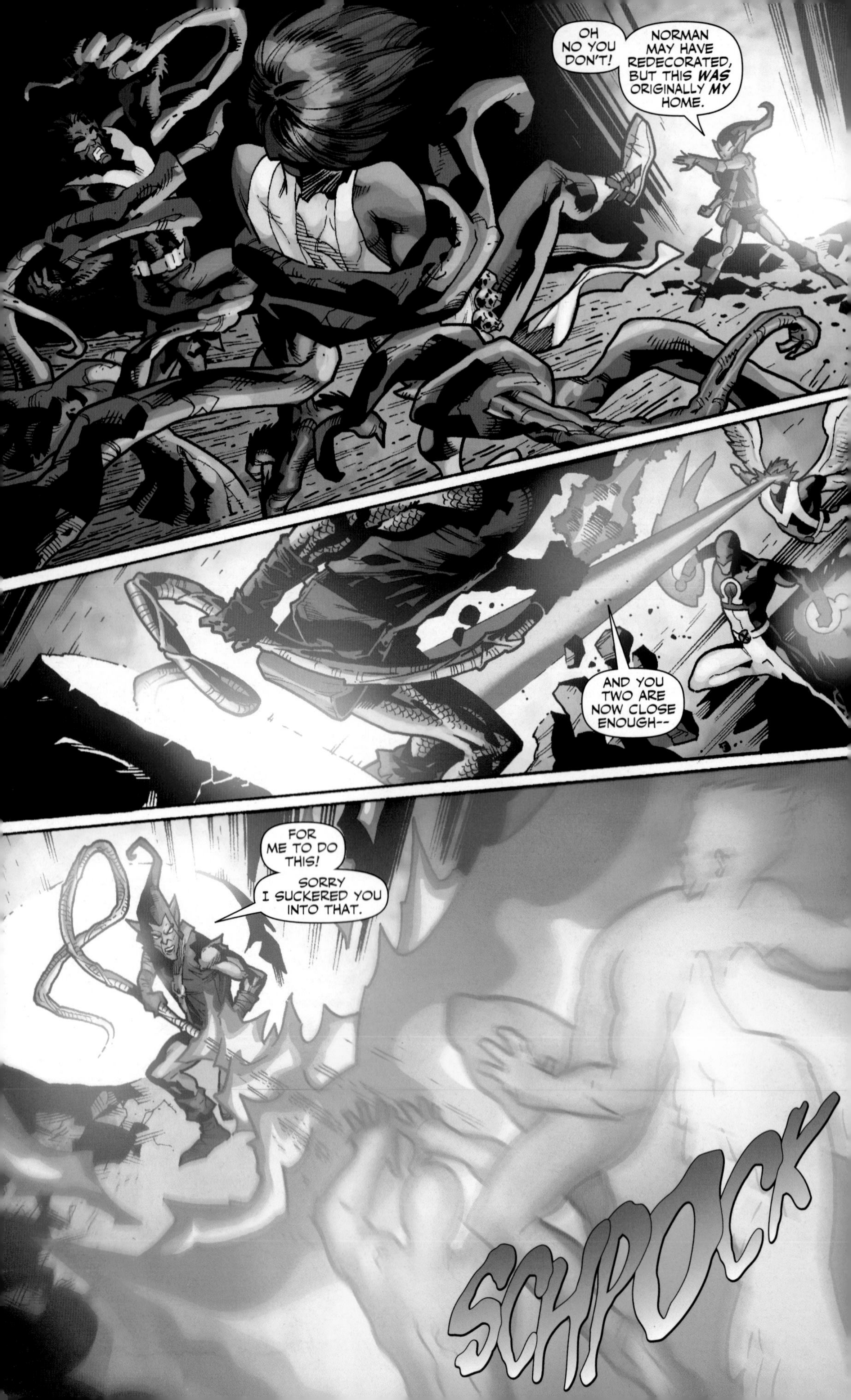
OH NO YOU DON'T!
NORMAN MAY HAVE REDECORATED, BUT THIS **WAS** ORIGINALLY **MY** HOME.
AND YOU TWO ARE NOW CLOSE ENOUGH--
FOR ME TO DO THIS!
SORRY I SUCKERED YOU INTO THAT.
SCHPOCK

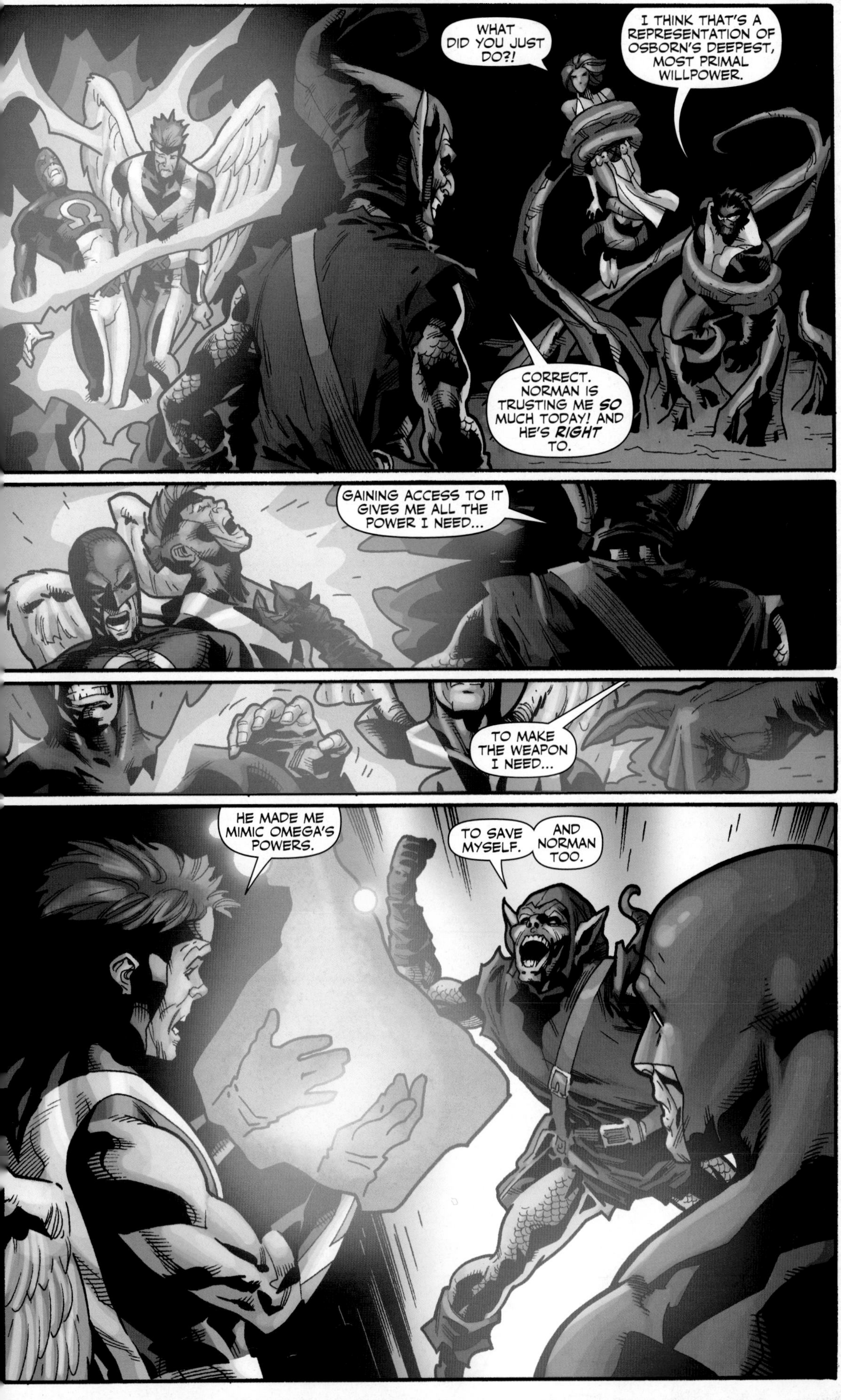
WHAT DID YOU JUST DO?!
I THINK THAT'S A REPRESENTATION OF OSBORN'S DEEPEST, MOST PRIMAL WILLPOWER.
CORRECT. NORMAN IS TRUSTING ME SO MUCH TODAY! AND HE'S RIGHT TO.
GAINING ACCESS TO IT GIVES ME ALL THE POWER I NEED...
TO MAKE THE WEAPON I NEED...
HE MADE ME MIMIC OMEGA'S POWERS.
TO SAVE MYSELF.
AND NORMAN TOO.

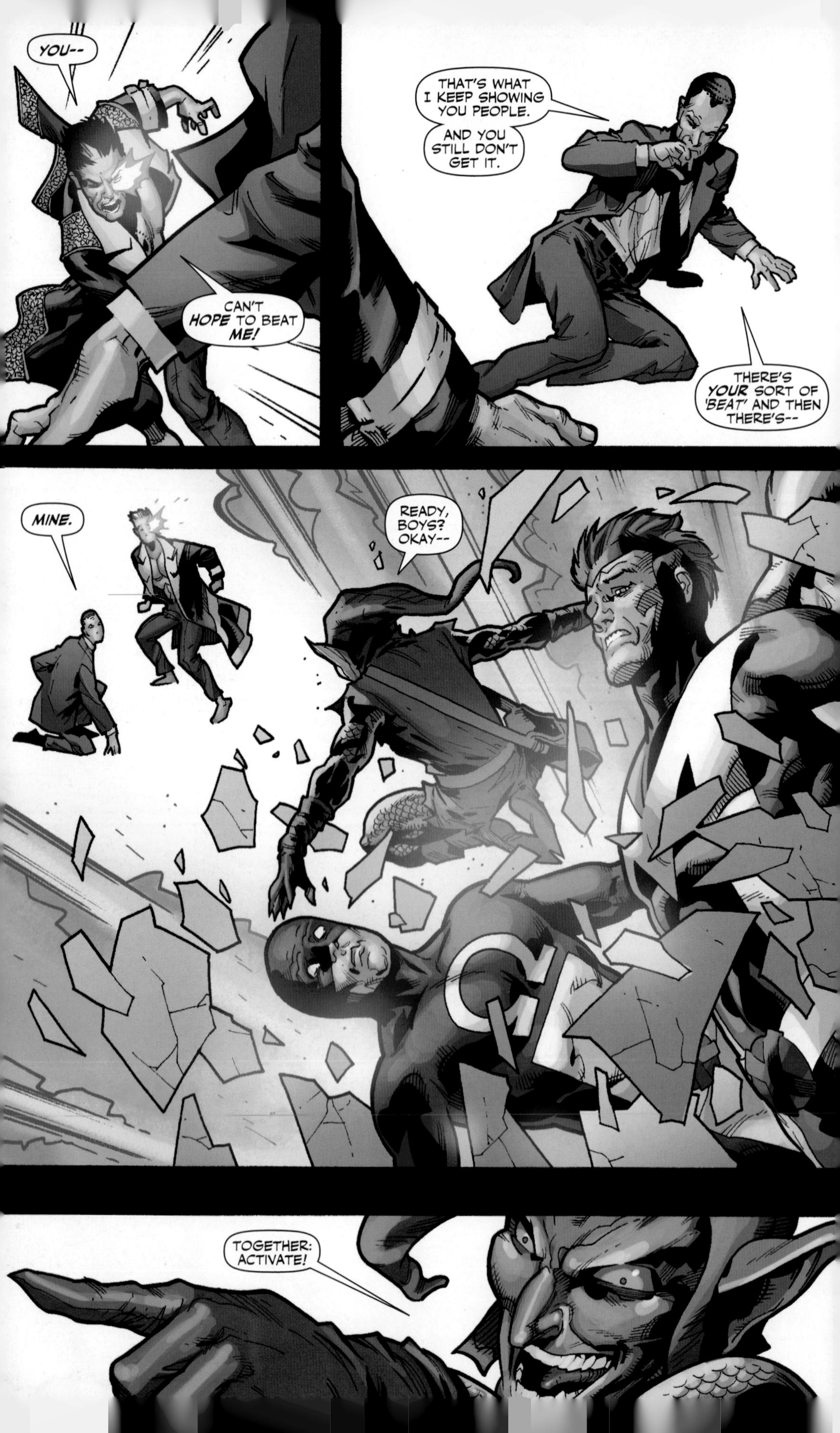
YOU--
CAN'T *HOPE* TO BEAT *ME!*
THAT'S WHAT I KEEP SHOWING YOU PEOPLE.
AND YOU STILL DON'T GET IT.
THERE'S *YOUR* SORT OF *'BEAT'* AND THEN THERE'S--
MINE.
READY, BOYS? OKAY--
TOGETHER: ACTIVATE!

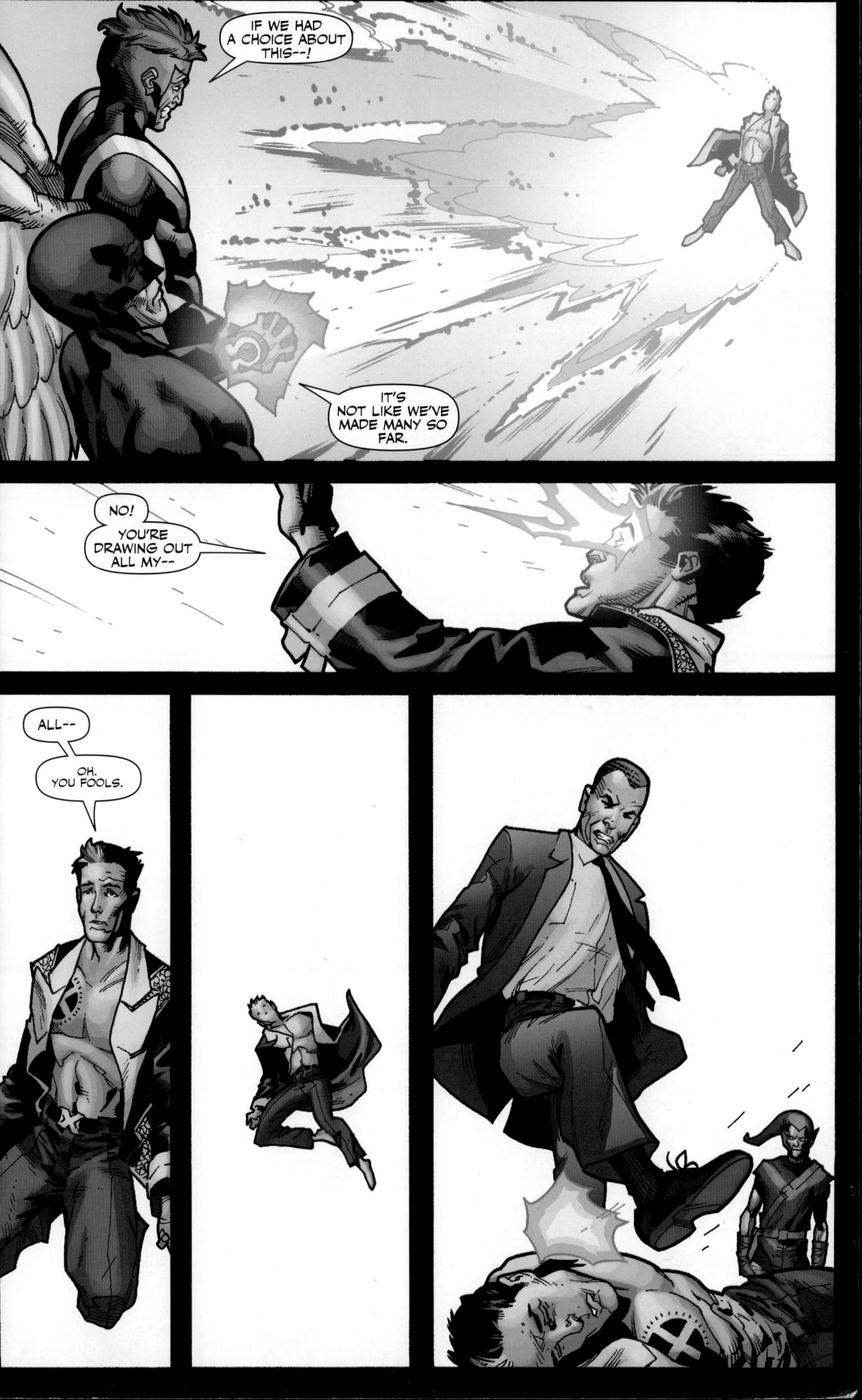
IF WE HAD A CHOICE ABOUT THIS--!
IT'S NOT LIKE WE'VE MADE MANY SO FAR.
NO!
YOU'RE DRAWING OUT ALL MY--
ALL--
OH. YOU FOOLS.

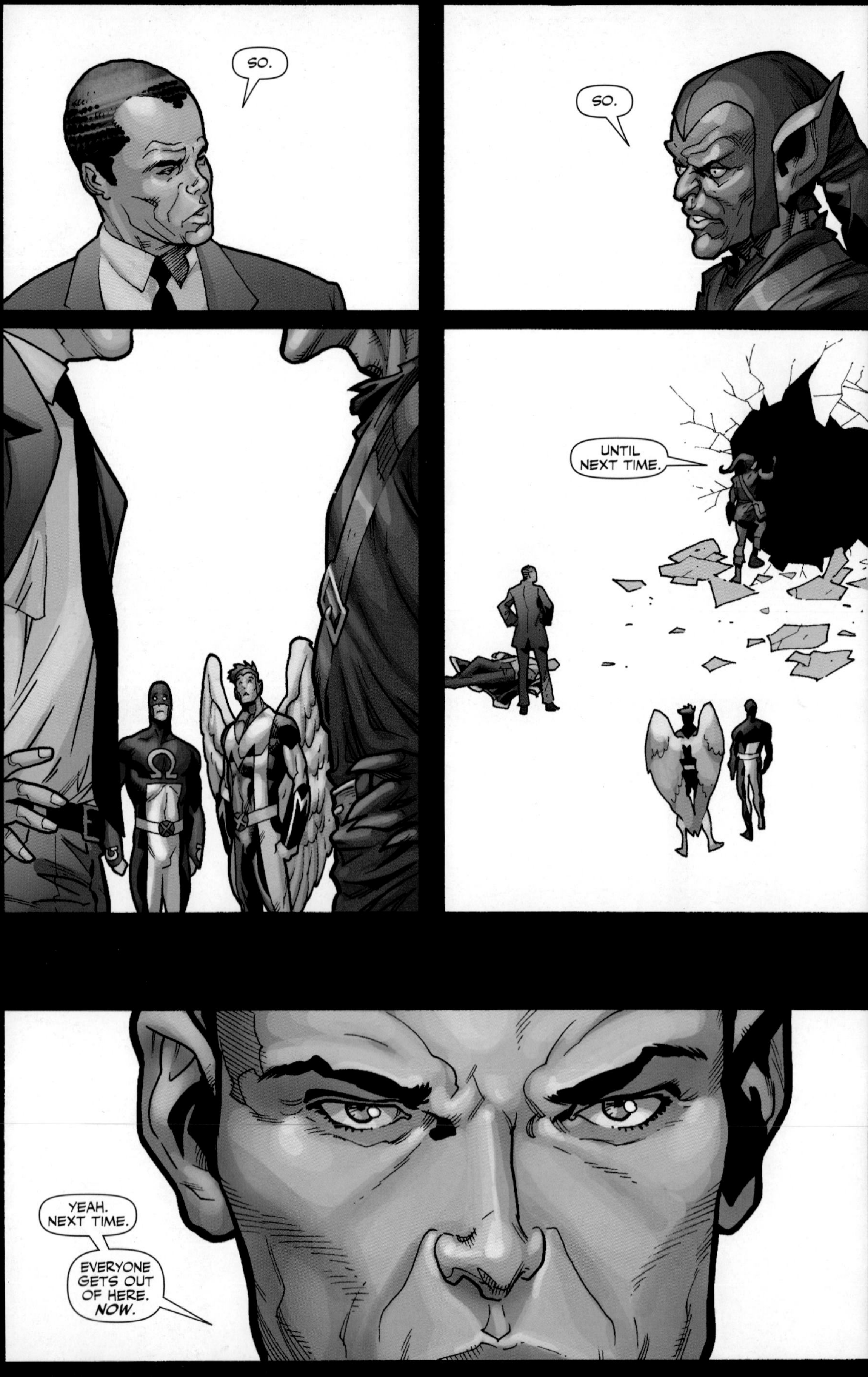
SO.
SO.
UNTIL NEXT TIME.
YEAH. NEXT TIME.
EVERYONE GETS OUT OF HERE. *NOW*.

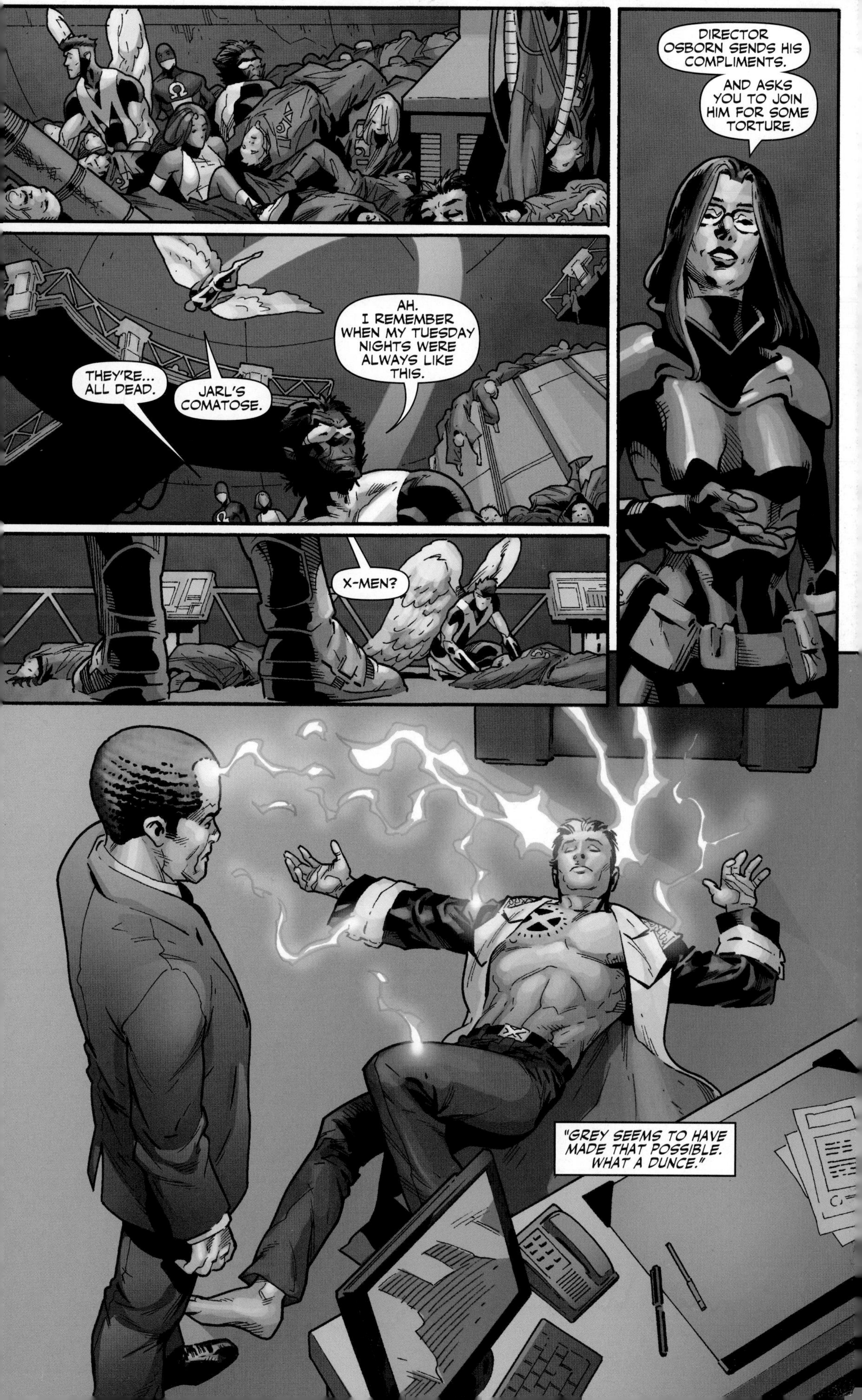
DIRECTOR OSBORN SENDS HIS COMPLIMENTS.
AND ASKS YOU TO JOIN HIM FOR SOME TORTURE.
THEY'RE... ALL DEAD.
JARL'S COMATOSE.
AH. I REMEMBER WHEN MY TUESDAY NIGHTS WERE ALWAYS LIKE THIS.
X-MEN?
"GREY SEEMS TO HAVE MADE THAT POSSIBLE. WHAT A DUNCE."

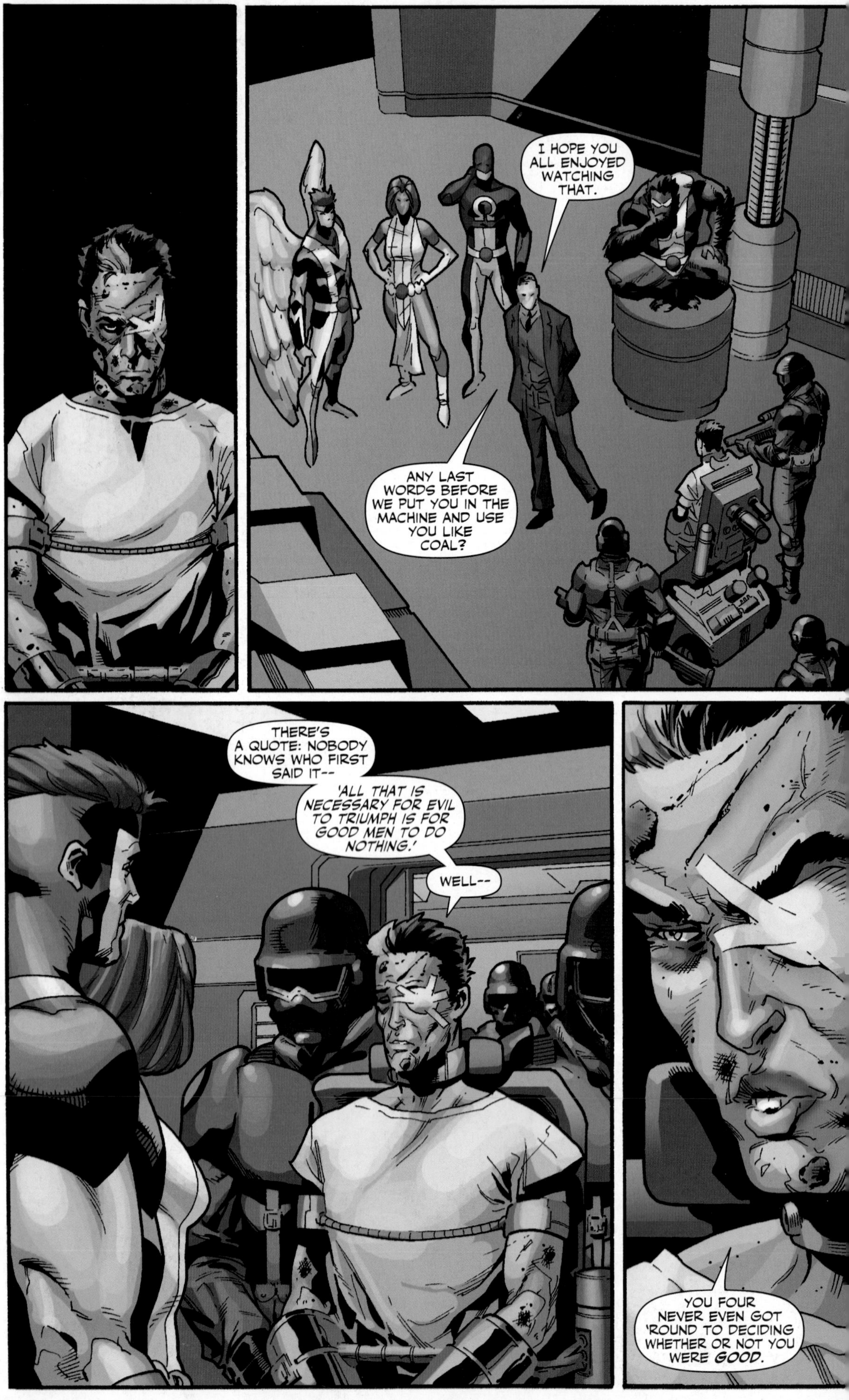
I HOPE YOU ALL ENJOYED WATCHING THAT.
ANY LAST WORDS BEFORE WE PUT YOU IN THE MACHINE AND USE YOU LIKE COAL?
THERE'S A QUOTE: NOBODY KNOWS WHO FIRST SAID IT--
'ALL THAT IS NECESSARY FOR EVIL TO TRIUMPH IS FOR GOOD MEN TO DO NOTHING.'
WELL--
YOU FOUR NEVER EVEN GOT 'ROUND TO DECIDING WHETHER OR NOT YOU WERE GOOD.

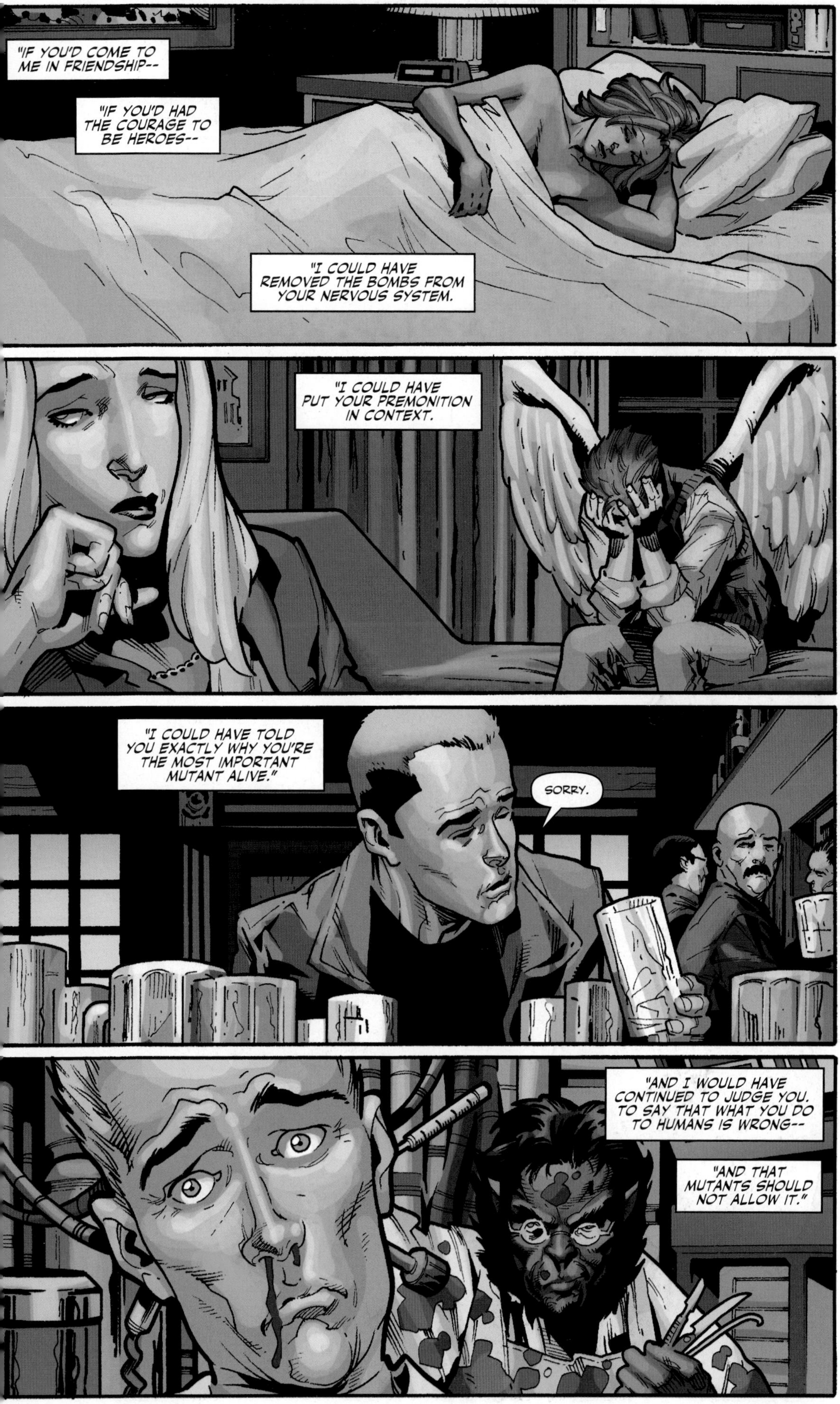
"IF YOU'D COME TO ME IN FRIENDSHIP--
"IF YOU'D HAD THE COURAGE TO BE HEROES--
"I COULD HAVE REMOVED THE BOMBS FROM YOUR NERVOUS SYSTEM.
"I COULD HAVE PUT YOUR PREMONITION IN CONTEXT.
"I COULD HAVE TOLD YOU EXACTLY WHY YOU'RE THE MOST IMPORTANT MUTANT ALIVE."
SORRY.
"AND I WOULD HAVE CONTINUED TO JUDGE YOU. TO SAY THAT WHAT YOU DO TO HUMANS IS WRONG--
"AND THAT MUTANTS SHOULD NOT ALLOW IT."

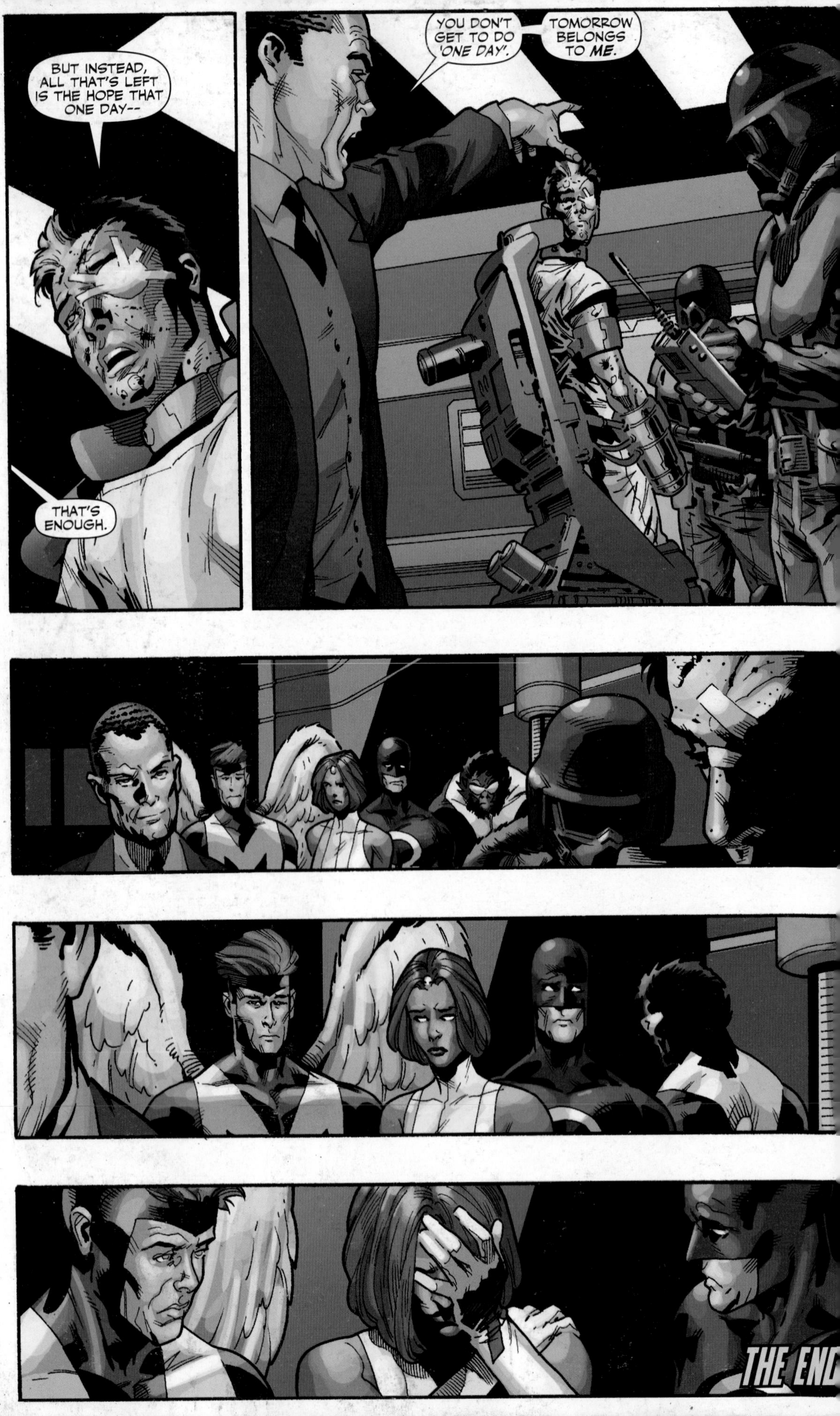
BUT INSTEAD, ALL THAT'S LEFT IS THE HOPE THAT ONE DAY--
THAT'S ENOUGH.
YOU DON'T GET TO DO 'ONE DAY'.
TOMORROW BELONGS TO ME.
THE END